W9-AUU-538

THE HIGHER CIRCLES:
THE GOVERNING CLASS
IN AMERICA

# The Higher Circles

## THE GOVERNING CLASS IN AMERICA

*by G. William Domhoff*

VINTAGE BOOKS
*A Division of Random House / New York*

*Vintage Books Edition, April 1971*
*Copyright © 1970 by G. William Domhoff*

*All rights reserved under International
and Pan-American Copyright Conventions.
Published in the United States by Random House, Inc.,
New York, and simultaneously in Canada by
Random House of Canada Limited, Toronto.
Originally published by Random House, Inc., in 1970.*

*Library of Congress Catalog Card Number: 79–102332*

*Acknowledgment is gratefully extended
to Monthly Review Press, 116 West 14th Street,
New York, N.Y. for permission to reprint
"Who Made American Foreign Policy: 1945–1963?"
published in* CORPORATIONS AND THE COLD WAR.
*Copyright © 1969 by Bertrand Russell Peace Foundation.*

*Manufactured in the United States of America*

TO MY PARENTS

# *Preface*

This book of empirically based essays is intended to deepen, extend and defend the picture of how America is governed that I presented in two previous works.[1] After a short introduction in which I show from our study of the social stratification literature that only a small percentage of it concerns the highest level of society, the four essays in the first section attempt to extend our understanding of the upper class as a social class. The three essays which compose the second section attempt to deepen our understanding of the upper class as a governing class; they explore the involvement of

1. *Who Rules America?* (Englewood Cliffs, N.J.: Prentice-Hall, Inc., 1967); "The Power Elite and Its Critics," in *C. Wright Mills and The Power Elite*, G. William Domhoff and Hoyt B. Ballard, eds. (Boston: Beacon Press, 1968).

members and organizations of the upper class in the governmental process. The third and final section, consisting of two essays, defends my views by contrasting them with those of pluralists and ultra-conservatives.

As in my previous work, the help of students has been indispensable, and I am grateful to the University of California, Santa Cruz, the Bertrand Russell Centre for Social Research and one private donor for the financial support that has made their assistance possible. First and most important among student research assistants has been Sonné Lemke; her role has been central throughout this project. Second only to Sonné in importance have been Mark Goldowitz and Allan Hunter, who also served as friendly critics on occasion. Other students who have worked on one or another aspect of the material in this book include Sharon Howser Moss, Duncan Graham, Tom Scott, Susan Scott, David Guggenhime, Tony Mohr, Kindra Kemp, Lee Hamilton, Ric Epstein, and Carl Gancher. Carolyn Brown and Charlotte Cassidy typed the final manuscript, with Charlotte also serving as a watchdog committee on misspelled words and misspelled names.

Several colleagues, too many to name here, have helped me in one way or another, some without recognizing the importance of their comments. Those to whom I am most indebted will be mentioned at various places in the essays, but here I want to single out Philip H. Burch, Jr., and Benjamin W. Smith for their role in the general development of my thinking about these matters, and Richard Hamilton, Robert Heilbroner and Ferdinand Lundberg for their critical reading of the essays. I also have benefited from my reading of hundreds of detailed research studies by a wide variety of social scientists; this work is gratefully acknowledged throughout the text.

I have invaded the special preserves of a great many specialists in my quest for a general picture of the American upper class and its involvement in the governing process, and I am painfully aware that I am not steeped in the literature of any of them. I apologize in advance for not having read all that I should have on each particular topic. I am sure that many social scientists can point out articles I have missed which would enrich my understanding and analysis, and I hope they will. At the same time, I hope my reading has been comprehensive enough that I have missed no source which presents a general viewpoint I had not previously encountered.

I also want to apologize in advance for any little errors in the spelling of names or in the listing of biographical details. We have checked and double-checked, but with so much material there are bound to be some slips of this nature. In any case, it is absurd to say, as some earlier critics implied, that such mistakes in detail cast doubt on a larger thesis. Having been sensitized to the prevalence of this mistaken belief, I tried unsuccessfully to forestall such commentary about *Who Rules America?* by pointing out one or two peccadilloes in generally accepted sources. Here I will add that I have found many more such minor errors in books presenting other viewpoints, so I hope we can start off by assuming that miscues of this nature are widespread and not germane to the larger issues that should be considered.

This book is dedicated to my parents, who only asked that I do my best at whatever I might undertake, but as before my wife Judy and our children—Lynne, Lori, Bill, and Joel—remain the essential sustenance to my work.

*G. William Domhoff*

Santa Cruz, California
April 25, 1969

# Contents

THE HIGHER CIRCLES:
THE GOVERNING CLASS
IN AMERICA

# Part One

# THE UPPER CLASS AS A SOCIAL CLASS

# Introduction

The investigation of the upper class as a social class is one aspect of the area of study called "social stratification." As several review articles over the years attest, social stratification is a burgeoning field. Perhaps to no one's surprise, however, very little of this work concerns the upper class. Our study of the bibliographies appended to books and articles on the subject published in 1940, 1952–53, 1953–54, 1958, and 1964 showed that by the most generous interpretation only 1–2% of the citations in each survey had anything to do with the highest levels of society.[1] Since

1. Charles H. Page, *Class and American Sociology: From Ward to Ross* (New York: Dial Press, 1940); Howard W. Pfantz, "The Current Literature on Social Stratification: Critique and Bibliography" (*American Journal of Sociology*, January, 1953); Donald G. MacRae, "Social Stratification: A Trend Report" (*Current Sociology*, V. 2, No. 1, 1953–54); Louis Wirth, "Social Stratification and Social Mobility in the

the bibliographies overlap somewhat, this is actually but a handful of research reports with information on the upper class, only two or three of which—on debutante rituals, on status after death, and on marriage announcements in *The New York Times*—were of any interest. The articles were isolated attempts on one specific topic, inspiring no further studies. Nor did any one author appear more than once or twice in our sample.

The situation was better, but not much better, for books containing information on the upper class. However, many of these were quite old, or were written by casual observers rather than social scientists. About the only exceptions to this statement are the well-known works of E. Digby Baltzell (*Philadelphia Gentlemen, The Protestant Establishment*); C. Wright Mills (*The Power Elite*); Robert and Helen Lynd (*Middletown, Middletown in Transition*); and W. Lloyd Warner (*The Social Life of a Modern Community, The Status System in a Modern Community*). Even here, only the studies of Baltzell and Mills are of prime importance, for the local upper classes are but one aspect of the work of the Lynds and Warner, who studied small towns which are of very little relevance in understanding the national upper class based in large cities across the country.[2]

Social stratification research sometimes touches on the

United States" (*Current Sociology,* V. 2, No. 4, 1953–54); Milton M. Gordon, *Social Class in American Sociology* (Durham: Duke University Press, 1958); Raymond J. Murphy, "Some Recent Trends in Stratification Theory and Research" (*The Annals of the American Academy of Political and Social Science,* November, 1964). This study was carried out for me by Allan Hunter.

2. Walter Goldschmidt, "Social Class in America—A Critical Review" (*American Anthropologist,* October, 1950), pp. 485–7, presents a good critique of the small-town studies from the point of view of the national class system. However, Baltzell points out in *Philadelphia Gentlemen* that many of the "upper uppers" from the small towns go to private boarding schools in the East, frequent exclusive summer resorts, and belong to gentlemen's clubs in the large cities, thus becoming part of the national upper class.

upper class in its concern with "social mobility," of which there always has been less than publicists claim. However, most social-mobility literature uses, for my purposes, rather crude indices of social origins and is not really interested in the upper class as such. The most important exception to this statement is the excellent work of historian William Miller and his associates, which has shown the continuity of the social upper class since at least the middle of the nineteenth century.[3]

In short, our survey shows that the upper class is the number one neglected aspect of a fast-growing area of inquiry. Blue collar, white collar, the professions, foreign countries and now the "other America" make regular appearances in the academic literature on social stratification, but *Fortune Magazine* and *Women's Wear Daily* remain more informative sources on the upper class. Thus, the general purpose of the four essays that make up this section is to rescue the upper class from this neglect by social stratification research. The first specific task in realizing this general aim is to present substantive information on several important topics in order to extend our understanding of the upper class as a social entity. The second specific task is to demonstrate a number of different methods by which research can be carried out on this small group which is hard to study by the usual methods used in this field of inquiry.

The first essay is "methodological" and descriptive, showing that several different approaches lead to the same conclusions as to which institutions can be singled out as indicators of the upper class. It thus provides the necessary anchoring point from which further research can develop, as well as providing a catalogue of institutions that could

3. William Miller, "American Historians and the Business Elite" (*Journal of Economic History*, November, 1949); "The Recruitment of the Business Elite" (*Quarterly Journal of Economics*, May, 1950); "American Lawyers in Business and in Politics" (*Yale Law Journal*, January, 1951); *Men in Business* (Cambridge: Harvard University Press, 1952).

be studied in order to gain an anthropological and psychological understanding of members of the upper class. It is the most technical essay in the book, but it is essential to what follows.

General readers who are willing to assume that certain "social registers," certain private schools and certain gentlemen's clubs are indicative of the upper class may want to begin with the second essay, which describes the life style of the feminine half of the upper class. It puts emphasis on the role played by upper-class women in the maintenance and operation of the entire society. The third essay tries to show that the "jet set," "café society," "international nomads," and other seemingly separate groups of "celebrities" are members of the upper class at play, and not just playboy members of the upper class. It suggests that C. Wright Mills, Cleveland Amory, and several others have led us astray on this point. The final essay in the section provides evidence for the "cohesiveness" and "consciousness" of the upper class. Such evidence is necessary in order to stress "consensus" rather than "conspiracy" when it comes to understanding how members and organizations of the upper class predominate in the political process.

# CHAPTER ONE

## *Social Indicators and Social Institutions of the Upper Class*

Even if everyone agreed on a definition of "social class," which they don't, and on the existence of an American "upper class," which they don't, there would still remain the problem of how to identify and study this tiny minority. For example, how would we decide who is a part of this privileged group? Many people may know of a few prominent examples, such as the Rockefellers and Vanderbilts, but a handful of well-known families is hardly adequate for systematic studies. Then too, just what would we study in order to find out more about the upper class? If it does not hold meetings or issue reports, are we reduced to observing certain select members—noting their activities and interviewing them about their opinions?

The answers to both of these problems—who is *in* the upper class and *what* do we study to find out more about it —are to be found in "blue books," private schools and social clubs. They are the starting points for studies of the upper class as a social group. On the one hand, the blue books, schools and clubs can be used as "social indicators," as handy and relatively objective (but not perfect) indices for deciding who is and who is not a member of the class. On the other hand, the schools and clubs are institutions— collections of individuals who organize together for some social or educational purpose on the basis of rules and traditions. By studying the history and activities of these institutions, along with others that will be discussed in later essays, it is possible to learn a great deal about the life styles, beliefs, and activities of members of the upper class.

The aim of this essay, then, is to identify the major indicators and social institutions of the American upper class. Building on the systematic studies of one or two sociologists and the hints of "high-society" writers, it provides the basis for a wide variety of detailed studies on various social and political questions about the upper class. Since no one method of determining social indicators is likely to be convincing to everyone, the ideal solution would be to attain the same results with several different methods. This is what has been done in this investigation, which can be presented in a rather brief way even though it took hundreds of hours of student power to complete it.[1] The primary methods used were "contingency analysis," "reputational analysis," and "positional analysis." Each will be explained in its turn, and the end result will be a guide to the social upper class that makes up at best .5 percent of the American population.

---

1. In particular, Sonné Lemke carried out a great deal of the computational work presented in this essay.

## CONTINGENCY ANALYSIS

Theoretically, contingency analysis is probably the best method for establishing the social indicators of the upper class. It is a statistical means of determining what is related to what. It is as free from bias as any method is likely to be, and it is relatively simple to use. For the purpose of an investigation of the upper class, it could be used by a completely naive social observer if he had a computer, a copy of *Who's Who in America,* and copies of the Social Register and other blue books which purport to list "high society" in the cities or states that they serve. He would need the computer because of the massive number of figures that must be processed through a relatively simple set of operations, the *Who's Who in America* as a source which provides a great deal of information on successful Americans from many walks of life and social backgrounds, and the Social Register because it has been shown by other investigations to be a reliable index of upper-class standing in thirteen major cities.[2] What this naive observer would do is to make a card for every person appearing in *Who's Who in America.* On this card he would note whether or not the person also appears in the Social Register (or any other blue book that he wanted to study) and the schools and clubs that are listed by the person in his *Who's Who* biography. He would then use contingency analysis to determine whether or not people who are listed in the Social Register or other blue books go to one set of schools and clubs, while people who are not so listed go to other schools and belong to different clubs. He would determine, in short, the "association," "contiguity," or "linkage" of the various blue books with various schools and clubs.

2. E. Digby Baltzell, *"Who's Who in America* and the *Social Register."* In Reinhard Bendix and Seymour M. Lipset, eds., *Class, Status and Power* (New York: The Free Press, 1966); G. William Domhoff, *Who Rules America?* (Englewood Cliffs, New Jersey: Prentice-Hall, 1967), pp. 13–16.

The way a contingency analysis works is actually more simple than the word "contingency" may make it sound. In this method the probability of two or more elements occurring together by chance is compared with the actual number of times they are observed to occur together. For example, if one in every ten *Who's Who* listees is in the Social Register, and if one in every ten went to, say, Groton, the chances of the Social Register and Groton appearing on the same card are one-tenth times one-tenth, or one in a hundred. If it is then found that the Social Register and Groton appear together, say, ten times in a hundred rather than once in every hundred, it can be suspected that there is a contingency or association between the Social Register and Groton. In fact, by use of what is called a statistical test of "significance," the probability of the Social Register and Groton appearing together by chance one time in ten instead of the expected one time in a hundred can be determined. If this test shows that the difference between the *observed* proportion (one in ten) and the *expected* proportion (one in a hundred) is so great that we would expect such a difference to occur by chance only one time in a hundred, we assume that the high contingency was not mere chance.[3]

By performing contingency analyses between all the various elements that appear on the cards, the computer could generate in moments the social institutions of the upper class without knowing a thing about that class. It could tell us which schools and clubs are related to each other and to social registers. It could separate the "ins" from the "outs" in a flash.

The study I have just described is the ideal one. It would take a great deal of time to put all the information on cards,

3. Charles Osgood, "The Representation Model and Relevant Research Methods," in I. deSola Pool (editor), *Trends in Content Analysis* (Urbana, Illinois: University of Illinois Press, 1959), pp. 55–78, for a discussion of contingency analysis. The statistical test used was the significance of difference between proportions.

and it would take money to buy time on the computer. Perhaps someone will undertake the task someday. In our case, we had to do the next best thing. I hypothesized that certain schools and clubs were institutions of the upper class, and then tested this hypothesis by means of contingency analysis. That is, if I am right in my guesses, which are based upon previous studies by myself and others, there should be statistically significant contingencies between the Social Register and certain schools and clubs. To check this, we went through 3,000 *Who's Who* biographies, noting which ones also were listed in the Social Register, which ones listed one of several private schools and which ones listed one of several social clubs. What we found was that being listed in the Social Register and attending certain private schools, or belonging to certain social clubs, were "contingent." For example, people who are listed in the Social Register are much more likely to have attended Groton or St. Paul's than would be expected by coincidence. Members of the Century Club are more likely to be listed in the Social Register than would be expected by accident. What is especially gratifying is that certain schools and clubs on our list that we did not consider exclusive did not have a significant relationship to the Social Register. It would seem that there is a social group we can call the upper class, and that previous investigations have given us a pretty good idea of where to look for it.

It is very important to state the limits of this study. Since a great many clubs and schools appeared only a small number of times due to the relatively small size of our sample, it was not possible to make a decision one way or another about them. Then too, the fact that the Social Register is limited to thirteen cities made it meaningless to compare it with clubs in certain cities. Nor did we take the next step, which the computer so easily could, and determine the contingencies among three, four, or more elements. These limitations admitted, I hope we have shown nonetheless what is obvious to most people, that the Social Register, certain private schools, and certain social clubs do involve the same people more than would be expected by chance, and that they are therefore justifiably used as indicators of the upper class. With this statistically determined anchoring point, we can expand our list of indicators and institutions by means of our second method.

## THE REPUTATIONAL METHOD — SOCIETY EDITORS AS INFORMANTS

Contingency analysis is the most impersonal and objective approach that is applicable to our problem. The second method has just the opposite qualities. It is personal and subjective. Simply put, I asked women's page and society page editors from major newspapers all over the country to give me their opinions as to the upper-class institutions of their respective cities. This is a variation of the reputational method in which knowledgeable people are asked to identify the important leaders or institutions that the researcher wishes to study. Anthropologists would call it the use of "informants." The following letter was sent to every daily newspaper in every city in the United States with a chapter of the Junior League. The Junior League was used as a starting point because it is one of the few nationwide organizations with a great many upper-class members and a reputation for being a very exclusive service organization. It is a lower benchmark from which we can build to an understanding of other, more exclusive upper-class organizations:

Dear Society Editor:

We are currently doing a research project on American High Society, and we want to determine if and how your city fits into the picture. We have sent this letter to all cities which have a chapter of the Junior League, and we hope you can take the five or so minutes necessary to answer the questions in this letter, and to return it to us in the self-addressed, stamped envelope that is enclosed.

1. Is the Junior League the most exclusive "High Society" women's organization in your city? _____ If not, what is the name of the one you would deem more exclusive? _____ Are there any similar exclusive clubs for women older than the Junior League age? _____ Name(s)? _____

2. Are there any exclusive gentlemen's clubs in your city that are parallel in social standing to the Junior League or the most exclusive club you named in question I above? _____ Could you list as many such clubs as you think relevant, from most exclusive to least exclusive? _____ _____

3. Is there a "blue book" or "social register" for your city? _____ Are its listees by and large the same persons as found in the Junior League and the exclusive gentlemen's clubs? _____ Could you give us its name and address so we might compare it to others we have purchased? _____ _____

4. Are members of "High Society" in your city likely to send their children to private preparatory schools previous to college? _____ What are the most popular preparatory schools for boys? _____ for girls? _____ Could you estimate how many (if any) sons of "High Society" parents from your city are likely to attend the following schools each year? Phillips Exeter _____, Phillips Andover _____, Groton _____, Choate _____, St. Paul's _____, Deerfield _____, Shattuck _____, Lake Forest _____, Webb _____, Episcopal High _____, Woodberry Forest _____.

If you have stayed with us to this point, we are deeply grateful, for you have given us the basic information we need. If you are pressed for time, please stop, check here (_____) if you wish to see the results of our study, and return this letter in the enclosed envelope with our thanks. But if you have another minute or so, perhaps you could turn over and comment on the question of whether or not rising corporation executives are assimilated into "High Society."

The following appeared on the back of the letter:

Along with your own comments on the relationship of rising corporation executives to "High Society," there are these questions which interest us:

1. At what level in the corporation (director, president, vice president, etc.) does one begin to join the highest social circles? _____ Or is salary level the important consideration? _____ If so, what salary level would you estimate for your city? _____

2. Into which exclusive organizations which you noted in the earlier questions are rising executives accepted? _____
   _____

3. Do rising corporate executives send their children to private schools? Circle one:  Very few,  Some,  Half and half,  Many,  Most.

4. Your own observations on rising executives and their relation to "High Society":

In all, 128 of our 317 questionnaire-type letters were returned. Some had very little information, but most were quite informative. In twelve cases we received two replies from a city, and in all but one—Tucson, Arizona—these multiple reports were in agreement. Some of the information reported, which often went well beyond what I had asked for, will be used in later essays. What is important here is that this method duplicates the results of the contingency analysis where the two overlap. For example, the Social Register was noted by the eight reports from cities covered by it. The reports also agree that Social Register listees tend to go to the schools and belong to the clubs found to be related to the Social Register in the contingency analysis. The agreement of the two methods gives greater confidence in our results, and encourages me to give credence to the reputational reports in the many cases where a contingency analysis was not attempted, either due to the limited size of our sample or because I did not know of the particular club or school.

## POSITIONAL ANALYSIS

Our final major approach in identifying indicators and social institutions was a positional analysis. That is, we studied the social backgrounds of men presumed from their occupational positions to be members of the upper class. Fifteen major cities were chosen for this study. In general, they were among the most important cities in the country for which there is no Social Register or for which we had little in-depth information on major social institutions. It was arbitrarily decided beforehand that we would study the following people:

1. All directors of companies in the given city that were listed in the August, 1965, *Fortune* survey as being among the top 500 industrials, top fifty insurance companies, or top fifty transports.

2. All directors of the five largest banks in the city.

3. All trustees of the five largest foundations in the city.

4. All partners of the five largest law firms in the city.

This study led to a list of 3,164 names. Using every available biographical source, at least some information was found on 46% of these people. The major source of our "no information" category was lawyers. They account for 47% of our failures, which is 27% of the sample. In the eleven cities where we had both reputational information and a large number of people in the positional analysis, the two methods were in agreement as to the most important clubs. For example, of seventy-five men on whom we found information for Seattle, fifty-eight were in the Rainier Club. In Portland, Oregon, forty of eighty-one were in the Arlington Club, and in Hartford, thirty-two of eighty-eight were in the Hartford Club. However, very little information was found on private schools for these men, so no comparison was possible on this score. What this study adds to the contingency analysis and reputational study is the assurance that big business leaders are members of the social clubs of the upper class.

One further benefit from this positional study was a comparison of these lists with the blue books which we learned about from society editor informants. Thus, 45% of our 349 Houston names were listed in that city's *Social Register;* 42% of our Detroit list was in that city's *Social Secretary;* 38% of our Seattle list was in that city's *Blue Book;* 28% of our Denver list was in that city's *Social Record;* and 21% of our San Diego list was in the *California Register.* The figures suggest that some of these books are as useful as Baltzell first showed the Social Register to be.

## OTHER STUDIES

There are other studies, by ourselves and others, which can be cited to extend our list of indicators and to provide further support for those already developed. First, the city of New Orleans afforded us the opportunity for a different type of study because we luckily came into possession of a little-known social register for that city as well as the membership lists for its two most exclusive clubs.[4] In this study we used the membership of the Boston Club as our starting

---

4. My deepest thanks to Robert Head and Darlene Fife of the NOLA *Express* for providing me with these invaluable raw materials. May all underground newspapers become as socially conscious as the NOLA *Express.*

point. We found that 22% of its members also were in the Pickwick Club (the other exclusive club whose membership list we have) and that 54% of its 1953 resident members were listed in the 1964 New Orleans *Social Register*. We also compared the New Orleans *Social Register* to a detailed social history of that city.[5] This study showed that virtually all the prominent names in the city's history have descendants who are registered. As another small example of the register's usefulness, we found it contained thirty-five of the forty-two New Orleans debutantes for 1968.[6] Having determined that the Boston Club and *Social Register* are indicative of the New Orleans social elite, we studied the brief biographies of the forty-eight Boston Club members from New Orleans who are listed in *Who's Who in America*. This study showed that most of the prominent businessmen of New Orleans are in that club. Thus, we moved from a leading social club to business leaders, whereas in the positional study we worked from business leaders to social clubs.

Our study of Los Angeles, undertaken by Kevin Fishburn, began with the 261 people who had donated enough money to the Los Angeles Art Museum, the Greek Theatre, the Music Center and the Hollywood Bowl to get their names inscribed within the august halls of these cultural shrines. At least some information was found on 180 of them. They were by and large big business leaders, with seventy-two belonging to the city's exclusive California Club. Sixty percent of them are listed in the Los Angeles *Blue Book,* as are 47% of the Los Angeles residents who are directors of the city's three largest banks.

Philadelphia, Chicago, and New York have been studied by other investigators. The most thorough study, of Phila-

<hr />

5. Robert Tallant, *The Romantic New Orleanians* (New York: E. P. Dutton and Company, 1950).

6. Lucile Griswold, "New Orleans Debutantes Are Revealed" (New Orleans *States-Item,* August 9, 1968), p. 20.

delphia, was done by E. Digby Baltzell.[7] It provides evidence for the usefulness of the Social Register as well as demonstrating the elite nature of the Rittenhouse and Philadelphia Clubs and several private schools. Dalton Potter studied the upper-class clubs of Chicago by means of interviews and the club listings of families who are in the Social Register.[8] Both methods suggested that the Chicago Club was the top men's club, the Fortnightly the top women's club, and the Casino the top family club. His study also showed that about one-third of the families in the Social Register listed themselves as members of one or more clubs. Supplementing our information on New York is the little-known dissertation by the well-known political scientist Gabriel Almond. It demonstrates that the Social Register is a good indicator of the upper class in that city as well as showing the overlapping leadership of the city's most exclusive social clubs.[9]

The work of society writer Lucy Kavaler provides evidence on upper-class social institutions across the country.[10] Although presented in a popular fashion, and interlaced with anecdotes of doubtful generality, its catalogue of social institutions is based on interviews with members of the upper class, private school teachers, Junior League officials, and observers and employees of society organizations. It has been an important starting point for some of our more systematic studies. The agreement between our work and hers gives me considerable confidence in her institutional findings.

In our final attempt to demonstrate the interrelationship

7. E. Digby Baltzell, *Philadelphia Gentlemen: The Making of a National Upper Class* (Glencoe, Illinois: The Free Press, 1958).

8. Dalton Potter, "Some Aspects of the Social Organization of the Elite in Chicago" (Unpublished M.A. thesis, University of Chicago, 1949).

9. Gabriel Almond, "Plutocracy and Politics in New York City" (Unpublished Ph.D. dissertation, University of Chicago, 1941), pp. 118–21, 146.

10. Lucy Kavaler, *The Private World of High Society* (New York: David McKay Co., 1960).

of our indicators, we compared the Social Register with certain private school alumni bulletins. For example, of those getting diplomas from Groton in 1967–68, 56% were in the Social Register. The percentage for St. Mark's for 1967 was 54. Of all living Hotchkiss alumni as of 1966, 26% were in the 1967 Social Register. On the other hand, only 3% of Loomis School graduates for the year 1967–68 were listed in the Social Register, so it should be dropped from the list of indicators that I used in my first study of the upper class. With that mistake in mind, let me present a revised list of social indicators of upper-class standing, fully expecting that further work once again will dictate revisions.

## SOCIAL INDICATORS OF THE AMERICAN UPPER CLASS

The following indicators are distilled from the several studies recounted above, with the exception that no Washington, D. C., social indicators are utilized because middle-class politicians are sometimes invited to join them upon their arrival in Washington. Each indicator is followed by one or more of the following symbols, which refer to the studies which justify the inclusion of that indicator: B—Baltzell's work; C—contingency analysis; D—Dalton Potter's work; K—Kavaler's work; P—positional analysis; R—reputational study; X—our special studies of Los Angeles and New Orleans. The indicators, then, are as follows:

1. A person is considered to be a member of the upper class if he, his parents, his wife's parents, or any of his siblings are listed in any of the following registers and blue books:

   a. The Social Register, which has editions for Boston, New York, Philadelphia, Baltimore, Buffalo, Pittsburgh, Cleveland, Dayton-Cincinnati, Chicago, St. Louis, and San Francisco. The Washington edition is not considered indicative of upper-class standing; it automatically lists senators, for example, and other middle-class politicians are sometimes included. This is not the case for other cities. B, C, K, R

b. Detroit *Social Secretary.* P, R
c. Houston *Social Register.* P, R
d. Los Angeles *Blue Book.* R, X
e. New Orleans *Social Register.* X
f. Seattle *Blue Book.* P, R

2. A person is considered to be a member of the upper class if he, his father, brothers, or father-in-law attended any of the following schools:

Asheville (Asheville, N. C.) K, R
Buckley (New York City) K
Cate (Carpinteria, Calif.) K, R
Catlin Gabel (Portland, Ore.) R
Choate (Wallingford, Conn.) B, K, R
Cranbrook (Bloomfield Hills, Mich.) K, R
Country Day School (St. Louis) K
Deerfield (Deerfield, Mass.) B, K, R
Episcopal High (Alexandria, Va.) B, K, R
Gilman (Baltimore) R
Groton (Groton, Mass.) B, C, K, R
Hill (Pottstown, Pa.) B, C, K, R
Hotchkiss (Lakeville, Conn.) B, C, K, R
Kingswood (Hartford, Conn.) R
Kent (Kent, Conn.) B, K, R
Lake Forest (Lake Forest, Ill.) K, R
Lakeside (Seattle) R
Lawrenceville (Lawrenceville, N. J.) B, K, R
Middlesex (Concord, Mass.) B, K, R
Milton (Milton, Mass.) K, R
Moses Brown (Providence) R
Pomfret (Pomfret, Conn.) K

Portsmouth Priory (Portsmouth, R. I.) B, R
Ponahou (Honolulu) K, R
St. Andrew's (Middlebury, Del.) K
St. Christopher's (Richmond) K, R
St. George's (Newport, R. I.) B, C, K, R
St. Mark's (Southborough, Mass.) B, C, K, R
St. Paul's (Concord, N. H.) B, C, K, R
Shattuck (Fairbault, Minn.) K, R
Taft (Watertown, Conn.) B, K, R
Thacher (Ojai, Calif.) K, R
University School (Cleveland) K, R
University School (Milwaukee) R
Webb (Bell Buckle, Tenn.) K
Westminister (Atlanta) R
Woodberry Forest (Woodberry Forest, Va.) B, K, R

3. A person is considered to be a member of the upper class if he, his father, brothers, or father-in-law belongs to any one of the following social clubs:

Arlington (Portland, Ore.) P, R
Boston (New Orleans) K, X
Brook (New York) K
Burlingame Country Club (San Francisco) C
California (Los Angeles) K, R, X
Casino (Chicago) C, K, R
Century (New York) C, K
Chagrin Valley Hunt (Cleveland) K
Charleston (Charleston, S. C.) R
Chicago (Chicago) C, K, R
Cuyamuca (San Diego) P, R
Denver (Denver) P
Detroit (Detroit) P, R
Eagle Lake (Houston) K
Everglades (Palm Beach) K, R
Hartford (Hartford, Conn.) P, R
Hope (Providence) P, R
Idlewild (Dallas) K
Knickerbocker (New York) C, K
Links (New York) C, K
Maryland (Baltimore) K

Milwaukee (Milwaukee) R
Minneapolis (Minneapolis) P, R
New Haven Lawn Club (New Haven) R
Pacific Union (San Francisco) C, K, R
Philadelphia (Philadelphia) B, K
Piedmont Driving (Atlanta) K, P
Piping Rock (New York) C
Racquet Club (St. Louis) R
Rainier (Seattle) P, R
Richmond German (Richmond) K, R
Rittenhouse (Philadelphia) B, K
River (New York) C, K
Rolling Rock (Pittsburgh) R
Saturn (Buffalo) R
St. Cecelia (Charleston, S. C.) K
St. Louis Country Club (St. Louis) R
Somerest (Boston) K, R
Union (Cleveland) K, R
Woodhill Country Club (Minneapolis) P, R

4. A person is considered to be a member of the upper class if his sister, wife, mother, or mother-in-law attended one of the following schools or belongs to one of the following clubs. The lists are based upon our reputational information, the work of Kavaler, and our study of upper-class women listed in *Who's Who of American Women*. The latter study will be presented in the next essay. This list probably can be expanded on the basis of more detailed studies:

*Schools:*

Abbot Academy (Andover, Mass.)
Agnes Irwin (Wynnewood, Pa.)
Anna Head (Berkeley)
Annie Wright (Tacoma, Wash.)
Ashley Hall (Charleston, S. C.)
Baldwin (Bryn Mawr, Pa.)
Beaver Country Day (Chestnut Hill, Mass.)
Berkeley Institute (Brooklyn)
Bishop's (La Jolla, Calif.)

Brearley (New York City)
Brimmer's and May (Chestnut Hill, Mass.)
Brooke Hill (Birmingham)
Bryn Mawr (Baltimore)
Catlin Gabel (Portland)
Chapin (New York City)
Chatham Hall (Chatham, Va.)
Collegiate (Richmond)
Concord Academy (Concord, Mass.)
Convent of the Sacred Heart (New York City)
Dalton (New York City)
Dana Hall (Wellesley, Mass.)
Emma Willard (Troy, New York)
Ethel Walker (Simsbury, Conn.)
Foxcroft (Middleburg, Va.)
Garrison Forest (Garrison, Md.)
Hathaway Brown (Cleveland)
Hockaday (Dallas)
Katherine Branson (Ross, Calif.)
Kent (Kent, Conn.)
Kent Place (Summit, N. J.)
Kingswood (Bloomfield Hills, Mich.)
Kinkaid (Houston)
Lake Forest Country Day (Lake Forest, Ill.)
Latin School of Chicago (Chicago)
Laurel (Cleveland)
Lenox (New York City)
Louise S. McGehee (New Orleans)
Madeira (Greenway, Va.)
Marlborough (Los Angeles)
Mary Institute (St. Louis)
Marymount Secondary (Tarrytown, N. Y.)
Master's (Dobbs Ferry, N. Y.)
Milwaukee Downer Seminary (Milwaukee)
Miss Hall's (Pittsfield, Mass.)
Miss Hewitt's (New York City)
Miss Porter's (Farmington, Conn.)
Mt. Vernon Seminary (Washington, D. C.)
Oldfield's (Glencoe, Md.)
Packer Collegiate (Brooklyn)
Radford (El Paso)

Rosemary Hall (Greenwich, Conn.)
Roycemore (Evanston, Ill.)
Salem Academy (Winston-Salem)
Shipley (Bryn Mawr, Pa.)
Spence (New York City)
St. Agnes Episcopal (Alexandria, Va.)
St. Catherine's (Richmond)
St. Katharine's (Davenport, Iowa)
St. Mary's Hall (San Antonio)
St. Nicholas (Seattle)
St. Timothy's (Stevenson, Md.)
Stuart Hall (Staunton, Va.)
Walnut Hill (Natick, Mass.)
Westminister (Atlanta)
Westover (Middlebury, Conn.)
Westridge (Pasadena)
Winsor (Boston)

*Clubs:*

Acorn (Philadelphia)
Chilton (Boston)
Colony (New York City)
Fortnightly (Chicago)
Friday (Chicago)
Mt. Vernon Club (Baltimore)
Society of Colonial Dames
Sulgrave (Washington, D. C.)
Sunset (Seattle)
Vincent (Boston)

5. A person is considered to be a member of the upper class if his or her father was a millionaire entrepreneur or a $100,000-a-year corporation executive or corporation lawyer, *and* (a) he or she attended one of the 130 private schools listed in the back of Kavaler's *The Private World of High Society or* (b) he or she belongs to any one of the exclusive clubs mentioned by Baltzell or Kavaler. The list of private schools and exclusive clubs can be larger here than for the second, third, and fourth criteria because it is known that the

person is a member of the second generation of a wealthy family. This criterion is useful in detailed studies where *Current Biography* and articles listed in the *Biography Index* are utilized in addition to such general sources as *Who's Who in America*.

## THE SOCIAL INSTITUTIONS OF SMALLER CITIES

Indicators are very important in the social sciences, but most of the indicators are not very good, even in the highly-developed field of economics.[11] Ours are no exception—they have their strengths and weaknesses, and there is a certain amount of arbitrariness in the lists I have presented despite the use of a large amount of information derived from several different studies. Many people may feel that one or another of the indicators should be excluded; others will know of indicators that should be added to the list. In any case, adding or subtracting one or two criteria makes very little difference in large-scale studies. For example, dropping Loomis School and the Harmonie Club from our previous lists changes nothing about the generalizations in my previous work. Both of the Loomis graduates in our earlier files are members of the upper class by other criteria (one is a Rockefeller), as are all but four of the very wealthy Jewish businessmen who were in the Harmonie Club. More generally, it can be said that the Social Register, five or six of the best-known private schools (e.g., Groton, St. Paul's, St. Mark's, Choate, Hotchkiss) and the clubs in major cities (e.g., Boston's Somerset, New York's Knicker-bocker, and Detroit's Detroit) include most of the upper-class people in the Eastern half of the United States.

11. Raymond A. Bauer, ed., *Social Indicators* (Cambridge, Mass.: MIT Press, 1966); Oskar Morgenstern, *On The Accuracy of Economic Observations* (Princeton: Princeton University Press, 1963).

Building on this base, this study has tried to extend our indicators to the rest of the country.

Those who look at the American upper class in terms of its classical base in New England prep schools and Eastern cities may find these expanded criteria too inclusive, picking up as they do some of the "new" wealth west of the Mississippi and some of the executives who have crawled the corporate ladders to positions of prominence. Such investigators can present their findings in terms of both inclusive and exclusive criteria. However, the results of our questionnaires to women's page editors, along with other evidence to be presented in the following essays, suggests that the upper class is now national in its scope and has developed a country-wide net of interrelated social and educational institutions.

From my point of view, the major arbitrariness comes in leaving out the Junior League and certain small-town clubs and schools that were uncovered in the reputational study. In essence, by leaving them out I have decided to err on the side of caution rather than include institutions which have at least a substantial minority of middle-class and upper-middle-class people. On the other hand, a brief consideration of our findings on the social institutions of smaller cities suggests that a great deal is not lost by this decision. Our first finding was that the Junior League is usually the most exclusive social organization in these cities, although it was often pointed out that it has middle-class members as well. Second, there is sometimes no male social club that is of the same high social standing as the Junior League. Third, the prominent families of these towns often send their children to the private schools in large nearby cities and in New England. For example, several society editors in the South mentioned St. Catherine's in Richmond as one of the most important girls' schools for local society, three in smaller New York cities mentioned the Emma Willard School, and one in Texas and one in

Arkansas mentioned the Hockaday School for girls in Dallas. Then too, a number of children from smaller cities went to the private schools listed in the questionnaire-letter to society editors. It should be added, however, that this varied from very few in the Southwest to quite a few in the South and New England. In the South, moreover, there was a much greater tendency for male children from the smaller towns to go to Woodberry Forest and Episcopal High than to the New England schools.

My conclusion from these results for the Junior League and smaller cities is that it is better to use only the most prominent private schools and the social institutions of major cities as indicators of upper-class standing. Since there is every reason to believe that prominent families from the smaller cities are in many ways affiliated with one or more of the upper-class social institutions of nearby major cities, little is lost by excluding minor schools and clubs about whose social standing there may be some doubt.

## TWO QUESTIONS

Two questions may have occurred to readers as they went along. First, what would members of the upper class think of these indicators? Second, why isn't there even more overlap among the indicators; why aren't all Hotchkiss graduates or Chicago Club members in the Social Register, for example?

There is only one study I know of which directly pertains to upper-class perceptions of these indicators. It was done in an unnamed town of over 50,000 population in upstate New York. It is obviously one of our towns with a Junior League chapter, although the author does not name the Junior League as the nationwide young women's service organization that she discusses. At any rate, interviews with upper-middle-class and upper-class women in this town made it quite clear that both groups used certain clubs as evidence of upper-class standing: ". . . 78% of elite respondents and 36% of peripheral respondents stated that the concrete evidence of elite position are membership in specific organizations and inclusion in the informal social functions of elite members."[12] The upper middle and the upper mingle at the country club, but only the upper are in the X Club. Anecdotal accounts suggest that there is a similar concern with club memberships in other parts of the country. And for all the snide comments made about the various social registers and blue books, it seems clear that many people take the trouble to fill out the necessary forms to be included in them. Then too, anyone who spends money on geneological searches, the "right" address, social secretaries, debutante balls, or a coat-of-arms is as indicator-conscious as the social scientist. In short, at least some members of the upper class are well aware of the assignative nature of these social institutions.

Turning to the second question, why isn't there even more overlap among the indicators? The answers are manifold, but not damaging. The important point was made earlier: no social science indicators are perfect, and they should be judged for their utility in large-scale studies and compared in their precision to similar indicators for other social science studies. On either score, I think these indicators stack up very well, but consider only the following reasons as to why they do not overlap perfectly:

1. The Social Register is published for only thirteen major cities; schools and clubs have members from all over the country.

2. An indeterminate number of upper-class people do not choose to list in the Social Register and other blue books for a variety of reasons. Some resent their anti-

---

12. Leila C. Deasy, "Social Mobility in Northtown" (Unpublished Ph.D. dissertation, Cornell University, 1953), pp. 47, 149.

semitism, some think the whole thing is "silly," and others are inverse snobs who are too good for the registers.

3. There is reason to believe that some people do not list their private schools in standard reference sources. Such is the case for Dean Acheson, Averell Harriman, and Adlai Stevenson, and for 37% of a representative sample of 168 Hotchkiss alumni listed in *Who's Who in America.*

4. Some people prefer to keep their children close to home in small private schools that are little known and hardly ever listed in standard biographical sources.

5. In some exclusive neighborhoods the suburban high schools are considered quite adequate, and only more subtle cues, such as debutante parties, socially separate the upper-middle from the upper class.

6. There are middle-class day students and scholarship students at many of the private schools. Some private schools are now recruiting among disadvantaged minority groups.

7. Some upper-class people seem to belong only to specialized clubs for fox hunting or horse showing which are not on our lists.

8. Some people may have made it big too late to have attended a private school. Our society-page respondents made it quite clear that a highly successful businessman with the right manners and attitudes could be accepted into some social clubs. (The rate of assimilation seems to vary from city to city, however.)

9. Some very middle-class people, such as university presidents and foundation officials, may be invited into one of the exclusive clubs by their employers.

None of the foregoing points casts any doubt on the value

of our social indicators. Rather, they raise interesting empirical questions about the upper class. Why are scholarship students sought by some private schools? Why aren't private schools listed in biographical sources by some members of the upper class? Is there a growing tendency to keep children in schools nearer to home rather than sending them "back East"? Why are middle-class persons asked to join the most exclusive club in the city when they become university presidents? Merely to ask these questions is to point to the complex psychosocial reality that is lying beneath this catalogue of social indicators. The indicators are the beginning, not the end, of detailed studies of the upper class.

## SUMMARY

I began by saying that not everyone agrees on the definition of social class or on the existence of an American upper class. This study sheds light on both of these problems. The consistency of our findings by different methods suggests the existence of an upper class which can be defined, operationally speaking, by its several indicators. Although I prefer a definition of "upper class" which points to the great wealth and unique life styles of these intermarrying and interacting families of high social standing, the social upper class can be defined as people who are listed in certain social registers and blue books, people who attend certain private schools, and people who belong to certain exclusive social clubs. These blue books, schools, and clubs can be used as social indicators, leading us to economic and policy-planning institutions of the upper class that are less well known than its social institutions. In the case of the schools and clubs, they also can be studied in their own right to develop a deeper understanding of the cohesiveness, consciousness and life styles of the privileged members of this group.

# CHAPTER TWO

# *The Feminine Half of the Upper Class*

There was a time, even in American history, when the wives of the rich and the well-born were mostly window dressing. This is not that time, nor has it been for over a century. The feminine half of the upper class plays a role in the functioning of the American system. In fact, upper-class women were very important between 1890 and 1920 in bringing into existence a more humane and paternalistic social system. If their role is less obvious since that time, it is perhaps even more pervasive. Among other things, the women of the upper class are fashion leaders, patrons of culture, directors of social welfare, and sustainers of the social activities that keep the upper class a social class.

Although this essay will describe the social activities and

life style of the feminine half of the upper class, it will stress the consequences of these activities for the overall operation of American society. Instead of speculating on the psychological motives of upper-class women, it will concentrate on the effects of their activities. In that sense it is a functional analysis: "Functionalism is a mode of social analysis that takes as its point of departure the notion that various social phenomena may be useful in the larger social context in ways that would not immediately strike the eye."[1]

What are some of the major ways in which the activities of upper-class women are useful in ways that would not immediately strike the eye? Most generally, their presence in a wide variety of institutions increases the participation of members of the upper class in all aspects of American culture. Assuming that these women have a somewhat unique outlook, the evidence for which will be presented shortly, this in itself is an important function when it is considered that there are only a few hundred thousand males in the country who are members of the upper class. In short, a distinctive point of view is brought to areas in which men of the upper class do not have the time or the inclination to participate.

More specifically, women of the upper class have three important functions. First, they are the mistresses of the social institutions that keep this collection of rich families an intermarrying social class. For example, they organize dancing classes, give parties, and plan charity balls. Some even serve as the "social secretaries" who organize the debutante season, counsel "new rich" families, and plan the large social functions of other wealthy families. In other words, they are the "gatekeepers" and "caretakers" of upper-class social institutions. They provide the framework within which the members of the class get to know each other.

A second function of women of the upper class is the

1. Raymond A. Bauer, Ithiel deSola Pool, and Lewis A. Dexter, *American Business and Public Policy* (New York: Atherton, 1963), p. 488.

setting of social and cultural standards for the rest of the population. They provide models for members of the underlying population to admire and emulate, whether it be in clothing or musical appreciation. Thus, for example, most if not all the Ten Best-Dressed Women of the Year are members of the upper class. This is not surprising, perhaps, for fashions are set by women of the upper class in conjunction with the magazines they work for and the designers they patronize.[2] Jackie Kennedy was the best recent example of an upper-class woman performing this function. She had a large following indeed, few of whom identified her with the less happy aspects of the social system until her recent remarriage. If anything, she was thought to be on the side of the angels on political matters, which leads directly to the third major function of the feminine half of the upper class: its involvement in welfare movements which attempt to improve the lot of the general population.

In blunt language, women of the upper class have served an important function by helping to take some of the roughest edges off a profit-oriented business system that has cared little for specific human needs. Beginning in the 1890's, some upper-class women argued for protective labor legislation, for minimum wages, and for a more respectful treatment of labor. They fought especially for these measures on behalf of their feminine counterparts from the other side of the tracks, but much of their activity also benefited male workers. As will be shown, well-known names such as Harriman and Morgan and Hanna were part of these developments. Today the daughters and granddaughters of these "progressives" are active in the Junior League, on hospital boards, and as directors of a wide variety of welfare organizations, thereby continuing this longstanding blueblood tradition of guiding social welfare and recreational activities for the less fortunate.

2. Marilyn Bender, *The Beautiful People* (New York: Coward-McCann, 1967), for evidence of this involvement in the fashion world.

These general functions stated, it is time to turn to a description of life in the feminine half of the upper class. This description will provide concrete evidence for the assertions I have made about the role these women play. It is based primarily upon a study of *Who's Who of American Women*, the alumnae bulletins of exclusive girls' schools, autobiographies and biographies, and popular books and magazine articles on "high society."

GIRLS' SCHOOLS

The little girl of the upper class tends to lead a very different life from her middle-class and lower-class peers. First, there is the possibility that she will have a nurse or governess in the early years. Then there is the exclusive kindergarten at the nearby Episcopal Church, accompanied or followed shortly by special dancing classes, riding lessons, and introduction to a foreign language. Perhaps the most obvious difference from other little girls is that she attends a private primary school in her city. There are few if any large cities where these "day schools" do not exist, and they are very important in bringing the young lady of the upper class to realize that she is set apart from the great number of people who attend the public schools.[3]

Not all girls may follow this regimen, and the Presbyterian Church or Unitarian Church may be substituted for the Episcopalian one in many cases. However, it does seem likely that most upper-class girls go off to boarding school for at least a year or two when they reach their early teens. There are several dozen such schools around the country, although only a handful are well known. It is at these schools that the young lady mingles with her "own kind"

3. "Private Schools Search for a New Social Role" (*The National Observer*, August 26, 1968), p. 5, reports that .5% of students attend private schools (exclusive of parochial schools) in the United States.

from all over the country in a relatively isolated setting, often learning distinctive sports and hobbies, and in the process, becoming even more aware of her unique class position. The schools make every effort to arrange social occasions with the private schools for males, thus providing some of the acquaintance circles within which upper-class intermarriages take place. Many of these schools also provide work on projects with the underprivileged, preparing the girl for her later activity as a volunteer and civic worker.

Most of these schools seem to be very good academically, with a great many of their students going on to further education. A survey of Chatham Hall alumnae, for example, showed that 90% of the graduates who returned the questionnaire had continued their education. About three-fourths of those who went on to four-year colleges had completed their degrees, while 70% of those entering junior colleges completed the two-year program.[4]

## COLLEGES AND UNIVERSITIES

There are some upper-class women at most major universities in the country, but they do tend to concentrate at a relatively small number of exclusive institutions. There are first of all such well-known girls' schools as Vassar, Smith and Wellesley in the New England-New York area, but there are also such places as Hollins and Sophie Newcomb in the South, and Colorado Women's College, Scripps, and Mills in the West. For girls desiring a less demanding atmosphere, there are a covey of "high-society" finishing colleges such as Finch, Pine Manor, Bennett, Bradford, and Briarcliff. As noted, some of the major co-educational universities also attract upper-class women, where they tend to be concentrated in certain exclusive sororities which are

4. Winston Case Wright and Louise Gillam Hopkins, "Questions & Answers," *The Chat* (circa 1966), p. 3.

well known on the respective campuses. A one best guess for many campuses would be Kappa Kappa Gamma.

If the girl remained in the private day school in her city rather than going off to boarding school, college is often her first major contact with counterparts from all over the country. Female graduates of Tulsa's Holland Hall in 1966 and 1967, for example, went to Briarcliff, Bradford, Mount Holyoke, Pembroke, Randolph Macon Women's College, Sophie Newcomb, Sullins, and Vassar, as well as universities in the Southwest. Needless to say, these exclusive girls' schools provide a variety of opportunities for their students to mingle socially with males of similar standing.

## THE DEBUT

Somewhere between her graduation from private school and the beginning of her sophomore year in college, the upper-class girl "comes out" at a debutante party. Basing their account on the reports of informants, two University of Pennsylvania sociologists have described this classic "rite of passage" in considerable detail for the city of Philadelphia.[5] What comparative information is available suggests that the occasion is not greatly different in other parts of the country.[6] Once again, the debut is an event almost completely distinctive to members of the upper class, and it further reinforces the sense of belonging to a separate social group.

The exact nature of the debut can vary slightly. For some it may involve a tea or small dinner dance; for others it may mean a very large party costing up to $250,000. In most cities there are also one or more debutante balls which the debs of the "season" attend. The debutante affairs usu-

5. James H. S. Bossard and Eleanor S. Boll, "Rite of Passage—A Contemporary Study" (*Social Forces*, March, 1948).
6. E.g., Lucy Kavaler, *The Private World of High Society* (New York: David McKay Co., 1960), Chapter 8.

ally take place in June, early September, or the Christmas holidays. The overall picture in each city is one of a considerable number of individual parties and two or three major dances at which upper-class youths between eighteen and twenty-two do a great deal of socializing.

## THE JUNIOR LEAGUE

The debut and the Junior League are often intimately related. In New York, for example, the Junior League sponsors a debutante ball, the proceeds of which go to charity. In smaller cities entrance into the Junior League may even substitute for the "coming-out" occasion. Founded in New York in 1901, the Junior League is one of the few nationwide organizations of the upper class. Mary Harriman, a sister of Averell Harriman, is the person most frequently credited with inspiring the organization, but she had the assistance of several other New York socialites. The league was meant to be a service organization, and it has maintained this objective throughout its history. Indeed, members of the Junior League do not like it to be considered as a society organization. They insist upon its assistance orientation. Nevertheless, it does have a very exclusive membership according to a great deal of testimony and evidence. Of two hundred Junior Leaguers in our sample of women listed in the 1965 *Who's Who of American Women* (a sample which consists of names beginning with the first nine letters in the alphabet), sixty were listed in the Social Register. When it is added that the Junior League has about 215 chapters with 95,000 members, this is a considerable overlap. On the other hand, it seems likely that the Junior League has a significant minority of upper-middle class women, particularly in smaller towns.

The Junior League is meant for young ladies between twenty and forty years of age. Shortly after the debut, the society matron is given a six-week training course and then accepted as a "provisional" member. Thus, she is early brought into the type of activities for which her private school training has prepared her. When she reaches the age of forty she often becomes a "sustaining" member of the league, contributing advice and money. At this time she also may become more involved in social welfare activities that are traditionally directed by older women.

The activities of the Junior League are varied. A good overview is provided in the 1966 annual progress report which appears in the *Junior League Magazine,* a bi-monthly publication of the league which keeps members informed about the activities of other chapters and presents information about national meetings and new projects. The progress report organizes league activities under the headings arts and humanities, health and welfare, education, films-TV-radio, and children's theater-puppetry.[7] As an example of an arts and humanities project, the Junior League of San Diego helped to coordinate programs at the city museums with the school curriculum, including the arrangement of bus trips to the museum for disadvantaged children. The Topeka chapter provides an example of service under health and welfare in its co-sponsorship with the county juvenile court of a community foster home, while the Leaguers in San Francisco are developing a program whereby volunteers can work with the city's Department of Social Services. Junior Leaguers are involved in education via tutoring programs in many cities, including a pre-school program in Dallas for disadvantaged children of Latin-American descent.

As noted, there were two hundred Junior Leaguers in

7. Rita McGaughey, "Annual Progress Report: Vitality Depends on Challenge and Response" (*Junior League Magazine,* September–October, 1966), pp. 16–21; Stephen Birmingham, *The Right People* (Boston: Little, Brown, & Co., 1968), Chapter 8, provides useful information and questionable anecdotes on the Junior League; Kavaler, *op. cit.,* Chapter 9, also gives details on Junior League activities.

the A-I listings of *Who's Who in American Women*. Their brief biographies suggest that for many of these women the Junior League is only one of their activities. They also are active in other welfare organizations, opera and symphony associations, alumni associations, and garden clubs. In short, as shall be elaborated in the next section, at least some members of the upper class are very much involved in the day-to-day management of American society.

## "WORK"

As might be expected, most upper-class girls marry and raise children. However, many also work at various stages in their life cycles. From our study of the upper-class women in our *Who's Who in American Women* sample and of the alumnae bulletins of several major private schools, the following occupations stand out:

1. "Civic worker." This means that the woman is a long-time volunteer worker or official in one of the many welfare and civic organizations in which women of the upper class participate. For example, Mrs. E. Roland Harriman, wife of the investment banker who once headed the American Red Cross, is listed as a civic worker. She is a member of the Women's Committee of the American Museum of Natural History and the former chairman of the Women's Committee of the Boy's Club of New York (1923–46).

2. Authors and artists. I have not tried to find out more about the work of women so designated, taking the report at face value. One such person added that she is a contributor to *The Saturday Review, The New York Times,* and the *Christian Science Monitor*. It seems likely that this classification shades into the next one, journalism.

3. Journalism. Upper-class women are involved in both the management and writing of newspapers and magazines. This includes society-page reporting, which may explain the usefulness of many of our reports from that source. Upper-class women also work for *Vogue* and other fashion and society magazines.

4. Academic positions. Women of the upper class are found as scholars, administrators and trustees at leading boarding schools and colleges for women. To take a prominent example, a recent chairman of the board of trustees at Radcliffe was Helen Homans Gilbert (*Social Register,* Boston), wife of a business leader, sister of a prominent sociologist and descendant on her mother's side of John Adams. Then, too, upper-class women sometimes teach in schools for the handicapped and underprivileged.

5. Business. A small number of women take part in the family business. The role they play probably varies from ceremonial to quite important.

6. Physicians. To our surprise, we have found a small handful of physicians in our samples. One of the most notable is Mrs. A. A. Berle, Jr. Although she inherited several million dollars, she still went on to earn a B.A. from Vassar, an M.A. from Columbia, and an M.D. from New York University. She has been very active in her field.

The aforementioned survey of Chatham Hall graduates provides further information on the occupational proclivities of upper-class women. With 32% of the 1,683 alumnae responding, it was found that 20% of those presently employed were involved in one way or another in education, while 16% were in business or banking, and 12% were in medicine as physicians, nurses, or technicians. Four-fifths of the respondents were involved in volunteer activities, 24% through churches and 23% through the

Junior League. Symphonies and operas were the concern of 29% of the sample; art museums and similar civic associations were helped by 27%.[8]

## "PLAY"

I do not want to imply that all women of the upper class are well-educated and hard-working. Obviously, many are neither. Some drop out after a year at a school like Briarcliff and become part of the "jet set," spending their time decorating their town houses, partying, buying clothes, and traveling around the world. Such clotheshorses and jet setters, who usually gravitate to New York from all over the country, provide many of the social settings within which harder-working members of the upper class often spend an evening or a weekend. They are sometimes celebrated in the newspapers and other mass media, and they love to be seen with and amused by entertainers, authors, artists, and certain kinds of athletic heroes.

The distinction between "civic workers" and "playgirls" is not clearcut and permanent. Many women are both, or have been one and then the other at different times in their lives. Some of the "new elegants" make a virtue out of their nighttime pleasures by donating the proceeds of their dances and parties to the charities and welfare groups that they work for and direct by day.[9] The Chatham Hall survey found that many of the women involved in other activities "play golf twice a week, tennis every afternoon . . ."[10]

Many of the social activities of upper-class women take place in and around a set of social clubs that parallel the

8. Wright and Hopkins, *op. cit.*, pp. 3–5; Joan W. Moore, "Exclusiveness and Ethnocentrism in a Metropolitan Upper-Class Agency" (*Pacific Sociological Review,* Spring, 1962) presents an excellent description of the activities of upper-class women in Chicago.
9. "The New Elegants" (*Time,* December 4, 1964), p. 54; Kavaler, *op. cit.*, p. 44.
10. Wright and Hopkins, *op. cit.*, p. 5.

male-only clubs of their husbands and brothers. The first one seems to have been founded in Philadelphia in 1889, with many others following along in the next several decades. Perhaps the most famous of such clubs is the Colony Club in New York, which was founded in 1903 by Mrs. Borden Harriman and her friends with the advice of a prominent clubman, J. P. Morgan.[11] Other chronicled clubs of this nature are the Chilton and Vincent in Boston, the Acorn in Philadelphia, and the Sulgrave in Washington, but there are similar exclusive organizations in many other major cities. In some places, garden clubs provide this social setting.

Jet setting, golfing, and spending time at the club do not exhaust the pleasurable possibilities available to the feminine half of the upper class. Rich ladies also relax with sports that involve boats, horses, and pedigreed dogs. One source summarizes a great deal of what I have been saying when it notes:

> This is the world of careful attention to "correct" dress (even though in certain groups that may mean carefully looking a little careless), of familiarity with certain forms of etiquette and social custom, of being on speaking terms with sailing, swimming, tennis, bridge, horseback riding, ballroom dancing, pedigreed animal breeding, and of facile social conversation.[12]

From birth to adulthood, then, whether at work or play, the feminine half of the upper class lives in a world apart from those without wealth.

## UPPER-CLASS WOMEN AND PROGRESSIVISM

At the outset of this essay I listed three sociological functions of upper-class women. The first two of these functions

11. Florence J. (Hurst) Harriman, *From Pinafores to Politics* (New York: H. Holt & Co., 1923), pp. 16, 75–6.
12. Bossard and Boll, *op. cit.*, p. 250.

—sustainers of the social institutions that help make the upper class a social class and fashion setters for the rest of the society—need not be belabored. Instead, I want to concentrate on their important role in social welfare, for their activities in this area are less obvious and less well known. The high point of this involvement was during the Progressive Era. An accounting of their involvement in this turn-of-the-century movement not only demonstrates the important role played by women but calls into question the notion that Progressivism was led by an old, status-frustrated middle class against a new plutocracy.[13]

Although upper-class women had taken a growing part in charity and welfare work throughout the nineteenth century, the best starting point for our purposes is the settlement house movement. In the late 1880's and early 1890's upper-class women in Chicago and New York, partly inspired by British experiments they had encountered in their European travels, founded missions to the poor in rambling old houses in crowded downtown tenement areas. Some of the women lived in these houses, providing a wide variety of services to the families in the neighborhood, services ranging from playgrounds and courses on hygiene to discussion groups on the problems of the day. The settlement houses served other functions besides their ministry to the day-to-day needs of the poor. First, they provided meaningful work for idealistic scions in their late teens and early twenties and for concerned young adults who wanted to do something significant with their considerable education. Jane Addams, the greatest leader of this movement, expressed this motivation very openly in discussing the events leading to the founding of her Hull House in Chicago in 1889. Similarly, the upper-class women who financed the activities of the houses often made it quite clear to the mothers of young socialites and to potential benefactors

13. Richard Hofstadter, *The Age of Reform* (New York: Alfred A. Knopf, 1956), Chapter IV.

that the movement was not entirely an idealistic undertaking. It also provided a place for oversensitive girls to gain perspective.[14]

A second function of the settlement houses was that they inspired hope in the leaders from other levels of the population. Heartened by the activities of Jane Addams and the many like her, leaders from the lower levels of society in effect concluded that a system which produced such decent and humane people could not be all bad. They were saved from despair over their incredible working and living conditions and perhaps from more radical action. This point is made most directly in the autobiography of Mary Anderson, a Swedish immigrant of peasant stock who rose to be head of the Women's Bureau of the Department of Labor:

> We began to feel that we were part of something that was more important than just our own problems. For me, and I think for many others too, Hull House and Jane Addams opened a door to a larger life.[15]

Closely related to this function was a third: the settlement houses provided a meeting ground for leaders of the upper and working classes. Members of the upper class such as Gerard Swope, Herbert Lehman and A. A. Berle, Jr., who were later to play important roles in the New Deal, learned about the masses at first hand from their settlement house experience, while working-class leaders such as Sidney Hillman made contact with the moderates of the upper class. It was in the settlement houses, for example, that an upper-class physician who was a leader in creating better working conditions, Alice Hamilton, learned things about the working class that are probably well understood by moderate leaders of the upper class:

14. John C. Farrell, *Beloved Lady* (Baltimore: Johns Hopkins Press, 1967), pp. 56–9.
15. Mary Anderson and Mary Winslow, *Woman at Work* (Minneapolis: University of Minnesota Press, 1951), p. 32.

If one's contact with the poor is only through their organizations, their clubs and trade-unions, one gets a very one-sided, distorted impression of the working class, which contains not only rebel youth but conservative middle age, not only the radical leader but his wife, who cares more for a nice flat and an electric refrigerator than for the emancipation of workers. . . . When I heard my wealthy friends speak of the spread of Bolshevism and the imminent danger of revolution, I would think of the families I knew, their devotion to their hard-won little properties, their reverence for property rights, their instinctive fear of change, their absorption in everyday life, and revolution seemed pretty remote. . . . I think it is the undying hope of better times coming which keeps our poor from the desperation that drives men to revolt.[16]

The importance of this meeting-ground function will be made even clearer when I describe the Women's Trade Union League, an upper-class women's organization closely related to the settlement house movement. However, as an example of the point I am making, it was Jane Addams of Hull House and the even wealthier Mary McDowell of University Settlement who interceded with their friend Ogden Armour when a deadlock developed in a stockyard strike of 1904. These young ladies knew the labor leaders from their settlement houses and the business leaders from their social activities and were able to convince Armour and his counterparts to at least discuss matters with the labor leaders.[17]

Most of the men and women who came to live in the settlement houses were young adults who stayed for only two or three years. They are described by one source as moderately well-to-do old-stock Americans, most of whom

16. Alice Hamilton, *Exploring the Dangerous Trades* (Boston: Little, Brown, and Co., 1943), p. 73. Dr. Hamilton recalls on the same page how Upton Sinclair told her with "quiet conviction" that the next President would be a socialist, but he turned out to be McKinley.

17. Allen F. Davis, *Spearheads for Reform* (New York: Oxford University Press, 1967), pp. 117–19.

were Presbyterians, Episcopalians, or Congregationalists.[18] However, where we have been able to find information on the people mentioned in these accounts, it would be more accurate to describe them as wealthy by the standards of their time. Socially, they were members of the upper class. Jane Addams, for example, was the daughter of one of the richest men in northern Illinois. She was a college graduate who had traveled widely in Europe and participated in the social life of Baltimore. Her friends in Chicago were of the social elite, and she was a member of the Friday Club, an exclusive club for women.[19] Her stepbrother, Harry Haldeman, who married her sister, was a socialite from Baltimore who went on to make a larger fortune in Kansas City. The situation is similar for Julia Lathrop, Mary McDowell, Alice Hamilton, Lillian Wald, Mary Simkhovitch, and many other of the leading names of the settlement house movement. Mary Kingsbury Simkhovitch, who married a Russian-born intellectual, was from an "old" family with varied connections. Her uncle had been with the Pennsylvania Railroad and the Interstate Commerce Commission, and she had a cousin who was the one-time head of Standard Oil of California.[20]

It there is doubt about the upper-class standing of women who ran the settlement houses, there is not the slightest about the men and women who financed their efforts. Very simply, they were the richest men and women of their day. In the case of Hull House, the names that would be best-known today are Anita McCormick of the harvester fortune and Julius Rosenwald of Sears, Roebuck.[21] Three of the key

18. *Ibid.*, pp. 14, 27, 33, 35.
19. James W. Linn, *Jane Addams: A Biography* (New York: D. Appleton Century Co., 1935); Hamilton, *op. cit.*, p. 67; Moore, *op. cit.*, p. 17.
20. Mary K. Simkhovitch, *Neighborhood* (New York: W. W. Norton & Co., 1938), Chapter 1 and p. 296. See pages 102, 179, 265, and 282–83 for the financial help given by Morgans, Harrimans, and Rockefellers to her work.
21. Linn, *op. cit.*, pp. 94, 104, 115; Robert M. Lovett, *All Our Years* (New York: Viking Press, 1948), p. 226. Another interesting backer

angels of the Henry Street Settlement in New York were Mrs. Solomon Loeb, Jacob Schiff (Mrs. Loeb's son-in-law), and John Crosby Brown, a leader of a finance house (now Brown Brothers, Harriman) that got its start in the early nineteenth century.[22] Foundations such as the Julius Rosenwald Fund and the Milbank Memorial Fund also were helpful.[23]

Closely related to the settlement house movement was the growth of social work as a profession. Originally the province of rich young ladies and charity organizations, such work is now institutionalized as a middle-class profession that was created by members of the upper class. As this transition occurred, the upper-class ladies became known as civic workers and the middle-class professionals took over the term "social workers." Although there are some people who separately from the settlement house movement helped to develop social work, there was considerable overlap in directors, and the settlement houses provided training grounds and personnel for the profession.

The social work movement developed in New York and spread across the country. It was first formalized and centralized in the Charity Organizing Services headed by New York members of the upper class. Many of the same people also were involved in the Russell Sage Foundation, which was started with a $10 million bequest by Mrs. Sage in 1907. This foundation played a leading role in the development of the social work profession, providing grants and office space for several organizations and financing various social work publications. In short, a history of social work in terms of leaders and financial backers

---

of Hull House was Mary H. Wilmarth, mother-in-law of New Dealer Harold Ickes. Her grandson, Raymond Ickes, is president of the American President Lines.

22. Beryl Williams, *Lillian Wald* (New York: Julian Messner, Inc., 1948), pp. 83, 108.

23. Lillian Wald, *Windows on Henry Street* (Boston: Little, Brown, & Co., 1934), p. 117.

makes it clear that the present involvement of upper-class women in welfare activities is not a new direction for the feminine half of the upper class.[24]

Two organizations were founded around the turn of the century that epitomize feminine involvement in making the social system less abrasive for its less privileged. The first was the National Consumers' League, the second the Women's Trade Union League. The NCL was founded in 1899, growing out of the New York Consumers' League that had been formed in 1891. It was the women's organization (there were some men involved) that worked most closely with the other upper-class organizations responsible for developing the reform measures that ameliorated working conditions in the early twentieth century. The rich and well-born leaders of the League looked to one of their own for the vigorous leadership necessary to put its programs into action. She was Florence Kelley, who is credited by many commentators as being second only to Jane Addams among the women who helped to better conditions for working families and their children in the industrializing cities. The fact that Florence Kelley considered herself a socialist of what she called the inch-along variety apparently did not deter the board, although it horrified more conservative members of the upper class who were a little suspicious of the League in the first place.[25]

Most settlement house workers and NCL members were very sympathetic to the problems of labor, but they were

24. Edward T. Devine, *When Social Work Was Young* (New York: Macmillan Company, 1939), pp. 21–23, 30–31; John M. Glenn, *The Russell Sage Foundation, 1907–1946* (New York: Russell Sage Foundation, 1947), pp. 8–9, 158, 223–24, 400; Roy Lubove, *The Professional Altruist* (Cambridge: Harvard University Press, 1965), pp. 180ff, 208ff.

25. Clarke A. Chambers, *Seedtime of Reform* (Minneapolis: University of Minnesota Press, 1963), pp. 4–8; Maud Nathan, *The Story of an Epoch-Making Movement* (New York: Doubleday, Page & Co., 1926); Josephine Goldmark, "50 Years—The National Consumers' League" (*The Survey*, December, 1949), p. 675; Josephine Goldmark, *The Impatient Crusader* (Urbana, Illinois: University of Illinois Press, 1953).

not all equally sympathetic to labor unions. Those who were pro-union banded together in one of the most interesting and least-known of upper-class organizations, the Women's Trade Union League. Formed and directed by upper-class men and women, it also included working-class girls.[26] Its most important leader from 1907 to 1921 was Margaret Dreier Robbins, Republican daughter of a wealthy Brooklyn businessman. She often worked closely with her socialist friend Florence Kelley, and it was difficult if not impossible to distinguish the goals and methods of the two leaders.[27] In addition to providing literature, finances and moral support, the socialites of the WTUL also went into the streets with their working-class sisters on at least one occasion. Some were even arrested.[28] However, I do not want to overstate the prevalence of that sort of activity. More typical were such things as Mrs. Franklin Roosevelt and her friend Mrs. Thomas Lamont (wife of a Morgan partner) raising $30,000 for the WTUL clubhouse in New York.[29]

The WTUL and its activities are significant for two reasons. First, they gave some workers hope of a decent life within the confines of the present system. Once again it was Jane Addams who best symbolized this hope for a member of the working class. In this case the person in question was Irish worker Mary Kenny O'Sullivan, a leader in the activities of the Women's Trade Union League as well as an early participant in the settlement houses:

> It was that word "with" from Jane Addams that took the bitterness out of my life. For if she wanted to work with me

26. Gladys Boone, *The Women's Trade Union Leagues in Great Britain and the United States of America* (New York: Columbia University Press, 1942); Allen F. Davis, "The Women's Trade Union League: Origins and Organization" (*Labor History*, Winter, 1964).
27. Davis, *op. cit.*, p. 15; Chambers, *op. cit.*, p. 7.
28. Davis, *op. cit.*, p. 16.
29. Eleanor Roosevelt and Lorena Hickok, *Ladies of Courage* (New York: G. P. Putnam's Sons, 1954), p. 262.

and [if] I could work with her, it gave my life new meaning and hope.[30]

All accounts of Mary Kenny O'Sullivan suggest that she was quite a person to have on your side, for she was a born agitator and organizer. She was the WTUL's first secretary; Jane Addams was vice president, and Mary McDowell of University Settlement, and Lillian Wald of the Henry Street Settlement were on the board.

The WTUL, then, interacted with the leaders of the female working class. It bound them to women in the upper class with pro-union sympathies. The relationship was not totally one-sided; the working-class girls did not give up something for nothing, for the second function of the WTUL was that it forced some corporate leaders to rethink certain of their positions. The silk-stocking labor agitators humanized and personalized the labor problem. No more was it a mere question of economics and principles, but a question of starving children and overworked women, and of the well-born women on whom so much conspicuous consumption was lavished calling into question the morality of their husbands. If this was not the most important variable in the complicated equation that led to a moderate thrust within the corporate leadership, it was certainly a factor. I agree with historian Allen Davis in lamenting the fact that historians of the Progressive Era have overlooked the significant role of the Women's Trade Union League.[31]

More generally, the role of upper-class women in the settlement houses, social work, the National Consumers' League and the Women's Trade Union League perhaps raises problems for the thesis that the Progressive movement was spearheaded by old-line members of the moderately wealthy middle class who were fighting the new plutocracy out of status envy. The presence of so many rich and very

30. Davis, *op. cit.*, p. 16.
31. *Ibid.*, pp. 16–17.

rich women, financially backed by the leading financiers and foundations of the day, suggests that moderate elements within the upper class are the key to the social reforms of Progressivism.[32] They were aided of course by middle-class professionals, but the money and prestige of the upper-class leaders gave the movement whatever reforming impetus it had. For those who might want to use the term "middle class" very broadly, thus restricting the term "upper class" to the handful of super-wealthy families within the upper class, the active presence of J. P. Morgan's daughter, E. H. Harriman's daughter, Mark Hanna's daughter, Jacob Schiff's mother-in-law, Cyrus McCormick's daughter, Borden Harriman's wife, and O. H. P. Belmont's wife, among others, still casts considerable doubt on any interpretation of Progressivism that does not recognize the central role played by the very rich in a movement which led to what Gabriel Kolko calls "the triumph of conservatism."[33]

The militancy of the settlement house movement died down in the 1920's. Several reasons can be adduced for this. First, in a certain sense the movement had accomplished what it had set out to do, and the time and energy of its supporters went elsewhere. Carnegie libraries, playgrounds, city museums, and professional social workers took over many of its functions. Second, and closely related, there was considerable prosperity during the twenties, and many key financial backers of the movement felt that their support was no longer necessary. Third, I suspect that many problems that remained required solutions which most members of the upper class were not willing to undertake or tolerate.

32. Chambers, *op. cit.*, p. 53, points, for example, to the role of the Russell Sage Foundation, Rockefeller Foundation, Commonwealth Fund, and many other foundations in financing child welfare programs.
33. Gabriel Kolko, *The Triumph of Conservatism: A Reinterpretation of American History, 1900–1916* (New York: Free Press of Glencoe, 1963); Gabriel Kolko, "Brahmins and Business, 1870–1914: A Hypothesis on the Social Basis of Success in American History." In *The Critical Spirit: Essays in Honor of Herbert Marcuse,* Kurt H. Wolff and Barrington Moore, Jr., eds. (Boston: Beacon Press, 1967).

Functionally speaking, reform-oriented leaders of the upper class had gone about as far as they were willing to go under the circumstances.[34]

However, the movement did not suddenly collapse overnight. It merely declined in importance and faded quietly into the background. Its most important leaders continued their programs and were leading figures in the New Deal. Among the most prominent names of the hundreds of settlement house-NCL-WTUL people who went to Washington in the thirties were Secretary of Labor Frances Perkins of the NCL, Social Security Board member Molly Dewson of the NCL, Assistant Secretary of the Treasury Josephine Roche of the NCL, and Labor Advisory Board member Rose Schneiderman of the WTUL.[35]

In recent years there have been no heroic efforts in the area of human betterment by any large number of upper-class women, who seem to have less direct contact with the poor than did their counterparts of the Progressive Era. However, routine efforts continue in this general area through the Junior League, the Red Cross, Planned Parenthood, hospital boards, and child welfare agencies.

## UPPER-CLASS WOMEN AND POLITICS

Contrary to my original expectations, the feminine half of the upper class does not seem to play a very prominent role in political parties. There are some very prominent exceptions, such as Eleanor Roosevelt, Mrs. Borden Harriman, Marietta Peabody Tree, Frances Bolton, Eugenie Anderson and Mary Pillsbury Lord, but very little systematic involvement in important positions within the parties. On the basis

34. Davis, *Spearheads for Reform, op. cit.,* pp. 230–35, discusses the first two points in this paragraph.
35. Chambers, *op. cit.,* pp. 254–57, for some of the many New Dealers who came out of this tradition.

of a statement by Mrs. Roosevelt, I had expected to find otherwise: "Too often the selection of a national committee-woman is based on her bank account, social prestige, or party service rendered by a deceased husband."[36] The national committeewomen may have to possess more than the usual amount of money, but our study of the one hundred women performing this function in 1966 turned up only one or two upper-class women among those on whom information could be found. Nor did our study of every woman listed in *Who's Who in American Politics* reveal more than a small handful of upper-class participants. Junior Leaguers were conspicuous by their absence in this middle-class population, and the few that did appear had very minor posts. Among our meager findings were the many upper-class credentials of TV performer Betty Furness, who served as President Johnson's Special Assistant for Consumer Affairs.

There is reason to believe that some upper-class women play a minor role at more mundane levels of the party struc-tures. For example, 41% of the respondents in the study of Chatham Hall alumnae "have done every conceivable job on local, state and/or national levels."[37] Of the 8% who have held a political office, most have done so in a party organization. There is also some indication that a study of the leadership of the League of Women Voters and the World Affairs Council might turn up a number of upper-class women with political interests, but we did not think the matter worth pursuing. The feminine half of the upper class does not seem to include a direct involvement in the political parties among its functions.[38]

36. Roosevelt and Hickok, *op. cit.*, p. 38.
37. Wright and Hopkins, *op. cit.*, p. 4.
38. Martin Gruberg, *Women in American Politics* (Oshkosh, Wisconsin: Academia Press, 1968) presents a very complete accounting of women's participation in all aspects of the American political process, including some biographical information on women who have served in important positions in Washington.

## SUMMARY

The American upper class is based upon large corporate wealth that is looked after by male members of the inter-marrying families that are its basis. However, it also includes a feminine half that must be taken into account if we are to understand the upper class as a social class. This essay has shown that the women of the upper class are socialized through a set of unique institutions that are quite distinctive to their social group, and that as adults they participate in a great many activities which sustain the upper class as a social class and help to maintain the stability of the social system as a whole.

# CHAPTER THREE

# The Jet Set, Celebrities, and the Upper Class

When most people think about the jet set, they picture rich playboys and movie stars, but they don't connect it with responsible big businessmen and the upper class. This, I believe, is an important mistake which publicists and writers of high society do very little to correct. However, it is not only publicists who make this misleading distinction. It also was made by one of this country's best and most critical social scientists of recent times, C. Wright Mills. In his *The Power Elite* he treats the celebrities as something apart from the power elite, except for the fact that they provide diversion and entertainment for the masses while the power elite go about their business. They have a function in bedazzling the populace. They provide the familiar "bread and circuses" offered by a successful ruling group, but they are not themselves an integral part of the power elite.[1]

In this instance I think Mills mistaken. I hope to show that more than he realized, what is now called the "jet set" remains very much based in the social upper class, and that many of its primary players also function as important businessmen. Mills' difficulties in his conception of the world of the celebrity were several. First, he felt there have been several changes over the past few decades which in fact have not occurred. For example, he distinguishes an "institutional elite" from the upper class. This essay will present evidence that such a distinction is not justified—much of the institutional elite comes from the upper class. Second, he equates upper class with the Social Register and then asserts that the number of upper-class people taking part in the high life is declining. Here I am afraid that he did not look closely enough at the names listed in the magazine sources that he cites. Then too, the Social Register is only one possible index of upper-class standing. In short, a careful study of the leading names in the world of café society and jet set society over the past thirty years shows that members of the upper class continue to play the lead role.

Mills also makes the mistake of defining the celebrities as a group apart from both the upper class and the institutional elite. In fact, this is not the case, at least for many of the celebrities mentioned in the sources he relies upon. Our studies suggest that many of the celebrities who are big names in high society have come from or married into the upper class. Nor did Mills inquire deeply enough into the attitude of members of the upper class toward publicity. He

1. C. Wright Mills, *The Power Elite* (New York: Oxford University Press, 1956), Chapter 4. The research and comments of Duncan Graham, an undergraduate assistant, were of great value in developing this essay.

seems to think that most members of the upper class are very concerned with publicity, and that many are upset over the rise of celebrities: "But it is also true that the old certainty of position is no longer so firm among those who 'do not care' to enter the ranks of the new celebrated."[2] I suspect that things are not nearly so uncertain here as Mills claims. The status of the wealthy is based upon much firmer foundations than newspaper and magazine publicity, and the style of the American upper class, going back into the early nineteenth century, has never been that publicity oriented. It may be true, as Mills claims with an approving quote from John Adams, that men thirst for admiration and esteem, but the important question is the reference group from which they seek it. It seems to me that the American rich are out to impress each other and the people with whom they come in contact, not the American populace as a whole through nationwide publicity.

Mills' emphasis on the importance of publicity to the status of members of the upper class leads him to mistake the fluff of the debutante ritual for its substance. He claims it has tried to compete with the movie stars, turning therefore to large subscription dances. In fact, the small coming-out parties are still given, with the large dances playing a unifying role for the debs of the season. That no debs appeared on the cover of *Life* during the war-torn forties, which Mills uses as evidence for the decline of the deb, is certainly not surprising. It also overlooks the thirteen articles on debutantes that appeared in *Life* between 1945 and 1955. More generally, our study of articles on debutantes listed in the *Reader's Guide* between 1930 and 1968 gives no reason to believe that debutantes are any more or less celebrated than they ever were. In any case, as made

2. *Ibid.*, p. 78. A few pages later Mills says the power elite may be content to let the celebrities have the stage. This is not a contradiction because Mills does not see a great overlap between the upper class and the power elite.

clear in the previous essay, the debutante ball never has been a search for publicity in the larger society; it is an in-group function. And when Mills quotes a magazine source as saying that modeling schools "have raised modeling to such a glamor pinnacle that eligible men would far rather have a Powers or Conover girl on the arm, or in the home, than one of the bluebloods," he is taking a mere journalistic puff much too seriously.[3]

Mills puts the cart before the horse in the case of "café society," the term for the high life that preceded the now-familiar jet set. Café society was not founded upon publicity, but rather café society made good copy. It was news when certain members of the upper class decided to go night clubbing and to hobnob with "the stars." Nor is it accurate to say that "Nowadays, café society often seems to be the top of such American society as is on national view."[4] A reading of any society page makes it quite clear that this is not so. Teas, parties, the races, dog shows, and charity balls are still considered much more chic. It also puts too much emphasis upon New York City, which is a mecca for rich playboys from all over the country. A society editor in the "hinterlands" volunteered the following information in reply to the questionnaire on upper-class schools and clubs that I sent to newspapers all over the country:

> . . . our stable society is liberally laced with fourth and fifth generation families, still decision-makers and leaders in both business and society. . . . Most of the Old Family money has been around long enough so that the descendants hardly think about it. If they want to SWING, descendants go to Europe, New York, or Somewhere Else to do it.

Let me now turn to the evidence on which I base these several criticisms of Mills. We first of all studied in great detail all the names listed in the 1937 *Fortune* article on café society, for Mills makes a great deal out of its testi-

3. *Ibid.*, p. 81.
4. *Ibid.*, p. 73.

mony.[5] Our study shows that it is not true that "its inhabitants do not have dinner rights in a few exclusive homes. . . ."[6] Out of 167 names in the article, 80% meet one or another of our criteria of upper classness. Aside from the presence of a great many members of very wealthy families, the first important finding is that several of the names on the list are leading businessmen of the time. These include George F. Baker, Walter P. Chrysler, Jr., James Forrestal and Averell Harriman, to name the most prominent corporate leaders who were frequenting the café circuit. The second finding is that even the celebrities in the group were often of the upper class. For example, cartoonist Peter Arno was a Hotchkiss graduate, Fred Astaire and Irving Berlin married upper-class girls, and Tallulah Bankhead and Cole Porter were from upper-class families.[7] When Mills says that boxer Gene Tunney could make it into society in the thirties whereas an earlier fight hero could not, he overlooks Tunney's marriage in 1928 to a wealthy and socially-connected member of the upper class, not to mention his subsequent career as a businessman.[8] There were of course people of middle-class standing on the list. One was the famous party-giver Elsa Maxwell, whose efforts were underwritten by a coterie of upper-class women. Another was actor Clifton Webb, a middle-class boy from Indiana who changed his name and became quite good at playing a well-mannered aristocratic type.

As noted, Mills claims there has been a decline in upper class participation in café society. The bases of this assertion are two. First, he accepts *Fortune's* statement that only two-thirds of café society are in the Social Register as

5. "The Yankee Doodle Saloon" (*Fortune,* December, 1937).
6. Mills, *op. cit.,* p. 73.
7. Leo Rosten, *Hollywood: The Movie Colony* (New York: Harcourt, Brace, and Co., 1941), p. 166, gives six examples of marriages between socialites and movie stars of that era.
8. Mills, *op. cit.,* p. 73; Frank Graham, Jr., "Double Image of a Champion" (*Sports Illustrated,* December 4, 1961).

evidence that only two-thirds are of the upper class. He then compares this with his casual study of Igor Cassini's "New 400" that was published in *Esquire* in 1953.[9] Unfortunately, Mills' study of that list was merely impressionistic: "I did not feel that Cassini's list warranted exhaustive analysis; in a cursory way, I was able to classify only 342 of the 399 names he listed: 102 professional celebrities; forty-one of the metropolitan 400; and 199 institutional leaders (ninety-three in government and seventy-nine in business)."[10] Furthermore, the list is not strictly comparable to the earlier one. The *Fortune* list consists of people said to be active in the social life of New York; the Cassini list claims to be an "aristocracy of achievement" whose members are loyal Americans of fine character who are leaders in their fields of work. However, despite the different basis for this list, our more detailed study gives a different picture than that painted by Mills, for 52% of its members can be classified as members of the upper class by our criteria. This is much higher than the 13% Mills classified in the "metropolitan 400," which is his label for the national upper class. A great many people on the list (140) are business-men and lawyers who are active as corporate leaders. This includes a dozen men from *Fortune*'s 1937 café list. There also are fifty-two entertainers; fifty columnists, writers and editors; twelve scientists; and nine athletes, but the main point is that this list does not pretend to delineate a group of people who interact socially.

There are several articles and books on the high society of the sixties. Most of them tell the usual story of allegedly ruinous taxes, new money, the influx of celebrities, and the openness of the new society. However, I decided to con-centrate on one book in particular, for it was written by a member of the upper class who is a public relations man.[11]

9. Igor Cassini, "The New 400" (*Esquire*, June, 1953).
10. Mills, *op. cit.*, p. 371.
11. Lanfranco Rasponi, *The International Nomads* (New York: G. P. Putnam's Sons, 1966).

Furthermore, his "in-ness" is vouched for by society photographer Jerome Zerbe (*Social Register,* New York), who writes columns on the jet set and appears on our 1937 *Fortune* list.[12] Aside from its anecdotes that must be taken with a grain of salt and its many glimpses of the incredible luxury in which these people live, Count Rasponi's book provides us with the names of 339 Americans who interact with dethroned royalty and wealthy European industrialists in New York, Paris, St. Moritz, Rome, Madrid, Palm Beach and the Riviera. Due to divorces and cases where the husband's first name is not mentioned, several people are difficult to trace or classify. Thus, our study of this list is not nearly so complete as our study of the earlier lists. Nevertheless, 62% of these American "nomads" are identifiable as members of the upper class. Twenty-five members of the café society of 1937 are still around, and there is an overlap of thirty-four with Igor Cassini's aristocracy of achievement for 1953. (Eight people appear on all three lists.) There are forty major businessmen on this female-dominated list of nomads, including platinum king Charles Engelhard, financier Robert Lehman, and corporation leader H. J. Heinz. The wives, ex-wives, and daughters of several other prominent corporate leaders are present. Only a small contingent of the jet set (36) is connected with the movie world as owners, directors, or stars. Rasponi plays down their importance, suggesting a decline in their role: "With a few exceptions, such as Audrey Hepburn, her husband Mel Ferrer, and George Hamilton, the new generation of screen stars rarely makes incursions into nomadic society."[13] People involved in the arts, fashion and mass media also

---

12. Jerome Zerbe, "Have You Heard: The Royal Marriage-Go-Round" (San Francisco *Chronicle,* June 17, 1967), p. 13. A reading of Zerbe's columns suggests that the jet set is very much rooted in the social upper class.

13. Rasponi, *op. cit.,* p. 133. He could have added that all three come from "good" families—Ferrer's family is in the Social Register, Hepburn's mother was a baroness, and Hamilton's mother married well several times.

mingle with the rich and well born. They are prominent among the fifty-six playwrights, fashion designers, and art patrons, and thirty-two columnists and editors on the list. One golfer, one evangelist, one educator, one beautician, and two plastic surgeons are among the anointed, along with a great many people (predominantly women) who are not classifiable occupationally.

Given the different sizes and origins of the lists, and our difficulties in finding information on many persons on the nomad list, I do not think a great deal should be made out of the 18% difference in upper-class participants between the 1937 and 1966 lists. To me, the important finding is that a very high percentage of those identified as high society or jet set are part of the upper class. Rich women, often aided by husbands active in the corporate world, are the jet set's most important functionaries. They are supplemented by luminaries from the glossy worlds of entertainment and fashion. Even if more detailed studies should show that there has been a slight increase in the size of the supporting entourage, the basic point is that members of the upper class are the substantial and sustaining core of café societies and jet sets.

## WRITINGS ON HIGH SOCIETY

Why did Mills go wrong on celebrity? I believe he took *Fortune* and high society writers too seriously. While these sources provide valuable raw material, they have several weaknesses and should never be accepted at face value. The first weakness of these sources is that they usually say that Society is dying. Things aren't what they used to be—the old ways are crumbling, new money is pushing in, and the younger generation has no manners and is marrying outside the upper class. *Fortune*'s 1938 article about debutantes, which is drawn upon heavily by Mills, tells us the sad tale of a declining rite. We learn that wealthy parents would spend $8 million on deb parties during that Depression year, but that "society is vanishing, leaving the debutante all dressed up with no place to go."[14] Today we hear similar claims from the "grandes dames" who came out in '38—only now they remember those times as the "good old days." The same myth is suggested in *Fortune*'s 1937 article on café society. It laments the passing of the "Knickerbocker Society" that is being replaced by celebrities and movie stars. Cleveland Amory, a Proper Bostonian turned celebrity, takes up these themes in *Who Killed Society?*. On the basis of a few sensational cases he chronicles the decline of the deb, and in spite of his own finding that every generation of American society has had some members who think Society is dying, he proceeds to say that Society is dead. Inflation; taxes; and the lack of servants, manners and morals finally killed it after all those premature announcements.[15]

Amory is not the first well-known writer on high society to make such a pronouncement. He was preceded by Dixon Wecter, the man upon whom later high society writers rely for many of their anecdotes and ideas.[16] Wecter begins with some colorful remarks about American high society, then sadly notes that it is fading away, "harrassed by levies, laws, codes, public criticisms, and gruelling committees of investigation . . ."[17] Wecter is saddened because the passing of the aristocracy would do "little good" and much "irreparable harm." "The distribution of a few dollars per capita and the conversion of a fleet of steam yachts into proletarian picnicboats would hardly compensate for the annihilation, among some members of that aristocracy, of gentle manners,

14. "The U. S. Debutante" (*Fortune,* December, 1938), p. 48.
15. Cleveland Amory, *Who Killed Society?* (New York: Pocket Books, 1960), Chapters 1 and 9.
16. Dixon Wecter, *The Saga of American Society* (New York: Charles Scribner's Sons, 1937).
17. *Ibid.,* p. 3.

beautiful speech, and the connoisseurship of gracious living."[18]

Perhaps it is the failure to be analytical and critical about such death-of-society claims that has led some academicians to overlook the continuity of the upper class, to make a distinction between the plutocrats of the turn of the century, and the more genteel wealth of earlier times. Henry Cabot Lodge, Sr., the grandfather of our present statesman, lays this trap for scholars when he says in his memoirs that "The persons who now fill Society, as depicted in the depressing phrases and strange language considered suitable to the subject by the daily press, are for the most part the modern, very modern plutocrats who are widely different from their modest predecessors of the middle of the nineteenth century."[19] There are two difficulties with this portrait of a Golden Past. First, the very modern plutocrats were mostly descendants of the highest levels of mid-nineteenth-century society. Second, anyone who reads about the "very modest predecessors" of the middle of the nineteenth century will know that they were just as money-seeking and eager as any twentieth-century plutocrat.

"Society is dead" is the first mistake of many high society writers. The second is artificial divisions of the upper class into "Plutocracy, Society, and Aristocracy" (Wecter) or "Publi-ciety and Aristocracy" (Amory). Plutocracy, Society, and Publi-ciety are more or less the bad guys. They are new-rich showboats and fast-rising celebrities. Aristocracy are the good guys—quiet, tasteful and old money. In this view, the inner core of the upper class tends to be aristocratic, the fringes tend to be new-rich and publicity-seeking. I do not think the distinction holds up. I believe it is really a distinction between "swingers" and "non-swingers" within the upper class, and has nothing to do with the age of their money. At least I have been able to find no other distinction on the various lists I have examined, in-

18. *Ibid.*, p. 5.
19. Amory, *op. cit.*, p. 22.

cluding social arbiter Maury Paul's list of "old guard" and café society for 1921.[20] "Café society," Paul's term for those who started to frequent night clubs after World War I, was simply those among the rich who were exploring new ways to enjoy their money, and it is not at all surprising that they would thereby mingle with movie stars and models. More generally, rich people who like excitement and publicity often end up in New York and on the café society trail. For every staid John Kimberly running the family store (Kimberly-Clark Company) and taking part in various policy-planning associations, there is a Jim Kimberly (his brother) who sails around the seven seas with a ring in his ear.[21] For every Cleveland Amory who becomes a celebrity by writing about celebrities and the upper class, there is a Robert Amory (his brother) who is busily keeping the country safe as a leading official in the CIA. Then too, being a part of the world of celebrity may occur only during one or another age level. John Lodge abandoned his motion picture career and later served as governor of Connecticut, a Boston deb who sang at a nightclub retired to become president of the Boston Junior League and the rich girl who joined the Ziegfeld Follies soon returned to the familiar haunts.[22] Society writer Stephen Birmingham provides the words that fit our impressions:

> There has always been a small but colorful segment of Real Society that has labored to see that its name and picture got in the papers, just as there has always been an element more fond of going to clubs and bars and bistros than of staying home. Café society, whether by that label or any other, is no new phenomenon, and the spiritual descendants of C. K. G. Billings's famous dinner-on-horseback at Sherry's dance today at the Electric Circus.[23]

20. *Ibid.*, pp. 127–9.
21. Maxine Cheshire, "Club for Impatient Rich" (*San Francisco Chronicle*, August 5, 1968), p. 8.
22. Cleveland Amory, *The Proper Bostonians* (New York: E. P. Dutton & Co., 1947), p. 347.
23. Stephen Birmingham, *The Right People* (Boston: Little, Brown and Co., 1968), p. 13.

Birmingham also suggests that a distinction between publicity-seekers and the more quiet types would have its uses for the upper class as a whole:

> It should never be assumed that publicity and Society are alien concepts, and that one can flourish only at the expense of the other. On the contrary, Society enjoys—and is grateful for—its publicity-seeking members. They, the few, in many ways protect and support the many. Far from killing Society, these busy few provide a façade and a showcase—a deceptively glossy showcase, to be sure—for what has become an enduring structure in America, the Social Establishment.[24]

A third weakness of many high society writers is that they overplay the role of stars and celebrities. Indeed, some say the influx of celebrities contributed to the death of Society. They have "stolen the show," says Wecter, although he qualifies his statement to a much greater extent than Mills does when he borrows it twenty years later.[25] The original Gibson girl, a lady of some notoriety herself, is among those who testify to high society writers that Society died due to the rise of celebrities. She goes on to admit, however, that there were celebrities present around the turn of the century, but that many were of some kind of social position.[26] It is well that she added this, for she happened to be, for all her celebrity, a Langhorne of Virginia whose sister was Lady Astor. Then what is the difference between yesterday and today? It seems that celebrities without social position are now invited to dinner, at least sometimes: "Of course, there were the others too, but one didn't have them for dinner. They came after dinner—to entertain."[27] Today, apparently, the celebrities entertain during meals as well, for they are invited to dinner. This may be a momentous change from the celebrities' point of

24. *Ibid.*
25. Wecter, *op. cit.,* p. 1.
26. Amory, *op. cit.,* p. 108.
27. *Ibid.*

view, as one of Amory's informants assures us, but it hardly signals the death of Society. Dru Heinz (*Social Register,* Pittsburgh), perhaps unknowingly, reveals one of the possible motives for this change:

> These people are now accepted by Society even though they never belong to it, and this is a wonderful improvement. You are not nearly so likely to get stuck at dinner between two scions of famous families who tell their golf scores or that they've given up drink. Now you have a good chance of being seated next to an author or artist or lecturer who is there because he has something to offer Society.[28]

Something to offer Society. In short, the presence of celebrities and entertainers at some of the parties and playgrounds of the rich is evidence for one thing only—the rich like to be entertained and stimulated.

A fourth weakness of writings about high society is that they tend to overemphasize the role of publicity and of high society arbiters in determining the upper class. Amory says that one such arbiter, Maury Paul, "soon became not only judge but also jury to Society not only in New York but, as his syndication spread, all over the country."[29] But Paul, as described by Amory, adds up only to a social climber, snob, and clotheshorse dandy who liked to show off his solid gold garter snaps. His lists, harangues, and accolades hardly determined who was in and out of anything—they merely provided amusement for some members of the upper class while satisfying the curiosity of untold numbers of more humbly situated newspaper readers. The same can be said about the Social Register. It does not determine who is *in* the upper class but merely lists many of its members. And being dropped from the Social Register for marrying an actress hardly removes one from the upper class.

A final weakness of high society writings is that they

28. "Society: Open End" (*Time,* July 20, 1962), p. 48.
29. Amory, *op. cit.,* p. 127.

ignore the business and political activities of high society participants, thus giving the impression that members of the upper class are incapable of looking after their own interests. Such writings leave us with the anomaly that people unable to take care of their affairs continue to prosper in spite of themselves. To take an example from one of the fountainheads of this bad practice, Wecter quotes de Tocqueville and Lord Bryce to the effect that the American rich do not involve themselves in politics.[30] There are the exceptions of course, but in fact Wecter has to overlook a lot of exceptions to make his point. To take one example, he mentions the various social antics of the first August Belmont, but nowhere does he note that the man was the head of the Democratic Party from 1860 to 1872.

In short, writings on high society provide much raw material for studies of the upper class, but their assumptions should not be accepted uncritically. They often obfuscate as much as they reveal, particularly because they divorce high society from economic and political life.

## SUMMARY

The "jet set" is a misleading term if it is thought to apply only to ne'er-do-wells, movie stars, and playboys. Rather, the jet set is a term for an activity: it is members of the American upper class at play. True, most members of the upper class probably are not jet setters, and not all jet setters are full time at the game. Nor do the upper-class members of the jet set play alone. Good-looking women and entertainers from all levels of society are often part of the entourage, as they always have been for the rich.

30. Wecter, *op. cit.*, p. 3n.

# CHAPTER FOUR

## *Cohesion and Consciousness: Is There an American Upper Class?*

Can we really speak of an American upper class? Or is the idea of an interacting and intermarrying upper crust the figment of a few imaginations? The purpose of this essay will be to present evidence affirming the existence of the upper class as a psychosocial reality. Such an undertaking is necessary because there are many who do not believe that something so vulgar as social classes exists in the United States of America. Indeed, this is the official view of many big businessmen and their publicists. They would have us believe we are all one big happy family with similar interests. However, I suspect they know quite otherwise, especially from the now available correspondence of their fathers and grandfathers, which shows their concerns about combating class consciousness and ideologies that supposedly promote class consciousness. I also believe they know better because of such dramatic confessions as this one by Mrs. Marietta Peabody Tree, a member of the upper class if there ever was one:

> . . . Mrs. Tree recalls that the "first and only" time her grandmother ever slapped her was when, as a young girl, Marietta referred to an acquaintance as "very middle class." After the slap came these stern, grandmotherly words: "there are no classes in America—upper, lower, or middle. You are never to use that term again."[1]

Closely related to the assertion of classlessness is the idea that this classlessness is in good part due to rapid social mobility. According to this view, our big rich were mostly farm boys and poor immigrants who "Horatio Algered" their way to the top, with no time to become part of or conscious of class.

Now, it is not my concern in this essay to trace the ways in which members and publicists of the upper class assiduously supported these closely related beliefs of One Big Happy Family and Horatio Alger. Nor will I attempt to judge how important their efforts have been in contributing to the weak class identifications in the American populace and the general acceptance of the Horatio Alger myth. Instead, I am concerned with what scholarship has to tell us about the truth or falsity of these conceptions. As will be seen, scholars do not share the publicists' theories. On the other hand, scholars have not given enough attention to the fraction of a percent making up the upper class, which places important limitations on their generalizations.

To take the claim of Horatio Alger first, the work of historian William Miller and his associates in the Research Center for Entrepreneurial History at Harvard has shown that important business leaders and corporation lawyers from the 1870's on have been native-born Anglo Saxons of

1. Stephen Birmingham, *The Right People* (Boston: Little, Brown and Co., 1968), p. 340.

"high-status" Protestant religions (Episcopal, Presbyterian, and Congregationalist) who were the well-educated sons of native-born businessmen and professionals. For example, in the study of 179 major businessmen at the turn of the century, fully half were from the upper class, only 5% came from the lower class.[2] The few cases of rags to riches which were trumpeted by publicists and uncritically accepted by some historians of an earlier generation were the rare exceptions rather than the rule. Miller's systematic data are rather embarrassing to the historical works he holds up to them. As to other work on the origins of big businessmen, it is summarized by Morroe Berger when he concludes that "there has been some movement from the bottom to the lower limits of the top, but very little to the upper limits of the top."[3] Thus, only one thing more needs to be asked about the slow ascendancy of a few individuals into the upper class of big businessmen and their descendants. Does this gradual infusion change the class? From all indications, the answer is no. The climbers seem eager to assimilate the values and styles of the class to which they aspire. This does not deny that there are changes within the upper class over a period of generations, but it does deny that upward mobility is one of the key factors in creating them. In short, social mobility is not central to the study of the American upper class of the twentieth century. For students of the upper class, the findings on the small amount of movement into the upper class are interesting because they provide a basis for re-evaluating the efforts of the upper-class publicists and upper-class historians. They also cast doubt on the value of the claim that rapid social mobility has inhibited the development of class consciousness or cohesion in the highest stratum of American society.

Scholars also have done away with the classless society

2. William Miller, "American Historians and the Business Elite" (*Journal of Economic History,* November, 1949), p. 206.
3. Morroe Berger, "The Business Elite: Then and Now" (*Commentary,* October, 1956), p. 370.

myth, but they have done so in a sophisticated way more relevant to other levels of society than the one of interest here. That is, they have decided that social "class" is not quite the right term to describe our hierarchical social structure. True, there are the highers and the lowers, and most people know about where they stand even if they don't understand the whole picture. However, there are no obvious or rigid boundaries, titles, or modes of dress that mark this continuum into classes. One level shades into the next in its social interactions and style of life. I do not want to quarrel with this overall conception of the American social structure except at its highest level. I hope to show that it is based upon studies of every level of society but the highest and that this level has in fact all the attributes which have traditionally marked off a group as a social class. In other words, the social structure is made up of strata that shade off one into the other until we arrive at the highest level, where the continuum hardens into a social class with more or less definite boundaries and class consciousness.

One of the best summary essays describing the view on social class which I have attributed to most American social scientists is by social psychologist Roger Brown. Entitled "Stratification," it provides an excellent starting point for this inquiry. Brown distills from previous writings three points which must be established to demonstrate the existence of a social class: patterns of in-group interactions to the general exclusion of out-group interactions; differences in style of life from other groups; and stratum consciousness, an awareness of oneself as a member of a specific social group.[4] After presenting these criteria, Brown summarizes a great deal of empirical research on social classes in America and then concludes that they do not exist, that what we have are status groups along a social hierarchy. However, his discussion is not relevant to the upper class. Indeed, it cites *none* of the references I will use in contradicting it for that level of

4. Roger Brown, *Social Psychology* (New York: The Free Press, 1965), pp. 102, 114.

society. Particularly conspicuous by its absence is the work of E. Digby Baltzell, which presents most of the points I will make using different empirical material.[5]

Before undertaking this exercise, it may be asked why I find it necessary to do so. The answer is that critics of the thesis that the upper class is a governing class or ruling class say that cohesion, consciousness, and conspiracy must be demonstrated within the group said to be the ruling class. It must be shown, according to this argument, that the members of the so-called ruling class are aware of each other and their common interests. Furthermore, if it is not shown that *they* meet (perhaps secretly) to designate leaders and plan strategies, then *they* are merely individuals participating as any other individuals in political activities. Members of the upper class are not a coherent force unless *they* are united by the "three C's"—cohesion, consciousness, and conspiracy.

The means by which various leadership groups within the upper class involve themselves as cohesive forces within the political process will be made clear in subsequent essays. The importance of *consensus* rather than *conspiracy* as the third of the "three C's" also will become apparent. For now, I want to concentrate on cohesion and consciousness to provide a context for assessing the involvement of members of the upper class in government and politics. Cohesion will be deduced from patterns of interaction and a unique life style.

## IN-GROUP INTERACTION

Roger Brown sets out our task for us in the following words:

> The reality of class in a community will be undeniable in the following circumstances: 1) the population is conscious of classes, agreed on the number of classes, and on the membership of them; 2) styles of life are strikingly uniform within

5. E. Digby Baltzell, *Philadelphia Gentlemen: The Making of a National Upper Class* (Glencoe, Illinois: The Free Press, 1958).

a stratum and there are clear contrasts between strata; 3) interaction is sharply patterned by stratum; 4) the boundaries suggested by the three kinds of data are coincident.[6]

Brown starts with class consciousness, but I prefer to build up to that problem by first considering in-group interaction and differential life styles, for they are the basis for whatever class consciousness might be found to exist.

## The Evidence of Intermarriage

Intermarriages are one of the key evidences of in-group interaction, and there is certainly a great deal of it within the American upper class. Indeed, a marriage outside the group is often the occasion for much tongue clucking or newspaper gossip. Intermarriage within the upper class defies simple description. It does not go too far to say that everyone is related to everyone else, and sometimes many times over. However, there is one general exception to this: Sons and daughters of the upper class can bring home a bright and well-polished youth of the upper-middle class whom they came to know because this arriviste was attending a school such as Vassar, Harvard, Smith, or Yale. Then too, it should not be forgotten that the beauties and charms of a small handful of models, actresses, and stewardesses often give them considerable social mobility. Brown may want to make something out of this small amount of boundary-crossing at Harvard and in the discothèque, but it does have the happy consequence of infusing more brains and beauty into the privileged class.

How do we know about this great amount of intermarriage? Through the reading of books about society, and through the study of family histories, biographies, and autobiographies. Let me cite just a few of the examples and authorities, leaving the quantification of this complex kinship system to an anthropologist and his computer:

6. Brown, *op. cit.*, p. 114.

1. First Families in Boston have tended toward marrying each other in a way that would do justice to the planned marriages of European royalty.[7]

2. Nathaniel Burt, an expert on the Philadelphia branch of the upper class, says there is nobody in the web of that city's financial and professional old-family elite who is not related.[8]

3. As members of the American aristocracy, over the years [the Bayards] have linked fortunes through marriage with the Washingtons of Virginia; the Carrolls, Howards, and Wirts of Maryland; the Bassetts and duPonts of Delaware; the Kembles, Kirkpatricks, Stevenses, and Stocktons of New Jersey; the Stuyvesants, DeLanceys, Jays, Livingstons, Pintards, and Schuylers of New York; the Bowdoins and Winthrops of Massachusetts.[9]

4. So intimately related by travel and actual multiple family connection was San Francisco with two of the watering places, Santa Barbara and Honolulu, that society news from those two bivouacs appeared regularly, from 1920 on, in more than one San Francisco newspaper in columns flanking Peninsula and East Bay Society News.[10]

5. "Through marriage, the Auchinclosses are now kin, in addition to Rockefellers, Sloans, Winthrops, Jenningses, Saltonstalls, and Smedbergs, to such other redoubtable families as the Frelinghuysens, the Van Rensselaers, the Cuttings, the Reids, the duPonts, the Grosvenors, the Truslows, the Tiffanys, the Bundys, the Adamses, the Ingrahams, the Burdens, the Vanderbilts, and, of course, the Kennedys."[11]

7. Cleveland Amory, *The Proper Bostonians* (New York: E. P. Dutton & Co., 1947), p. 20.
8. Nathaniel Burt, *The Perennial Philadelphians* (Boston: Little, Brown & Co., 1963), p. 43.
9. Stephen Hess, *America's Political Dynasties* (New York: Doubleday & Co., 1966), p. 297.
10. Julia Cooley Altrocchi, *The Spectacular San Franciscans* (New York: E. P. Dutton & Co., 1949), p. 319.
11. Birmingham, *op. cit.*, p. 327.

Histories of, among others, the Rockefellers, Roosevelts, duPonts, Morgans, Astors, Vanderbilts, and Kennedys point in the same direction. In each case one can find a few people who went outside the class for a marriage partner, but the overall picture is one of marriage to other wealthy people of the upper class.

## The Evidence of Schools

We have studied the publications of expensive private schools. Attendance patterns at these schools suggest that rich children from all over the country interact at this handful of exclusive institutions. For example, Hotchkiss graduates are listed in the Social Register for the following cities: New York, 552; Chicago, 125; Philadelphia, ninety-four; Cleveland, sixty-four; Pittsburgh, sixty-four; Boston, fifty-nine; San Francisco, forty; Washington, thirty-five; and St. Louis, thirty-four. St. Marks, which is twenty-three miles from Boston, had 214 boarding students and twenty-six day students in 1967. In addition to sixty-nine students from Massachusetts, forty-four from New York, twenty-two from New Jersey, and fourteen from Pennsylvania, there were eighteen from the Midwest, eighteen from the South, and fifteen from the Far West. Foxcroft, a school for girls, had students from twenty-nine states in 1967, while Eaglebrook, a school in Massachusetts for younger boys, had forty-seven from New York, twenty-two from Connecticut, thirteen from Pennsylvania, seven from Illinois, six from Florida, and three from California. Chatham Hall, a girls' school in Virginia, had sixteen students from New York, sixteen from Ohio, fifteen from Connecticut, and eight from Texas, in addition to seventy-three from the South. The picture would not be different if we looked at exclusive girls' colleges and junior colleges, for a few girls from each of the private schools are found in each of the classes at these schools.

## The Evidence of Clubs

Upper-class clubs have nationwide memberships. This is particularly true of such strategically located clubs as the Links, Brook, and Century in New York, and the Bohemian and Pacific Union in San Francisco, but it is true to a certain extent for other clubs as well. As of 1953, for example, the Boston Club in New Orleans had thirty-one non-resident members from Texas, twenty-two from New York, ten from Washington, D. C., and six each from Chicago and San Francisco, in addition to the dozens of non-resident members from Mississippi and the rest of Louisiana.

A very interesting club meets once a year on the 3,700-acre Abercrombie Ranch in Santa Barbara, California. The Ranchero Visitadores "are a group of 500 wealthy businessmen, industrialists, and ranchers who get together once a year for a week of horseback riding, partying, games, relaxation—and just plain fun."[12] The article goes on to note that they come from all over the country, and that they bring their own equipment and "fine horses" with them. There are many such nationwide clubs. For example, the finely bred and highly trained dogs of rich men and women from all over the country are the basis for get-togethers by the National Retriever Field Trial Club. At the 1963 national championship stake one could mingle with upper-class people from all over the country, including the president of Olin Industries of St. Louis and the wife of a San Francisco shipping magnate.

## The Evidence of Summer Resorts

The work of Cleveland Amory and E. Digby Baltzell suggests that summer residences in exclusive resort areas are good evidence for the cohesiveness of the national upper

12. Jack Lind, "The Good Life in Santa Barbara" (*Mainliner*, November, 1967), n.p.

class. We attempted to systematize the anecdotal hints of Amory and to extend the systematic study of Philadelphia by Baltzell.[13] This was done by geographically classifying the summer residences of every person who takes the trouble to list in the *Summer Social Register,* which is a compendium of summer addresses for the thirteen city editions. It does not include the summer residences of a great many listees, but it is indicative of where vacations are spent by the upper class. This study shows that the summer homes of the rich who live in the eastern half of the United States are on islands and secluded coastlines. In Maine, for example, there are Social Register listees in many of the little towns along the coast. The greatest concentration, however, is on two tiny islands, Mt. Desert and Vinalhaven. The several towns on Mt. Desert, such as Northeast Harbor, Seal Harbor, and Southwest Harbor, are the summer addresses of Social Register listees from the following cities: Philadelphia, ninety-two; New York, eighty; Boston, forty; Washington, twelve; Chicago and Baltimore, seven; Cincinnati–Dayton, six; and St. Louis, five. North Haven, on Vinalhaven Island, is another prominent Maine address, with forty-two from Boston, twenty from New York, eight from Philadelphia, and three from St. Louis.

Further down the Atlantic Coast, two islands off the Massachusetts cape are popular summer respites. The first is Nantucket, which has seventy-one families from New York, thirty from Philadelphia, twenty-six from Boston, fifteen from Washington, eight each from Baltimore and Cincinnati–Dayton, four each from Buffalo and Pittsburgh, and three from San Francisco. The second is the better-known Martha's Vineyard, particularly at Edgartown, where 121 New Yorkers, twenty-five Bostonians, ten Philadelphians, eight Washingtonians, and seven each from Chicago, Cincinnati–Dayton, and Pittsburgh make their summer

13. Cleveland Amory, *The Last Resorts* (New York: Harper & Row, 1952); Baltzell, *op. cit.,* pp. 220–2.

home. The Osterville–Hyannisport area on the cape itself is also popular. Pittsburgh's *Social Register* provides the largest contingent with thirty-three families, but these families are joined by twenty-three from Boston, twelve from New York, nine from Philadelphia, eight from Washington, four from Chicago, and three each from Buffalo and St. Louis.

Little Rhode Island turns out to be a summer haven for the well-to-do listed in the Social Register. One favorite spot is Jamestown, which is on Conanicut Island in the Narragansett Bay. There are twenty-eight families from Philadelphia, six each from Boston and Washington, three from Buffalo, and two each from New York and St. Louis. The Watch Hill area, on the southern-most coast of Rhode Island, can boast of thirty families from New York, eleven from Philadelphia, six each from Pittsburgh and Cincinnati–Dayton, five from Washington, four from Boston, and three from St. Louis.

Watch Hill is only a short yacht ride from Fisher's Island, which is offically part of the state of New York. It is a long-standing retreat for the wealthy. Most of the residents seem to be New Yorkers, with seventy-seven families from that city, but there are also nine Philadelphians and one or two families from Boston, Pittsburgh, Chicago, Baltimore, Buffalo, and St. Louis. Below Fisher's Island, on an island that is the eastern-most tip of Long Island, the cities of Southampton, Bridgehampton, and East Hampton provide summer homes for 353 New Yorkers, ten Philadelphians, seven Washingtonians, and seven from the Cincinnati–Dayton area. There are several other minor gathering places in the East, but none are of the significance of the nine detailed in the preceding paragraphs. One more that might be mentioned is the isolated coastal town of Rehoboth Beach, Delaware, which has nineteen St. Louis families in addition to eleven from Washington, nine from Baltimore, and six from Philadelphia.

As seen, there are Midwesterners in most of these Eastern retreats. However, many Social Register listees from Chicago (17) and Cincinnati–Dayton (12) are also partial to a covey of small towns on the Northern Michigan coast that borders on Lake Michigan. From Kavaler's work we know they are joined there by several well-to-do families from Detroit.[14] Three Philadelphians and two Clevelanders also go to this area. In general, very few Clevelanders list themselves as being part of the summer resort circuit.They tend to stay in the gently rolling and wooded hills east of their home city. Social Register families from Buffalo have their own area across the lake in Ridgeway, Ontario, but some of them join a handful of Social Register listees from ten other cities in journeying to small towns in northern Ontario. Except for one or two families at Edgartown, Nantucket, Long Island, and Watch Hill, very few San Franciscans are found in any of the resorts mentioned. They summer on Lake Tahoe on the California-Nevada border, on the Monterey Peninsula below San Francisco, and in little towns north of the city.

Members of the upper class spend their summers in a great many other places, including Europe, but the general point has been made. There are a handful of summer resort areas, on islands and secluded coastlines, which provide evidence for in-group interactions among families from every Social Register city except Cleveland and San Francisco. The next step would be "field studies" of these areas to determine how many wealthy families are in attendance from cities without Social Registers. Paul Sweezy made this suggestion many years ago to those who question the existence of an upper class, but no one has taken him up on it.[15]

---

14. Lucy Kavaler, *The Private World of High Society* (New York: David McKay Co., 1960), p. 37.
15. Paul Sweezy, *The Present As History* (New York: Monthly Review Press, 1953), p. 130.

## The Evidence of Winter Resorts

During the winter two areas in the United States are the principal meccas for members of the upper class from all over the United States. The first is Palm Beach–Hobe Sound in Florida, the second is Palm Springs in southern California. Observers stationed in these two places alone might be able to convince skeptics of an interacting national upper class. Indeed, the membership lists of the Everglades in Palm Beach and the Thunderbird in Palm Springs might save them the trouble of being there physically, but such membership lists are not easy to come by.[16] In any event, both of these areas have been treated anecdotally by Stephen Birmingham in *The Right People*.[17] Among the examples he uses to show the rich visitors to Palm Springs are corporate leaders Paul Hoffman, Benjamin Fairless, Conrad Hilton, Leonard Firestone, William Ford, and J. J. McCloy.[18] As for Palm Beach, society from the eastern half of the United States has been joined there by "invasions from Middle Western cities, and from the oil lands of Oklahoma and Texas."[19]

Palm Springs and Palm Beach, of course, do not exhaust the winter spas. Members of the upper class from all over the country can be found on "Millionaires' Row" in Naples, Florida. Others settle down among their counterparts in Fort Lauderdale, or in the "other Miami"—Coral Gables— wherein live "the best of Miami's year-round Society, whose lives are led with quiet elegance, whose sons go North to New England prep schools, whose daughters come out at

16. The phrase "but such membership lists are not easy to come by" is obviously added with the hope that mavericks and youthful rebels will send me every membership list they can obtain on any upper-class organization. Perhaps the most valuable prize would be the membership list for the Junior League.
17. Birmingham, *op. cit.*, chapters 18 and 19.
18. *Ibid.*, pp. 295, 303.
19. *Ibid.*, p. 284.

the Debutante Ball at the Surf Club, and who speak with the 'social voice'. . . ."[20]

## The Evidence of Acquaintance Patterns

In the 1950's sociologist Floyd Hunter sent questionnaires to and interviewed one hundred men from all over the country who had the reputation of being top leaders. Among the questions he asked them was how well they knew the other men on his list. Whether they are top leaders or not, these men did know each other.[21] Since we have found that many of Hunter's top leaders are members of the upper class by our criteria, he has provided evidence for nationwide in-group interactions among rich men of considerable prominence in the business world.

We decided to attempt a variation of Hunter's "acquaintance" study by sending questionnaires to prominent social families in San Francisco, Los Angeles, and Beverly Hills. With the help of informants, Tony Mohr selected twenty-five of the most prominent Christian families and twenty-five of the most prominent Jewish families in San Francisco. (The reason for separating Christian and Jewish families was that the study was concerned with anti-Semitism within the upper class as well as inter-city acquaintance patterns, but that aspect will not be pursued here.) All of the Christian families were listed in the Social Register, as were seven of the Jewish families. Also working with informants, David Guggenhime, in a parallel study, selected twenty wealthy families who were quite active in civic affairs in Beverly Hills. Sixteen of the families were Jewish. Guggenhime also selected twenty prominent Los Angeles Christian families. He did not have the help of informants for this city, but all those selected were in both the Los Angeles

20. *Ibid.*, p. 293.
21. Floyd Hunter, *Top Leadership, USA* (Chapel Hill: University of North Carolina Press, 1959), pp. 167–72.

*Blue Book* and the California Club. Most of the names
are quite well known, but several not known to us were
selected on the basis of their several upper-class credentials
in addition to being listed in the *Blue Book* and belonging
to the California Club. In short, there is every reason to
believe that our four groups are part of any elite social circle
that exists in their respective cities.

The ninety names so selected were later arranged alpha-
betically on a questionnaire that was sent to each person on
the list. It was introduced by a letter asking cooperation in
a study of how well various prominent families in California
know each other. Respondents were asked to indicate be-
side each name their degree of acquaintance with the family
by writing "1" (know well); "2" (know casually); "3"
(know by reputation only); "4" (do not know). We did
not try to control whether one or both members of the
family answered the questionnaire, assuming that any differences in husband and wife acquaintance patterns were too
minor to make any restrictions on answering that might
reduce the number of questionnaires returned.

The subjects were very cooperative. Seventy-six percent
of the San Francisco Christians returned the questionnaire.
The figures were 88% for San Francisco Jewish families,
70% for Los Angeles Christian families, and 75% for
Beverly Hills civic families. The results can be expressed
in what I call an "acquaintance percent." That is, the
number of families scored "1" or "2" are divided by the
number of families rated. For example, if twenty San Francisco Christian families rated twenty Los Angeles Christian
families, there would be 400 ratings; 400 is then divided
into the number of "1" and "2" ratings. The decision to
use both "1's" and "2's" is based upon the assumption that
it is enough for these people to know each other casually
to be considered part of the same social class.

As to our findings, it can first of all be said that our
informants were correct that the prominent families within

San Francisco and Beverly Hills respectively are well acquainted with each other. The acquaintance percent for San Francisco Christians was ninety-one, for San Francisco Jewish families, ninety-seven, and for Beverly Hills civic leaders, seventy-eight. The acquaintance percent for the Los Angeles group was sixty-four, which suggests that California Club members are well known to each other.

Of greater interest were the acquaintance percents between local elites. First, there is a considerable degree of acquaintance between the prominent Christian and Jewish families of San Francisco in spite of the exclusion of most wealthy Jewish people from the *Social Register* and all Jewish people from the Pacific Union and Bohemian Clubs. The acquaintance percent between the two groups was fifty-nine according to twenty-two Jewish respondents who rated the twenty-five Christians, sixty-five according to the nineteen Christian respondents who rated the twenty-five Jewish families. The similarity of the acquaintance percents as judged from different sides of the fence reinforces the credibility of both of them.

There is a modest amount of acquaintance between the Los Angeles Christians and the San Francisco Christians. The acquaintance percent is thirty-one according to nineteen San Francisco raters, twenty-seven according to fourteen Los Angeles respondents. Again, the similarity of the two percentages lends to the credibility of both of them. On the other hand, the Jewish families of San Francisco and the Christian families of Los Angeles are less well known to each other. According to the twenty-one Jewish families who rated twenty Los Angeles Christians, the acquaintance percent was only seven, while the fourteen Angelenos who rated twenty-five San Francisco Jewish families thought the percentage of acquaintance somewhat higher at fourteen.

Our Beverly Hills sample is not part of the national upper class. The Beverly Hills group is known to neither the Los

Angeles nor the San Francisco groups, and its members do not claim to know members of the Los Angeles and San Francisco groups except by reputation. The acquaintance percents in question are fifteen, eight, seven, three, two, and one. As further evidence for this negative finding, we found there is very little overlap of the clubs and schools of the Beverly Hills group with those assumed to be institutions of the upper class. If there is a branch of the national upper class in Beverly Hills, it is not known to the Beverly Hills insider who served as our informant.

## Summary on In-Group Interaction

The picture that emerges for me from these various types of evidence for in-group interaction within the upper class is one of overlapping social cliques that have a considerable amount of intermarriage and social interaction among them. It is quite clear that everyone does not know everyone else, but it is also highly probable that everyone has friends and relatives who interact in one way or another with one or more persons in other cliques. The person thus has entrée into the highest social circles all over the country. For some it is the Junior League that fills this function. For others it is graduation from Groton or membership in the Piedmont Driving Club. Or perhaps a brother rides to the hounds in Virginia and summers in Watch Hill, or a fellow member of Hasty Pudding at Harvard is in the Woodhill Country Club in Minneapolis. If all else fails, there is even the letter of introduction. Lucy Sprague Mitchell, raised in the Chicago branch of the upper class, had friends in Los Angeles where she went to Marlborough School, in Boston where she attended Radcliffe, and in San Francisco-Berkeley where she was the first dean of women at the University of California, but she knew very few people in New York. When she got ready to go to New York, however, she had "a suitcaseful of letters of introduction ranging from Anne Morgan to Lillian Wald." They came from a friend she had met in Boston.[22]

And then there are the more subtle bases of cohesion, such as the feeling of belonging and the comfortableness of being among one's own kind. This brings us to a consideration of the rather unique style of life that is typical of members of the American upper class.

## DIFFERENCES IN LIFE STYLE

Brown believes that life style differences in America "arborealize into the flimsiest trivia."[23] However, he mentions none of the following points that distinguish members of the upper class—from birth to death—from the rest of the population. If the perception of differences leads to cohesion and consciousness, the pattern of activities and experiences unique to the upper class are evidence for its reality.[24]

### Early Years

Upper-class babies are seldom born in the general hospital, but the first distinctive difference I want to stress is the presence of nurses, governesses, or maids in the houses in which the babies are raised. This rather unusual situation is followed by special pre-schools and a private day school. Indeed, many members of the upper class have never been in a public school in their lives, which distinguishes them from a considerable percentage of the population. Special dancing classes, riding lessons, and tutoring in a foreign

22. Lucy Sprague Mitchell, *Two Lives* (New York: Simon & Schuster, 1953), p. 207.
23. Brown, *op. cit.,* p. 132.
24. Unless otherwise specified, the following account is based upon Baltzell, *op. cit.,* and Kavaler, *op. cit.* Many of these points were made in more detail for the feminine half of the upper class in the second essay.

language are some of the other unusual experiences that may be part of the early years for upper-class children.

## Adolescence

Adolescents of the upper class continue their private schooling, often at boarding schools far from home. Summers are spent at exclusive summer camps, at the family summer home, and in traveling. One of the unique experiences of late adolescence is the round of debutante parties that occur in June, early September, and the Christmas holidays. Many of the affairs are fairly routine parties costing only a few thousand dollars, but every once in a while someone celebrates the occasion in a way not likely to be emulated by middle-class pretenders. A recent example would be the party held on a chartered Braniff jetliner as it flew from Dallas to New Orleans; the proud father is part of a syndicate that owns one-third of the land area in that Louisiana city.[25]

## Adulthood

Maturity finds members of the upper class in such prestigious occupations as businessman, financier, and lawyer, occupations which suggest the common interest of ownership and management of business enterprises. Others function as museum directors, architects, art collectors and physicians, which are among the most prestigious pursuits on the occupational ladder. The lady of the house is in the Junior League or is a volunteer for any one of a number of agencies and charities. The daily routine of both men

25. "Debs Put Party on Jet" (San Francisco *Chronicle*, December 18, 1965), p. 2. "Hostesses wearing the Emilio Pucci-designed ensemble served a nonstandard menu that ranged from *mumms cordon rouge, brut vintage, cruse t. Emilion,* to *empandana,* rumaki, roast heart of tenderloin, broiled lobster and Italian rum cake."

and women is supplemented by directorships, trusteeships, and association memberships.

Upper-class families live in town houses or large apartments in an exclusive area of the city, or in an exclusive suburb. Chances are they will have a second home—perhaps a farm or ranch, more likely a summer home. While the city home is usually quite plush, the reverse snobbery of casual tastefulness is well understood. The most conspicuous consumption—often conspicuous only to those who can recognize quality—is more and more reserved for the interior of the home. Expensive art may be part of the decor.

The upper-class man is a member of one or more male-only clubs in the city. There may or may not be a parallel club for women, but it is likely that there is a country club for the family. Club memberships outside one's home city are not unusual.

The leisure activities of the upper class also show distinctiveness. Charity balls and jet setting may be part of the nighttime activities. Weekends may be spent on a boat, or chasing foxes at one of the ninety-some hunt clubs across the country. The breeding and raising of horses is another activity that has an upper-class bias. So does the showing of dogs and the training of dogs for bird retrieving. Many of these people annually spend more money on their animals than most people earn in a year.

## Status After Death

Finally, after all this, there is death, but it is not the great leveler it is claimed to be when it comes to differences in life style. For example, a study of post-war Philadelphia showed that its *Social Register* listees had distinctive funeral and burial customs.[26] First, they were much more likely to practice cremation. Second, they had a shorter elapsed time between death and burial than any other group. They

26. William M. Kephart, "Status After Death" (*American Sociological Review*, October, 1950).

showed the greatest control of emotion, and they were more likely to restrict viewing of the body. Most interesting, they also have their own burial grounds, which are usually simple and uniform churchyard cemeteries.

According to Cleveland Amory, Proper Bostonians also seem to have a concern with status after death:

> Great attention is also paid to the final resting place of the deceased. In Boston's early days Old Granary, across from the ancient Park Street Church, was a sort of Proper Bostonian Westminster Abbey. . . . In more recent times Forest Hills and Mount Auburn . . . have risen to positions of high favor.[27]

And some families, such as the duPonts, have private burial grounds, which truly completes the circuit from private school through exclusive club and exclusive neighborhood.

There are many other things that could be shown to be rather unique about the life style of the upper class, but I believe the general point has been made. Members of the upper class not only have *more,* they have *different.* And it would be amazing, defying laws of discrimination and perception, if some of these differences did not register somewhere, consciously or unconsciously, in the psyches of most members of the upper class. As political scientist Gabriel Almond noted many years ago, "The elaborate private life of the plutocracy serves in considerable measure to separate them out in their own consciousness as a superior, more refined element."[28] It is now time to confront the problem of class consciousness directly.

## CLASS CONSCIOUSNESS

American social scientists, who put a great deal of emphasis on class consciousness in determining the existence of social

27. Amory, *op. cit.*, p. 257.
28. Gabriel Almond, "Plutocracy and Politics in New York City" (Unpublished Ph.D. dissertation, University of Chicago, 1941), p. 108.

classes, have done a number of studies which show that there is not much of it in the United States. I think the emphasis on such an ephemeral thing as consciousness is mistaken in an age of behaviorism and psychoanalysis; people's behavior—e.g., interaction patterns and life styles —and their implicit, unverbalized conceptions are much more important than their ability to verbalize about their class positions in a brief interview with a polltaker. Then too:

> "Economic position" and the control over the life chances of others are matters of social fact, which are relatively independent of subjective recognition. They can and frequently do exist outside popular awareness; sometimes, they exist though they are denied explicitly.[29]

Nonetheless, the problem of class consciousness can be met on its own terms. As Seymour Lipset and Reinhold Bendix point out, not even Marx expected the lower levels of society to develop class consciousness except under certain unusual conditions. However, Marx did claim there was class consciousness in the upper stratum, and that is precisely where it can be demonstrated.[30] Starting once again with Brown, he asks that the population be conscious of classes, agreed on the number of classes, and agreed on the membership of them.[31] However, to expect everyone in the population to understand the entire class structure, as Brown does, is clearly too demanding. No one carries around a complete conception of his own social stratum, let alone the entire social structure. Indeed, social scientists

29. Seymour M. Lipset and Reinhold Bendix, "Social Status and Social Structure: A Re-examination of Data and Interpretations: II" (*British Journal of Sociology*, October, 1951), p. 249.
30. *Ibid.*, p. 241n. "Marx never suggested that any but the members of the dominant controlling class would by themselves develop a consistent, class-conscious ideology. It is significant to note that most of American sociological research on class, as well as the reports of perceptive journalists, tend to confirm this hypothesis."
31. Brown, *op. cit.*, p. 114.

who have studied the problem often have a better overview of a social class than any of their informants. C. Wright Mills once noted that he had never studied a group which had "an adequate view of its own social position."[32] For my purposes, then, it would be necessary to show only that the population is conscious of the upper class and its membership. Such consciousness is suggested by the fact that 82% of respondents place big businessmen in the upper class, that 67% of respondents reply that wealth and income are the key factors in being a member of the upper class (those who say they are upper class play those factors down), and that only 3% of those who call themselves middle class and .2% of those who call themselves working class consider big businessmen to be part of their class.[33] In short, people have a pretty good idea of the upper class.

However, what non upper-class people think is not the real issue. The question is the class awareness of members of the upper social class. Are they class conscious? Unfortunately, the major work on class consciousness is of little use on this question, for it included few if any persons from the top .5% of the social hierarchy.[34] Any arguments on the matter therefore have had to rely on the testimony of an insider–expert such as Baltzell, the novels of a perceptive observer such as J. P. Marquand, and remarks about the "mobility" and "peasants" that used to slip from cultured tongues. Then too, every once in a while an upper-class writer will drop a remark that implies class consciousness. For example, Lewis Lapham (*Social Register*, New York) noted in the *Saturday Evening Post* that "the old rich recognize one another by small and elusive signals: a tone of voice, a name in common, a summer once at Fisher's

32. C. Wright Mills, "Comment on Criticism," in *C. Wright Mills and the Power Elite*, G. William Domhoff and Hoyt B. Ballard, eds. (Boston: Beacon Press, 1968), p. 230.
33. Brown, *op. cit.*, p. 130; Richard Centers, *The Psychology of Social Classes* (Princeton: Princeton University Press, 1949), pp. 80–3, 94–5.
34. Centers, *op. cit.*, pp. 48–9.

Island, the recollection of a bunker below the 13th green at a course in Southampton."[35] Stephen Birmingham, a graduate of Hotchkiss, devotes a whole chapter to "How Shall We Tell the Children."[36] The concern with ancestry, family emblems, and club memberships also implies class consciousness, but it does not carry us much beyond arguments based on life style and anecdotal testimony.

## The Testimony of Psychoanalysts

I thought I had the perfect coup, the ace of them all on class consciousness in the upper class, when I wrote to the men I hoped would know its members best, the psychoanalysts. A questionnaire was sent to one-third of the 912 Freudian analysts and all of the seventy Jungian analysts. Unfortunately, very few psychoanalysts replied, and only thirty-six of the sixty-nine who did felt they could speak on this subject. The low rate of return may reflect the fact that few analysts see upper-class patients. The typical psychoanalytic patient is a professional man making $10–15,000 per year. Only 22% have incomes over $20,000; 40% are Jewish; occupationally, 18% are psychiatrists or psychiatric residents, 17% academic professionals, 11% students, and 10% social workers and psychiatric nurses.[37] It also may reflect hesitancy due to the criticism psychiatrists and psychoanalysts received for their part in a sensationalist story on Barry Goldwater's sanity that appeared several years ago.[38] At any rate, thirty-six psychoanalysts were willing to comment on the class consciousness of patients who listed in the Social Register or graduated from such

35. Lewis H. Lapman, "Old Money, New Money" (*Saturday Evening Post*, December 30, 1967), p. 22.
36. Birmingham, *op. cit.*, Chapter 3.
37 ."Who's In Analysis?" (*Trans-Action*, November, 1968), p. 7.
38. Ralph Ginzburg, "Goldwater: The Man and the Menace"; Warren Boroson, "What Psychiatrists Say About Goldwater" (*Fact*, September/October, 1964).

schools as Groton and St. Paul's. Fifteen of the thirty-six circled the highest option, 90–95%, in answer to a question asking what percent of their upper-class patients "could be described as class conscious in terms of being aware of themselves as members of a social group distinct from others." Another twelve believed that 70–80% of such patients were class conscious. One said 60% were, three said 40–50%, and two said 25%. Only three took the lowest choice, 5–10%. In short, most of the psychoanalysts who have seen such patients believe that most of them are class conscious.

There is some speculation that women of the upper class are more class conscious than the men. However, most of the psychoanalysts saw no difference. Those who did were evenly divided as to whether men or women were more class conscious. The analysts also were asked what they thought created any class consciousness that they discerned. The most frequent answer was the family, with schools running a distant second. Several of the psychoanalysts were kind enough to send further comments on the psychology of their upper-class patients. These comments suggest that in-depth discussions with psychoanalysts could be very useful.[39] For now, it is enough to say that the testimony of several psychoanalysts hopefully in a position to know supports the observations of insiders and novelists.

## The Testimony of an "Informant"

Perhaps the most interesting result of the questionnaire to psychoanalysts was that it brought me into correspondence with a person who is both a psychologist and a member of the upper class. This person, whose credentials are impeccable and go back several generations, gave me detailed

39. Herbert E. Krugman, "The Role of Hostility in the Appeal of Communism in the United States" (*Psychiatry*, August, 1953) demonstrates the usefulness of careful interviews with psychoanalysts.

comments on class consciousness as well as differences in life style. Basing comments on the observation of "$x^N$" fellow members of the upper class, this observer believes that 95% of them are class conscious. There is agreement with the psychoanalysts in seeing neither men nor women as more class conscious, and in believing that class considerations are important for both men and women when it comes to a marriage partner. The family is given great importance in inculcating the feelings that are part of this class consciousness. This participant also testifies to the ability of upper-class people to recognize one another, which implies some sort of awareness:

> UC individuals certainly do recognize one another, by many variations of "the old school tie"; accent; understatement in dress and behavior frequently; common assumptions and values; maintenance of standards of behavior; and by a characteristic sense of "noblesse oblige" which is really a *sine qua non* . . .

Nationwide contacts are documented in passing:

> One of the ways that UC members know people all over the country is by keeping up with those they knew at schools and colleges typically attended by their number. And of course, when they move around, their friends write and alert friends in the new locality, who show hospitality, and tend to incorporate them into the local UC.

The letters of this correspondent also make it clear that the subjective sense of "upper classness" does not correlate perfectly with our institutional indicators, at least in this person's mind. Looking at it from the perspective of a family that has been in the upper class for several generations, this participant-observer sees many very wealthy private school graduates and club members as upper-middle class. Right or wrong, the comments of this sophisticated informant are very interesting. They raise questions that should be broached with other members of the upper class. If cooperation could be obtained, in-depth interviews and free association sessions might go beyond questionnaires and polls in determining the consciousness of the American upper class.[40]

## SUMMARY

I think the evidence I have presented on in-group inter-actions and life style demonstrates the cohesiveness that makes the American upper class a sociological reality. As my psychologist–informant assured me in the unexpected letter offering an insider's lifetime of observations: "[Members of the upper class] are not a figment of the imagination, nor a machination of the unconscious, and need to be defined and evaluated if the record is to be complete." Unfortunately, I am not able to put a quantitative stamp on the degree of cohesiveness that characterizes the upper class. Nor am I able to compare it quantitatively with the cohesiveness of other social layers in America or with upper classes in other countries. It would take very subtle and expensive studies to make such comparisons, probably involving extensive interviewing and field observation. However, I believe it can be argued that the upper class is more cohesive than any other level of the American social hierarchy. Its smaller size, greater wealth, different sources of income (stocks and bonds), different schooling, different leisure activities, and different occupations, not to mention its complicated web of intermarriages, are among the evidences for this statement.

I also think there is ample evidence for asserting that

40. Herbert Hendlin, Willard Gaylin, and Arthur Carr, *Psychoanalysis and Social Research: The Psychoanalytic Study of the Non-Patient* (Garden City: Doubleday & Co., 1965), introduction and pp. 103ff, demonstrates the possibilities of this approach.

an upper class exists in American consciousness. *We* know *they* exist, even if society page readers are the only Americans who know of very many examples by name. And *they* know *they* are members of a privileged social class. *They* also know *they* have a good thing going, which no doubt sets certain limitations on the activities and verbalizations of most of *them*; surely we do not need a smug multi-millionaire like William F. Buckley, Jr., to remind us of that truism.[41]

Psychoanalyst Theodore Reik once told his great mentor, Sigmund Freud, that the psychoanalytic method reminded him of the detective work of Sherlock Holmes. Freud said no, it was more like the work of a certain art historian, Giovanni Morelli, who had developed a method of identifying paintings by studying their unimportant and irrelevant aspects. Instead of studying the choice of subjects or the use of colors, this astute art detective turned to minor details such as fingernails and ear lobes in order to determine whether or not the painting was by a given person. The details of an eyelid, like a slip of the tongue, give the whole game away. In this spirit, I offer in conclusion the following irrelevancies to support the case for the existence of a national upper class that is cohesive and conscious:

1. The ninety bands of Meyer Davis and the twenty-five bands of Lester Lanin play at society parties and debutante balls all over the country.[42]

2. "The same style of decoration can be found in the homes of socialites all over the country. And the reason again is that a handful of decorators gets all the society trade. Most of these designers, as they like to be called, live in New York, but wealthy clients

41. William F. Buckley, Jr., "God Bless the Rich" (*Saturday Evening Post*, December 30, 1967), p. 4.
42. Personal communications from Meyer Davis Productions and Lester Lanin Orchestras. The number of "bands" the two organizations maintain is lower during certain times of the year.

do not hesitate to fly an approved decorator to Houston, Cleveland or Los Angeles."[43]

3. The maid's night out is Thursday throughout the United States from Portland, Oregon to Norwich, Connecticut.

43. Kavaler, *op. cit.,* pp. 26–7.

# Part Two

# THE UPPER CLASS
# AS A
# GOVERNING CLASS

# Introduction

The essays in the previous section provide the sociological and psychological context within which to consider the question of the involvement of members of the upper class in the political process. By emphasizing the bonds of wealth, education and friendship that unite this group, we can put political disagreements among its members within their proper perspective. That is, we can comprehend why journalist Douglass Cater is probably right when he says that there is often more smoke than fire in Washington disputes, with a good part of the theatrics for the benefit of home audiences.[1]

1. Douglass Cater, *Power in Washington* (New York: Random House, 1964), p. 241.

It might be said that the essays in this section are concerned with "power," but that word is so fraught with ambiguities that I prefer by and large to ignore it except as part of the phrase "power elite," which will be defined shortly. "Power," as we all know, is "clout," or "juice," or "what it takes," but when we have to define it or measure it we stumble badly. For myself, I prefer to infer power from various indicators which tell us something about the relative distribution of things people seek as valuable, but except for a few asides I will content myself in this book to say that I am exploring the involvement of members of the upper class in the political process. Readers can decide for themselves whether or not the use of the term "power" is appropriate.

While it is easy to avoid the word "power," it is not possible to avoid certain other words. In my first book, I used "control," by which I meant that a person or group of persons had legal authority over a given institution or organization. I then presented evidence purporting to show that members of the upper class control major corporations, foundations, policy-planning associations, and the executive branch of the federal government. However, my use of the term got me in trouble with several reviewers, one of whom, a sharp-eyed Marxist, even found two or three places where I had used the word in passing in a slightly different sense. Since "control" as I used it caused so many problems, I would like to try again. I begin with the friendly criticisms of a former colleague, political scientist Benjamin W. Smith:

> Domhoff chose to single out "control" as a crucial relational component. The concept of control is used for two different types of institutions—corporations and the federal government. As I said earlier, in the case of economic institutions, authority over personnel based on legal ownership is sufficiently clear. However, the same criteria of control cannot legitimately be used to argue control of government, which legitimates ownership in the first place. . . .

This said, Domhoff does offer the initial steps toward an adequate grounds for establishing the continuity of "control" between corporate and governmental institutions in his chapter on "policy-planning" institutions of the upper class. Here he clearly implies that the evidence substantiating "control" of the federal government must have an independent institutional base which shapes the ways in which the selection and replacement of political personnel takes place. The "policy-planning" upper-class institutions seem to govern *access* to the policy-forming process and to shape and provide the personnel recruited to key institutions of the government. However, he does not fully develop this analysis. . . .

*Who Rules America?* will be criticized on this account by academic pluralists who will never allow his use of the term "control" for the federal government on the basis of power elite personnel in government office. In any case, his governing-class model does not need the term. Political recruitment, political resources, elaborate channels of intra-class and power elite communication, personnel participation in historic issue decision, and frequency and ease of access to decision centers are quite sufficient types of data to justify typing the American, political order as a governing-class system.[2]

I think Smith's comments are well taken, and they provide a good starting point for restatement. Henceforth I will use the term "control" to mean legal authority over non-governmental organizations and institutions. "Control" will refer to what various members of the upper class have over most major corporations, foundations, and private universities. What word, then, should we use to characterize the great involvement of members and organizations of the upper class in the political process? I propose "dominance." By this I mean members of the upper class sit in pivotal government offices, define most major policy issues, shape the policy proposals on issues raised outside their circles,

2. Benjamin W. Smith, "Who Rules America?: A Review" (Unpublished text prepared for the Government Affairs Research Center, California State College, Los Angeles), pp. 24–6.

and mold the rules of government. Legally, the government is of all of us, but members of the upper class have the predominant, all-pervasive influence. In short, they dominate it, as the following three essays will make clear.

Just how members of the upper class dominate the political process is of great concern to social scientists. They want to know the specific mechanisms by which members of the upper class formulate and communicate political issues, reach a degree of consensus, and act as a relatively cohesive force in the arena of policy formation. I hope the essays that follow will contribute to a satisfactory answer to these concerns. Although relatively few members of the upper class concern themselves with political matters, and although members of the upper class are not elected or appointed by their compatriots to secret ruling committees, it is the case that there are a variety of foundations, associations, committees, and institutes within which members of the upper class participate if they wish to be active in determining policy. These foundations, institutes, and associations—along with corporate board rooms and gentlemen's clubs—are the citadels wherein consensus is reached and from which natural leaders emerge. If the process of developing upper-class leaders is not what would be expected by those who focus on the formal operations of representative government, perhaps it is something like what would be expected by social psychologists and sociologists who have observed leadership in gangs, clubs, universities and informal groups.

Leaders within the upper class do not labor alone in dominating the political process. They have the help of hired employees: high-level managers and officials in corporations, law firms, foundations and associations controlled by members of the upper class. Together, these upper-class leaders and their high-level employees constitute the power elite. I define the power elite as active, working members of the upper class and high-level employees in institutions controlled by members of the upper class. The power elite has its roots in and serves the interests of the social upper class. It is the operating arm of the upper class. It functions to maintain and manage a socioeconomic system which is organized in such a way that it yields an amazing proportion of its wealth to a minuscule upper class of big businessmen and their descendants.

To speak of a power elite is not to say that its many thousands of members are in agreement on each and every issue. Far from it. There are conservative and moderate tendencies within the power elite. These two tendencies dominate the major coalitions in American society, which means that some groups among the underlying population are more in sympathy with the moderates while other groups find the conservatives more deserving of their loyalty. Simply put, the moderates have been extremely internationalist in foreign policy and moderately welfare-oriented on domestic policy, while the conservatives have been somewhat isolationist on foreign policy and extremely opposed to any welfare spending or concessions to labor unions. To help readers keep these and other disagreements in mind, I will usually refer to the power elite in the plural "they" rather than the singular "it." However, what should be clear is that the limits of most policy disputes in the United States are defined by the limits of differences within the power elite. Other groups in the population are sometimes taken into account, especially when they are angry, but they are seldom an integral part of the deliberations.

The implicit protagonist throughout this section is a viewpoint called "pluralism." The final essay in the book will have a great deal to say about one version of this view, but for now it is enough to let a leading spokesman for it present a concise summary of its major tenets:

> At the other extreme [from C. Wright Mills] are neo-pluralists like Truman, Key, and Latham (and perhaps Berle) who suggest that there are a number of loci for arriving at political decisions; that businessmen, trade unions, politicians, con-

sumers, farmers, voters, and many other aggregates all have an impact on policy outcomes; that none of the aggregates is homogeneous for all purposes; that each of them is highly influential over some scopes but weak over many others: and that the power to reject undesired alternatives is more common than the power to dominate over outcomes directly.[3]

The first essay in this section presents in considerable detail a model of how members and organizations of the upper class initiate and carry out foreign policy with very little pressure or involvement on the part of any group within the underlying population. It provides a framework within which studies of foreign policy formation can be made. Such a framework has been lacking in all the literature I examined on this subject. The second essay shows how members and organizations of the upper class, faced with considerable pressure from other elements of the population, shaped the important welfare legislation of this century. It has greater historical depth and goes into more detail on specific decisions than does the first essay. The final essay in this section recounts certain CIA activities, revealing another face of the upper class and casting a different light on the mentality of many of its members.

In re-reading the three essays of this section as a preparation for writing this introduction, I was struck once again by the two empirically-based generalizations that emerge from them: Moderate leaders within the upper class, somewhat restrained by their more conservative brethren, have made the key decisions of the twentieth century; these moderate leaders have been helped in every area—foreign policy, domestic policy, propaganda and espionage—by a small number of highly-respected academic experts who are situated in a handful of prestigious and richly endowed universities.

The research presented in this section has reinforced me

3. Robert A. Dahl, "Business and Politics," in *Social Science Research on Business* (New York: Columbia University Press, 1959), p. 36.

in my belief that the American upper class is a governing class, by which I mean a social upper class which owns a disproportionate amount of the country's wealth, receives a disproportionate share of the country's yearly income, contributes a disproportionate number of its members to governmental bodies and decision-making groups, and dominates the policy-forming process through a variety of means to be discussed in the following essays. The governing class manifests itself through a power elite which is its operating arm. It is with this power elite that the next three essays are concerned.

# CHAPTER FIVE

# How the Power Elite
# Make Foreign Policy*

This essay will attempt to show that American foreign policy is initiated, planned, and carried out by members and organizations of a power elite that is rooted in and serves the interests of an upper class of rich businessmen and their descendants. It will be claimed that none of the factors often of importance in domestic issues—Congress, labor, public opinion—has anything but an occasional and minor effect on foreign policy. If there is one issue-area truly and solely

* I wish to thank undergraduate research assistant Mark Goldowitz for his help in gathering and organizing material for this essay, an earlier version of which appeared in *Corporations and the Cold War,* David Horowitz, ed. (New York: Monthly Review Press, 1969). This new version benefited from the comments of Douglas Fox, David Horowitz and Richard Hamilton.

the domain of the power elite, it is foreign policy. Given the great importance of foreign policy in determining the framework within which all types of policy-making take place, power elite dominance of this single issue-area gives them a great influence on all aspects of the political process.

The making of foreign policy takes place within an environment or setting: the international community of nations, American public opinion, mass media, political interest groups, agencies of the executive branch and committees of Congress. However, it is possible to suggest that public opinion is rarely felt and that Congress is usually bypassed. Moreover, it is possible to be much more concrete in spelling out the specific mechanisms within which the decision-makers function. In general, the most important institutions in foreign policy decision-making are large corporations and banks, closely intertwined charitable foundations, two or three discussion and research associations financed by these corporations and foundations, and the National Security Council, State Department, Defense Department, and specially appointed committees of the federal government. Admittedly, this is only the most important core, for there are several other private and university-affiliated research and opinion-molding organizations, as well as several other agencies of the federal government.

## THE COUNCIL
## ON FOREIGN RELATIONS

To give empirical flesh to these generalizations, there is no better starting point than the Council on Foreign Relations (CFR). It is the key middle term, so to speak, between the large corporations on the one hand and the federal government on the other. By studying its connections in both directions, it is possible to establish the first link we are looking for in showing the specific mechanisms by which the power elite formulate and transfer their wishes into government policy. While it would be hard to underestimate the importance of this organization in understanding the overall framework for American foreign policy, I do not want to overemphasize it, and we will see that there are other links between big business and big government.

The Council on Foreign Relations is a nonpartisan research and discussion group dedicated to informing citizens about world affairs and creating an interest in international relations. Despite its reputed prominence and the fact that it was founded in 1921, most information on it comes from its own publications: a fifteen-year history, a twenty-five-year history and annual reports. One of the few who has written on it, Washington journalist Joseph Kraft, noted in 1958 that it was mentioned only five times in *Time* magazine in the period 1953–1958.[1] We can go one step further and say that there never has been any research paper on it in any scholarly journal indexed in the *Social Science and Humanities Index*. While this may suggest it is not very important, there are several ways to establish its crucial role, including testimony by journalists and scholars, the acknowledged preeminence of its journal (*Foreign Affairs*), the nature of its financial backing, the composition of its leadership and membership, and the presence of its members in federal government positions.

To begin with expert testimony, CFR was called by Kraft a "school for statesmen [which] comes close to being an organ of what C. Wright Mills has called the Power Elite— a group of men, similar in interest and outlook, shaping events from invulnerable positions behind the scenes."[2] Douglass Cater, a journalist from Exeter and Harvard who

---

1. Joseph Kraft, "School for Statesmen" (*Harper's Magazine*, July, 1958), p. 64.
2. *Ibid.*, pp. 64, 68.

served on the staff of President Lyndon B. Johnson, has noted that "a diligent scholar would do well to delve into the role of the purely unofficial Council on Foreign Relations in the care and breeding of an incipient American Establishment."[3] *The New York Times* calls it "a testing ground for new ideas, with enough political and financial power to bring the ideas to the attention of the policy makers in Washington."[4] Political scientist Lester Milbrath notes that "The Council on Foreign Relations, while not financed by government, works so closely with it that it is difficult to distinguish Council actions stimulated by government from autonomous actions."[5]

Empirically speaking, such reputational testimony is the least important of our evidence. Far more important is CFR's financing and leadership. Aside from membership dues, dividends from invested gifts and bequests, and profits from the sale of *Foreign Affairs,* the most important sources of income are leading corporations and major foundations. In 1957–58, for example, Chase Manhattan, Continental Can, Ford Motor, Bankers Trust, Cities Service, Gulf, Otis Elevator, General Motors Overseas Operations, Brown Brothers, Harriman, and International General Electric were paying from $1,000 to $10,000 per year for the corporation service, depending upon the size of the company and its interest in international affairs. (The benefits of subscribing to this corporation service are as follows: free consultation with all members of the CFR staff, subscriptions to *Foreign Affairs* for leading officers of the corporation, the use of the Council's excellent library which is second to none in its field, and the right to nominate one

3. Douglass Cater, *Power in Washington* (New York: Random House, 1964), p. 247.
4. "Experts on Policy Looking to Youth" (*The New York Times,* May 15, 1966), p. 34.
5. Lester Milbrath, "Interest Groups and Foreign Policy" in James N. Rosenau, ed., *Domestic Sources of Foreign Policy* (New York: Free Press, 1967), p. 247.

"promising young executive" to participate in seminars whch the Council conducts each fall and spring for the benefit of the corporations.)[6] More generally, in 1960–61, eighty-four large corporations and financial institutions contributed 12% ($112,200) of CFR's total income. As to the foundations, the major contributors over the years have been the Rockefeller Foundation and the Carnegie Corporation, with the Ford Foundation joining in with a large grant in the 1950's. According to Kraft, a $2.5 million grant in the early 1950's from the Ford, Rockefeller, and Carnegie foundations made the Council "the most important single private agency conducting research in foreign affairs."[7] In 1960–61, foundation money accounted for 25% of CFR income.

The foundations which support the CFR are in turn directed by men from Bechtel Construction, Chase Manhattan, Cummins Engine, Corning Glass, Kimberly-Clark, Monsanto Chemical, and dozens of other corporations. Further, to complete the circle, most foundation directors are members of CFR. In the early 1960's, Dan Smoot found that twelve of twenty Rockefeller Foundation trustees, ten of fifteen Ford Foundation trustees, and ten of fourteen Carnegie Corporation trustees were members of CFR.[8] Nor is this interlock of recent origin. In 1922, for example, former Secretary of State Elihu Root, a corporation lawyer, was honorary CFR president as well as president of the Carnegie Corporation, while John W. Davis, the corporation lawyer who ran for President on the Democratic ticket in 1924, was a trustee of both the Carnegie Corporation and CFR.

A consideration of the leadership and membership of CFR is equally conclusive in establishing its relationship to

---

6. *Annual Report of the Council on Foreign Relations,* 1957–58.
7. Kraft, *op. cit.,* p. 68.
8. Dan Smoot, *The Invisible Government* (Dallas: The Dan Smoot Report, 1962), pp. 168–71.

the power elite. Its founders included two lawyers and two bankers from Wall Street. The single permanent official of CFR at its outset, Hamilton Fish Armstrong, and the first editor of *Foreign Affairs,* Archibald Coolidge, were both from well-known, upper-class families. Indeed, Hamiltons, Fishes and Armstrongs have been involved in American foreign policy since the beginnings of the Republic. Nor has anything changed since the early 1920's, with fourteen of the twenty-two recent or current directors as of the early 1960's being listed in the Social Register. Among the most prominent of the recent directors highly visible in the corporate elite are Frank Altschul, Elliott V. Bell, Thomas K. Finletter (one-time Secretary of the Air Force), Devereaux C. Josephs, John J. McCloy, David Rockefeller and Adlai E. Stevenson.

The CFR limits itself to 700 New York area residents and 700 non-New York residents (no women or foreigners are allowed to join). As of the mid-sixties, 46% of the resident members and 49% of the non-resident members, most of whom are big businessmen and lawyers, were listed in the Social Register.[9] The Council's only other formal associates are the Committees on Foreign Relations that have been formed in about thirty cities across the country. These committees come together at dinners and other occasions to hear speakers (mostly supplied by CFR) and exchange ideas. This committee program has been financed since 1938 by the Carnegie Corporation.[10] We were able to locate information on 509 committee members from twenty-nine cities ranging in size and importance from Philadelphia, Detroit and Atlanta to Albuquerque, Boise and Little Rock. A significant minority of those studied (41%) were corporate executives and bankers. Twenty-one percent were lawyers, almost half of whom (44%) were also corporate directors. Thus, a small majority

9. John F. Whitney, Jr., "The Council on Foreign Relations, Inc." (Unpublished research paper, Texas A and I University, January, 1968).
10. Smoot, *op. cit.,* p. 21.

(51%) were directly involved in business enterprises. Another significant group consisted of educators (22%), most of whom were college presidents, political scientists, economists, and deans. Seven percent of those studied were editors or publishers, with the remainder being small numbers of government officials, politicians, church leaders, physicians, accountants and museum directors.

Turning to the all-important question of government involvement, the presence of CFR members in government has been attested to by Kraft, Cater, Smoot, CFR histories and *The New York Times,* but the point is made most authoritatively by John J. McCloy, Wall Street lawyer, former chairman of Chase Manhattan, trustee of the Ford Foundation, director of CFR and a government appointee in a variety of roles since the early 1940's: "Whenever we needed a man," said McCloy in explaining the presence of CFR members in the modern defense establishment that fought World War II, "we thumbed through the roll of council members and put through a call to New York."[11] According to Kraft, "When John McCloy went to Bonn as US High Commissioner, he took with him a staff composed almost exclusively of men who had interested themselves in German affairs at the Council."[12] CFR members also were prominent in the US delegation to the founding of the United Nations, and several dozen have held high posts in postwar administrations. One *Annual Report* spoke as follows in an obituary notice:

> [John Foster] Dulles was a member of the Council almost from the start. He wrote an article on "The Allied Debts" for the first issue of *Foreign Affairs* and six more articles thereafter, including two while Secretary of State. He participated in numerous study and discussion groups over the years and spoke often at Council afternoon meetings and dinners, twice as Secretary of State.[13]

11. Kraft, *op. cit.,* p. 67.
12. *Ibid.,* p. 68.
13. *Annual Report of the Council on Foreign Relations,* 1958–59, p. 4.

Theodore White, in recounting how Lyndon Johnson won the Presidency in 1964, wrote as follows about the relationship of the Council to government:

> Its roster of members has for a generation, under Republican and Democratic administrations alike, been the chief recruiting ground for Cabinet-level officials in Washington. Among the first eighty-two names on a list prepared for John F. Kennedy for staffing his State Department, at least sixty-three were members of the Council, Republicans and Democrats alike. When, finally, he made his appointments, both his Secretary of State (Rusk, Democrat) and Treasury (Dillon, Republican) were chosen from Council members; so were seven assistant and undersecretaries of State, four senior members of Defense, . . . as well as two members of the White House staff (Schlesinger, Democrat; Bundy, Republican).[14]

Now that we have located the CFR in sociological space as an institution controlled by members of the upper class, we are in a position to see what it does and how effective it is in shaping foreign policy. As to what the CFR does, in addition to serving as a talent pool and training ground for government service, it is a tax-exempt, non-partisan organization which sponsors education, discussion and research on all aspects of foreign affairs. As part of its educational effort, it brings before its exclusive membership leading scholars and government officials from all nations to make off-the-record speeches and to answer questions from the members. And, as Kraft notes, this not only educates the members, it gives them a chance to size up important leaders with whom they will have to deal.[15] Also under the heading of education, CFR publishes *Foreign Affairs,* by far the most important journal in its field,

---

14. Theodore H. White, *The Making of the President 1964* (New York: Atheneum Publishers, 1965), pp. 67–8.
15. Kraft, *op. cit.,* p. 66. A perusal of any annual report of the CFR will show that a foreign official visiting in New York who is anyone at all will be speaking or meeting with members of the Council.

and three annual surveys: *Political Handbook of the World, The United States in World Affairs,* and *Documents on American Foreign Relations.*

Despite the importance of speeches and publications, I think the most important aspects of the CFR program are its special discussion groups and study groups. These small groups of about twenty-five bring together businessmen, government officials, military men and scholars for detailed discussions of specific topics in the area of foreign affairs. Discussion groups explore problems in a general way, trying to define issues and alternatives. Such groups often lead to a study group as the next stage. Study groups revolve around the work of a Council research fellow (financed by Carnegie, Ford and Rockefeller) or a staff member. This group leader usually presents monthly papers, which are discussed and criticized by the rest of the group. The goal of such study groups is a detailed statement of the problem by the scholar leading the discussion. In 1957–58, for example, the Council published six books which grew out of study groups. Perhaps the most famous of these was written by Henry Kissinger, a bright young McGeorge Bundy protégé at Harvard who was asked by the CFR to head a study group. His *Nuclear Weapons and Foreign Policy* was "a best seller which has been closely read in the highest Administration circles and foreign offices abroad."[16] As to his study group, it included "two former chairmen of the Atomic Energy Commission, a Nobel Prize winner in physics, two former civilian secretaries in the Defense Department and representatives just below the highest level from the State Department, the Central Intelligence Agency and the three armed services."[17] When economist Percy Bidwell of the CFR staff led a discussion on foreign tariff, an issue that will be discussed later, the study group included ten corporate representatives, ten economists, two

16. *Ibid.*
17. *Ibid.*

communications experts from MIT's Center for International Studies, a minor Defense Department official and a foreign service officer.[18]

It is within these discussion groups and study groups, where privacy is the rule to encourage members to speak freely, that members of the power elite study and plan as to how best to attain American objectives in world affairs. It is here that they discuss alternatives and hash out differences, far from the limelight of official government and mass media. As *The New York Times* says of these unpublicized luncheons and closed seminars: "Except for its annual public Elihu Root Lectures, the Council's talks and seminars are strictly off the record. An indiscretion can be grounds for termination or suspension of membership. . . ."[19] Such discussions also help to reduce the effect of political changes. In Kraft's language: ". . . the Council plays a special part in helping to bridge the gap between the two parties, affording unofficially a measure of continuity when the guard changes in Washington."[20]

Given its privacy as to discussions (it is quite open about everything else), can we know the relationship between CFR and government policy? Can we go beyond the fact that CFR conducts research and discussions and that its members hold responsible positions in the federal government? It is not only secrecy which makes this question hard to answer; there is also the problem that CFR as an organization does not take a partisan stand. To even begin to answer such a question completely would require a large number of studies of various decisions and their outcomes. In lieu of such studies, the most important and easy of which would be on the origins of the bipartisan foreign policy of postwar years, several suggestive examples will

18. Percy W. Bidwell, *What the Tariff Means to American Industries* (published for the Council on Foreign Relations by Harper & Row, New York, 1956).
19. "Experts on Foreign Policy Look to Youth," *op cit.,* p. 34.
20. Kraft, *op. cit.,* p. 68.

have to suffice, along with the general testimony of Kraft ("It has been the seat of some basic government decisions, has set the context for many more") and *The New York Times* ("Discussion groups, scholarly papers and studies sponsored by the Council laid the groundwork for the Marshall Plan for European recovery, set American policy guidelines for the North Atlantic Treaty Organization, and currently are evolving a long-range analysis of American attitudes toward China").[21] More concretely, Kraft claims that CFR action was responsible for putting Greenland out of bounds for the Nazis, for shaping the United Nations charter, and for softening the American position on German postwar reparations, among others. One of the most impressive evidences is that four CFR planning groups, set up in 1939 with aid from the Rockefeller Foundation, were taken (along with most of the personnel) into the State Department in 1942 "as the nub of its Advisory Committee on Postwar Planning Problems."[22] And it was supposedly a special CFR briefing session in early 1947 that convinced Undersecretary of State Robert Lovett of Brown Brothers, Harriman that "it would be our principal task at State to awaken the nation to the dangers of Communist aggression."[23]

Despite the fact that the CFR is an organization most Americans have never heard of, I think we have clearly established by a variety of means that it is a key connection between the federal government and the owners and managers of the country's largest financial institutions and corporations. It is an organization of the power elite. If it is not all-embracing in its importance, it is certainly a consider-

21. *Ibid.*, p. 64; "Experts on Foreign Policy Look to Youth," *op. cit.,* p. 34.
22. Kraft, *op. cit.,* p. 67. Much of Kraft's information on CFR involvement in specific issues seems to be drawn from CFR's self-published 25-year history. It contains further details and information on other issues as well. See *The Council on Foreign Relations, A Record of Twenty-five Years,* New York, 1947.
23. Quoted in Kraft, *op. cit.,* p. 68.

able understatement to speak of CFR members and members of similar power elite associations, as one scholar does, as "external bureaucrats" who supply the government with information, perspectives, and manpower.[24] In my view, what knowledge we have of CFR suggests that through it the power elite formulate general guidelines for American foreign policy and provide the personnel to carry out this policy. But I also know that the evidence I have presented is not enough for those scholars who prefer to analyze actual decisions. Then, too, skeptics can point out that CFR has no policy (other than the all-important policy of international involvement, as opposed to isolationism, for which it is called "Communist" and "Un-American" by older-fashioned, nationalistic critics). Furthermore, skeptics can say that CFR's members have other institutional and associational affiliations that may be more important in determining their outlook. For all of these reasons, I will let the case for CFR rest at this point, noting the presence of its directors and members only in passing, and instead emphasizing the direct corporate connections of important decision-makers. In closing this discussion of the CFR as an organization of the power elite, it should be noted that Kraft is among the skeptics. Despite all the comments we have quoted from him on the importance of CFR, he concludes that "even that cock will not fight" as far as the CFR being part of any power elite. This is because CFR has assumed "semi-official duties only in emergencies," because it "has never accepted government financial support" and because its recommendations "have subsequently all stood test at the polls or in Congress." Furthermore, there are "divergent views" within the Council, and such an organization is necessary because issues are too complicated for the ordinary citizen, who is all wrapped up in his private life. Kraft's concluding sentence seems to be a challenge

24. Chadwick F. Alger, "The External Bureaucracy in United States Foreign Affairs (*Administration Science Quarterly*, June, 1962).

to those who might criticize—he quotes Voltaire, asking, "What have you got that's better?"[25]

## OTHER POLICY-PLANNING GROUPS

The Council on Foreign Relations is by no means the only power elite link between the corporations and the federal government in the issue-area of foreign policy. There are many others, perhaps the most important of which are the Committee for Economic Development, the RAND Corporation and a handful of research institutes affiliated with elite universities. Turning to the first of these, the Committee for Economic Development (CED) is a tax-exempt research organization which is in many ways the counterpart on economic policy of the Council on Foreign Relations. While its concentration on monetary and economic problems makes it more prominent on issues involving the Departments of Treasury and Commerce, it has on several occasions played a major role in shaping foreign policy.[26] Organized in the early 1940's to prepare for postwar reconversion to a civilian economy, the leaders in its formation were financier Jesse Jones, then Secretary of Commerce, and millionaires Paul Hoffman and William Benton. These three men brought together corporation executives and bankers with outstanding economists for weekend study sessions which were intensified versions of the CFR study groups. Out of these sessions came the guidelines for American economic policy in the postwar era, including some of the provisions of the Employment Act of 1946, the stabilized budget concept, long-range fiscal and monetary policy, and certain aspects of the Marshall

25. Kraft, *op. cit.*, p. 68.
26. Karl Schriftgiesser, *Business Comes of Age* (New York: Harper & Row, 1960).

Plan. Perhaps the most impressive evidence for CED prominence in foreign policy is that its corporate elite members and hired economists were the men who moved into the government to administer the Marshall Plan. That CED head Paul Hoffman of Studebaker and the Ford Foundation became administrator of the Marshall Plan is only the surface of the iceberg.

The relationship of the CED to the corporations really does not need to be established, for membership is limited to big businessmen and a handful of university presidents. Among its original and most active members have been Ralph Flanders, the Vermont toolmaker and Boston banker; Thomas B. McCabe, head of Scott Paper Company; Clarence Francis of General Foods; Marion B. Folsom of Eastman Kodak; William L. Clayton of Clayton, Anderson; William L. Batt of SKF Industries; Charles E. Wilson of General Electric; Eric A. Johnston of the Brown-Johnston Company; Chester C. Davis of the Federal Reserve Bank of St. Louis; and S. Bayard Colgate of Colgate-Palmolive-Peet. As with the CFR, many CED members become officials of the federal government: thirty-eight of the trustees during the first fifteen years of CED held elective or appointive positions.[27] Flanders and Benton became senators, McCabe became head of the Federal Reserve Bank under President Truman, and Folsom, Clayton, William C. Foster, and Wayne C. Taylor held important posts in major departments. As of the early 1960's, forty-eight of 190 CED trustees were at the same time members of CFR.

Perhaps the best known of the power elite's large research organizations is the RAND Corporation, a name which is an acronym for "research and development." It has been credited with many technical innovations and operational suggestions. Started after the war with government research contracts and Ford Foundation money to

27. *Ibid.*, pp. 25, 62, 162.

"think" for the Air Force, it has since expanded its staff and facilities to provide this service for the entire federal government. Its 500-man professional staff is well-paid and well-educated (150 have Ph.D.'s) due to the fact that RAND was purposely set up as a non-governmental agency so that civil service rules and salary scales could be avoided in order to attract the finest talent money could buy. It is governed by a board of trustees which is made up of members of the power elite. In 1963, when RAND published a report on its first 15 years, the board included executives from CBS, Hewlett-Packard, Owens-Corning Fiberglas International, Monsanto Chemical and New England Electric System, as well as the president of one of the Carnegie foundations, a leading official in the Council on Foreign Relations, the former vice president of the Carnegie Corporation (then president of Cornell) and the presidents of MIT and Rice University.[28] Seven of the seventeen trustees were members of the CFR. Of fifteen former trustees, seven were leading figures in the corporate world. The rest were university administrators or physicists. The most important of these former trustees was H. Rowan Gaither, a West Coast attorney, banker, and Ford Foundation trustee who was one of the key organizers of RAND. His legacy is seen in two of the 1963 trustees not with one of the companies listed above: Frederick Anderson is a partner in the investment firm of Draper, Gaither, and Anderson; Edwin E. Huddleson, Jr., is a partner in the law firm of Cooley, Crowley, Gaither, Godward, Castro, and Huddleson.

In addition to CFR, CED, and RAND there are many other associations and research organizations controlled by members of the power elite. About 300 study centers consult for the Defense Department alone.[29] Rather than try-

---

28. RAND Corporation, *The First Fifteen Years* (Santa Monica, California: The Rand Corporation, 1963).
29. Arthur Herzog, *The War-Peace Establishment* (New York: Harper & Row, 1965), p. 54.

ing to outline any more of these specific links, I want to turn instead to a more general, less direct link between the power elite and the federal government: the world of academic scholarship. As we have seen in the case of CFR, CED and RAND, members of the power elite are not averse to seeking advice from professional researchers, a fact which has led some to claim that "experts" control the country. Without emphasizing the direct power of these scholars, for they are often ignored and seldom have decision-making roles, it can be added that the power elite pay for their training and encourage them by monetary inducements to study certain questions rather than others. This is accomplished, first, by the general framework created at major universities through financing and through service on boards of trustees. Second, it is accomplished by foundation grants which encourage research on specific questions. Thus, Rockefeller, Carnegie, and Ford money are responsible in one way or another for almost all American research in non-Western areas.[30] While many of these grants are to universities to provide scholarships and to individuals to undertake specific research projects, the foundations also provide money for institutes affiliated with universities. For example, Ford and Carnegie money finance a Russian Research Center at Harvard, Rockefeller money finances a Russian Research Center at Columbia. Scholars from these institutes are frequent consultants to the Council on Foreign Relations.

The interrelationship of corporate-controlled foundations, think factories, and university research institutes can be demonstrated by studying the prefaces to leading books in the field of foreign affairs. For example, Gabriel A. Almond, of the very prominent Princeton Center of International Studies (publisher of *World Affairs,* which is second only to CFR's *Foreign Affairs* in this field), offers

30. George M. Beckmann, "The Role of Foundations" (*The Annals of the American Academy of Political and Social Science,* November, 1964).

thanks to the Carnegie Corporation for the funds which made possible his study of *The Appeals of Communism.* Carnegie also supplied the funds for *The Civic Culture: Political Attitudes and Democracy in Five Nations,* co-authored by Almond and Sidney Verba. Thomas C. Schelling of the Center for International Affairs at Harvard wrote *The Strategy of Conflict* during a year-long stay at the RAND Corporation, and Herman Kahn did most of the research for *On Thermonuclear War,* published by the Princeton Center, while at the RAND Corporation. Lucian Pye's *Aspects of Political Development* was written while at the MIT Center for International Studies, with the help of Carnegie money. Walt W. Rostow of the MIT Center, a leading adviser to Democratic presidents during the 1960's, wrote his "non-communist manifesto," *Stages of Economic Growth,* during a "reflective year" grant provided by the Carnegie Corporation. Harry Eckstein edited *Internal War* for the Princeton Center with the help of Carnegie funds; an earlier version of Eckstein's own contribution, "On the Etiology of Internal Wars," was published in *Social Science and National Security,* a book which had government circulation only. Apparently, such secret books are not unusual. According to one source, it is "standard procedure at MIT and elsewhere" to publish two versions, "one classified for circulation within the intelligence community, the other 'sanitized' for public consumption."[31] While I do not believe for a minute that the power elite dictate to these scholars as to what to say, it should be clear that members of the power elite see no reason to discontinue their support of such efforts. The relationship has been explained by political scientist David Easton:

> . . . a deeper social reason for the failure of political science to transcend its limitations . . . lies in the proximity of political research to social forces that determine social policy.

31. David Wise and Thomas D. Ross, *The Invisible Government* (New York: Random House, 1964), p. 243.

. . . Entrenched power groups in society, those who have a firm hold on a particular pattern of distribution of social goods, material and spiritual, have a special reason to look askance at this probing into the nature and source of their social positions and activities. They are prone to stimulate research of a kind that does not inquire into the fundamentals of the existing arrangement of things.[32]

## THE NATIONAL SECURITY COUNCIL

To this point I have approached our problem from only one direction. That is, I started with various non-governmental institutions known to be involved in foreign affairs and showed through studies of their financing, membership, and leadership that they are controlled by the power elite. I then presented evidence as to the importance of these arms of the power elite in determining government policy. As impressive as the evidence from this approach is, it is not sufficient in and of itself. It is also necessary to start from the other direction, the important institutions and agencies within the government that are concerned with foreign policy, and work back to their ties with the power elite. It is to this task that I turn in this section. Its goal is to complete the framework within which specific foreign policy events must be analyzed. As with the non-governmental institutions, there are too many governmental units to analyze them all in any detail. Fortunately, as with the non-governmental side, there are some that are more important than others. These include a coordinating agency called the National Security Council (NSC), the Departments of State and Defense, and specially-appointed Presidential and departmental committees consisting primarily of non-governmental personnel.

The NSC was developed by the power elite, after much

32. David Easton, *The Political System* (New York: Alfred A. Knopf, Inc., 1966), pp. 50–1.

debate among the armed services and their various protagonists in Congress, on the basis of experience in attempting to coordinate departments and military units during
World War II. It is strictly an advisory group that is headed
by the President and now includes as statutory members
the Vice President, the Secretary of State, the Secretary of
Defense, and the director of the Office of Civil and Defense
Mobilization. However, "the President can also ask other
key aides to take part in Council deliberations," and in
practice this has meant the Secretary of the Treasury and
personal advisers.[33] As statutory advisers it has the director
of the Central Intelligence Agency and the Chairman of
the Joint Chiefs of Staff. The machinery of the NSC is
very flexible and has been used in different ways by different Presidents. President Eisenhower, for example, enlarged
and formalized the NSC, giving to it many powers traditionally thought of as belonging to the various departments.
President Kennedy dismantled much of this machinery,
gave more responsibility for carrying out NSC decisions to
the departments, cut its size to a minimum, and met with
it less frequently. President Johnson reduced the NSC to a
foursome that included the Secretaries of State and Defense,
but President Richard Nixon criticized this informality and
made plans to establish the agency as the key instrument
on foreign policy.[34] Thus, this formally important institution
can vary greatly in its actual usefulness in bringing about
the necessary coordination among various departments.

---

33. Henry M. Jackson, *The National Security Council: Jackson Subcom-
mitte Papers on Policy Making at the Presidential Level* (New York:
Frederick A. Praeger, 1965), p. 31. This book contains details on the
NSC and its use by various Presidents, as well as testimony on its usefulness by members of the power elite and scholars.

34. Stewart Alsop, *The Center* (New York: Harper & Row, 1968), pp.
278–80; "The Nixon Plan For Overhauling Foreign Policy" (*San Francisco Chroncile*, January 2, 1969), p. 1. "Convinced that the country's
foreign policy machinery needs an overhaul, President-elect Nixon plans
to convert the long dormant National Security Council into the central
decision-making instrument of his administration."

Who are the men who sit on the National Security Council? *Who Rules America?* partially answered this question by showing that the heads of State, Defense, and Treasury during the postwar years have been almost without exception members of the power elite. For example, Robert Lovett of Brown Brothers, Harriman served as Secretary of Defense, as did Charles Erwin Wilson of General Motors, Neil McElroy of Procter and Gamble, Thomas S. Gates, Jr., of Drexel & Co. (in 1961 he became president of Morgan Guaranty Trust) and Robert McNamara of Ford Motor. Treasury Secretaries have included John Snyder of the First National Bank of St. Louis, George Humphrey of M. A. Hanna Company, Robert Anderson of the W. T. Waggoner oil estate, and C. Douglas Dillon of Dillon, Read; heads of State have included John Foster Dulles of Sullivan and Cromwell, Dean Rusk of the Rockefeller Foundation, Dean Acheson of Covington and Burling, General George C. Marshall, and Boston aristocrat Christian Herter. It is possible to be more specific by looking at the composition of the NSC when it was studied by journalists during the Truman, Eisenhower and Kennedy administrations.

When John Fischer of *Harper's Magazine* wrote of "Mr. Truman's Politburo" as "the most powerful and least publicized of all government agencies," it included in addition to Acheson, Marshall, and Snyder the following wealthy leaders: Averell Harriman of Brown Brothers, Harriman; Charles Edward Wilson of General Electric; and Stuart Symington of Emerson Electric.[35] The secretary of the NSC was a big businessman from St. Louis, Sidney Souers. His assistant was James Lay, a former employee of utilities companies, whom Souers had met during World War II. Others present for NSC meetings were Alben Barkley, Vice President; General Walter Bedell Smith, director of the

35. John Fischer, "Mr. Truman's Politburo" (*Harper's Magazine*, June, 1951), p. 29.

CIA and General Omar Bradley, Chairman of the Joint Chiefs of Staff.

When *U.S. News & World Report* ran a story in 1956 on "How Ike Makes the Big Decisions,"[36] the following were regularly a part of the NSC in addition to Dulles, Humphrey and Charles Erwin Wilson:

Richard Nixon, Vice President, who was selected and financed for a political career by top corporate executives in Southern California

Arthur S. Flemming, a lawyer, who was formerly president of Ohio Wesleyan University

Percival Brundage, a partner in Price, Waterhouse & Company

Allen Dulles, a former partner in the large corporate law firm of Sullivan and Cromwell

Lewis Strauss, investment banker and personal financial adviser to the Rockefellers

William H. Jackson, a lawyer who managed the investment firm of John Hay Whitney, as well as sitting on the boards of Great Northern Paper and Bankers Trust

Dillon Anderson, a Houston corporation lawyer who was the President's Special Assistant for National Security Affairs

Harold Stassen, former governor of Minnesota and former president of the University of Pennsylvania

Admiral Arthur W. Radford, Chairman of the Joint Chiefs of Staff

Managing the NSC for President Kennedy was aristocrat McGeorge Bundy, who played a leading role in foreign

36. (*U.S. News & World Report*, April 20, 1956).

affairs throughout the 1960's until he left government service to become president of the Ford Foundation. His staff included Walt Rostow of the MIT Center for International Studies, Harvard economist Carl Kaysen, Michael Forrestal (son of the former Secretary of Defense who was also the one-time president of Dillon, Read) and Robert Komer (a government official). The following were members of the Executive Committee of the NSC which met regularly over a period of two weeks to determine American reactions during the Cuban missile crisis of 1962:[37]

Lyndon Johnson, Vice President, representative of Texas oil interests

Dean Rusk, formerly president of the Rockefeller Foundation

Robert McNamara, formerly president of Ford Motor

Robert F. Kennedy, a multimillionaire from Boston

C. Douglas Dillon, a former president of Dillon, Read

Roswell Gilpatric, a corporation lawyer from New York

McGeorge Bundy, a Boston aristocrat who was formerly a dean at Harvard

Adlai Stevenson, a corporation lawyer from Chicago

John McCone, a multimillionaire industrialist from Los Angeles

Dean Acheson, a corporation lawyer and former Secretary of State

Robert Lovett, an investment banker with Brown Brothers, Harriman

37. Wise and Ross, *op. cit.*, p. 293.

General Maxwell Taylor, a presidential adviser at the time, and former chairman of the Mexican Light and Power Company, Ltd

Major General Marshall S. Carter, Deputy Director of the CIA

George Ball, a Washington corporation lawyer, later to become a partner in Lehman Brothers

Edwin M. Martin, a State Department official specializing in Latin America

Llewellyn Thompson, a foreign service officer

Theodore C. Sorensen, presidential speechwriter and adviser

## STATE AND DEFENSE DEPARTMENTS

The policies decided in the NSC or an informal coordinating equivalent are often discussed in terms of information and options developed in the Departments of State and Defense. There is thus no question but that they are an important part of the process by which foreign policy is created. As noted, we have found the men who hold the key positions in these departments to be members of the power elite. We also can recall White's statement that seven assistant and undersecretaries of State and four senior members of the Defense Department during the Kennedy administration were members of the Council on Foreign Relations. There is every reason to believe that his findings for the Kennedy administration are prototypical. In the case of the State Department, at least, there also is evidence that the involvement of members of the upper class reaches even deeper than the policy-deciding levels. For example, a study of all foreign service officers for 1951–52 showed that 36% had attended private schools.[38] Lawyers and businessmen, drawn in large numbers from the upper class, with the assistance of academic experts they met at policy-planning associations, are the important decision-makers in these departments. However, as the next section suggests, they are aided and supplemented by prominent persons from private life on many crucial issues.

## SPECIAL GOVERNMENT COMMITTEES

It is important to look at one other "institution" of the federal government which is absolutely essential in under-standing how the power elite are involved in foreign policy. These are the special commissions, "blue ribbon" citizen committees, and "task forces" appointed by the President and the executive departments to make recommendations on specific problems:

> Despite the extensive government apparatus for policy-making on problems of national security, the American President in the postwar period has, from time to time, appointed groups of private citizens to investigate particular problems and report to the National Security Council. Some of these groups have performed their task without the public's ever becoming aware of their existence; others have in one way or another come to public attention. Among the latter are those which have become known under the names of their chairmen: Finletter, Gray, Paley, Sarnoff, Gaither, Draper, Boechen-stein, and Killian.[39]

These committees are almost without exception headed by members of the power elite and staffed by the employees

38. James L. McCamy and Alessandro Corradini, "The People of the State Department and Foreign Service" (*American Political Science Review*, December, 1954).
39. Morton H. Halperin, "The Gaither Committee and the Policy Process" (*World Politics*, April, 1961), p. 360.

and scholars of the foundations, associations, and institutes outlined in previous sections. For example, among the eight committee heads mentioned in the previous quotation, seven are corporate leaders and the eighth is the chairman of MIT. All are affiliated with the Council on Foreign Relations, three with the Committee for Economic Development. I believe it is by means of these committees that the policy recommendations of the power elite's non-governmental groups are given official sanction: they become the "reports" of the specially appointed committees. The circuit between corporations (and their foundations and associations) and the government is thus completed.

Two such committees, the Gaither Committee and the Clay Committee, have been studied in detail by social scientists. The Gaither Committee was appointed in the late 1950's by President Eisenhower to reconsider American military preparedness. H. Rowan Gaither, its head, is the aforementioned attorney and Ford Foundation official who was instrumental in organizing the RAND Corporation. Other members of the corporate elite on the eleven-man committee were Robert C. Sprague, William C. Foster, and William Webster, the latter also being a trustee of RAND. Two other prominent members were James A. Perkins, a vice president of the Carnegie Corporation at the time, and scientist Jerome Weisner, who became a "wealthy man" as one of the owners of the Rockefeller-financed ITEK Corporation.[40] Other members were James Baxter, a college president; Robert Calkins, an economist who had consulted for CED before becoming head of The Brookings Institution (yet another research organization founded, financed, and directed by the power elite); John Corson, research director for the Cooperative League of America; Robert C. Prim, a mathematician who directed research for Bell Telephone; and Hector Skifter, a radio engineer who con-

40. Lester Tanzer, *The Kennedy Circle* (New York: David McKay Co., Inc., 1961); "Rocky Ride on Route 128" (*Forbes*, September 1, 1965).

sulted for the Department of Defense. Six of the eleven are members of CFR.

Much of the detail work of the Gaither Committee was assigned to technical staff members drawn from the military and the various non-governmental institutes, including RAND and the Institute for Defense Analysis. The committee also had an advisory panel of corporate and military leaders. The final report, highly critical of the emphasis on nuclear weapons and the de-emphasis of conventional ground forces, was discussed at a special meeting of the NSC on November 7, 1957. Over forty people attended, including financiers Robert Lovett and John J. McCloy. President Eisenhower was hesitant, but it is interesting that the Kennedy administration adopted an approach much like that advocated by the Gaither Report. Among President Kennedy's appointees who had been on the Gaither Committee or its advisory panel were arms control chief Foster, disarmament negotiator McCloy, and science adviser Weisner. However, the military stance of the 1960's also may derive from a special Rockefeller-financed panel on international security of the late 1950's, which is said to be very similar to the still-secret Gaither Report. In any case, there were four people who participated in the Gaither Committee work who also helped with the Rockefeller Report. More generally, the first three of six Rockefeller-financed panels were directly concerned with foreign affairs. Members of those three panels who became part of the Kennedy administration were A. A. Berle, Jr., Chester Bowles, Harlan Cleveland, Roswell Gilpatric, and Dean Rusk.[41]

Equally impressive was the composition and effect of the Clay Committee, selected by President Kennedy to recon-

---

41. Halperin, *op. cit.*, p. 382; Samuel P. Huntington, *The Common Defense* (New York: Columbia University Press, 1961), p. 456; The Rockefeller Panel Report, *Prospect for America* (Garden City, N.Y.: Doubleday, 1961), pp. 8, 94, 160.

sider US foreign aid policy. In addition to Lucius Clay, a retired upper-class army general who sat on the boards of a half-dozen major corporations, the committee consisted of financier Robert Anderson, financier Robert Lovett, banker Eugene Black, corporation lawyer Herman Phleger, corporate leader L. F. McCollum, college president and Rockefeller foundation trustee Clifford Hardin, economist Edward S. Mason (a member of CFR, a consultant to CED), physician Howard A. Rusk (no relation to Dean Rusk) and labor leader George Meany. All but Lovett, Rusk and Meany are in the CFR. With Meany dissenting, the committee suggested large cuts and other changes in foreign aid. Although the cuts were apparently more than President Kennedy expected, "in an aid message to the Congress President Kennedy deferentially referred to the Clay Report seven times, setting forth in detail how the new aid program was based on the application of standards 'affirmed by the Clay Committee'."[42]

## THE MILITARY AND FOREIGN POLICY

Up to this point, I have presented what could be termed "positive evidence" for control of foreign policy by the power elite, first from the direction of prestigious non-governmental institutions, then from the direction of the governmental institutions most involved in foreign policy. I now want to approach the problem from another angle, by considering the possible power of other groups. This gives us a chance to utilize the detailed research of a great many social scientists, the upshot of which is that there are really no other possible candidates that could be claimed to have any great effect on the making of foreign policy. Congress gets in the act on immigration policy, and the

42. Usha Mahajani, "Kennedy and the Strategy of Aid: The Clay Report and After" (*Western Political Quarterly*, September, 1965), p. 657.

military in the design of weapons and the letting of defense contracts, but neither is responsible for the policy decisions which guide American foreign policy.

The most detailed consideration of the military in important policy decisions has been in the case studies coming out of the Institute of War and Peace at Columbia University, particularly the study of *The Common Defense* by Samuel P. Huntington. Summarizing his own work and that of his colleagues on several postwar defense decisions they analyzed in detail, Huntington concludes that:

> Perhaps more striking is the relatively unimportant role which they played in proposing changes in policy. In no case did they effectively prevent major new policies and in no case did they effectively prevent changes in old ones . . . more than anything else, one is struck by the tendency of the military to embrace the broad policy *status quo*. . . . General Landon was much more ready to accept existing policy than the State Department members of the NSC-68 drafting group . . . even in the New Look the initiative for a new strategy and its principal ideas came as much from the President, Humphrey, and Dulles as from Radford. . . . A year later it was the civilian Gaither Committee, not the Joint Chiefs, which challenged existing policy and succeeded in producing minor changes in it. The initiative in military policy rested with the civilian executives, the decision on military policy with the President.[43]

It is difficult to go beyond Huntington's emphatic and unequivocal conclusion, but we might say that the key civilians in each case were members of the power elite. We already have seen this in the Gaither Report; here I will add only brief comments on the all-important National Security Council document NSC-68, formulated shortly before the Korean War. This position paper, calling for a general rearmament, was, according to Huntington, the US reaction to the first Soviet nuclear test and the Com-

43. Huntington, *op. cit.*, p. 115.

munist take-over in China.[44] The initiative for the study came from corporation executive Sidney Souers, secretary of the NSC at the time, and corporation lawyer Dean Acheson, Secretary of State. The chairman of the study was Paul Nitze, head of the State Department's policy-planning staff. Nitze, who was later to play an important role in the Kennedy administration, had been a partner in the finance house of Dillon, Read, which had already contributed Forrestal and William H. Draper to the postwar effort, and was later to contribute C. Douglas Dillon as Ambassador to France, Undersecretary of State, and Secretary of the Treasury.

In short, if the United States in the postwar era has adopted what Mills called a military definition of reality, it is because this was chosen by leading big business members of the power elite on the basis of their understanding of national goals and international events, not because it was somehow foisted on them by the military men with whom they interact at high-level military "colleges," promote and retire within the Department of Defense, and hire into large corporations upon retirement.

## CONGRESS AND FOREIGN POLICY

Although involved in foreign affairs through certain constitutional powers and through final authority for financial appropriations, Congress is seldom put forth as a significant factor in the making of foreign policy. Nevertheless, the possibility must be considered. One political scientist concerned with Congress, James A. Robinson, concludes, "Congress's influence in foreign policy is primarily (and increasingly) one of legitimating and amending policies initiated by the executive to deal with problems usually identified

44. *Ibid.*, pp. 47–50.

by the executive."[45] Roger Hilsman and H. Field Haviland, Jr., both conclude that superior information and other resources give the executive the initiative over the legislators.[46] Further, it seems that Congress has given up some of its determinative powers on foreign matters. In the 1930's, with the Reciprocal Trade Act, it turned over much of its power on tariffs. In the postwar era it has by and large lost its right to declare war.

In a summary of the role of Congress in sixteen postwar foreign policy issues that have been the object of case studies, Robinson is able to find only one that was initiated by Congress and three where Congress had "major influence." The one clear case where a member of Congress both initiated and was the major influence in a policy issue was the Monroney Resolution, which was merely "a simple Senate resolution suggesting that the administration study the possibility of proposing to other governments the establishment of an international development association as an affiliate of the World Bank."[47] The interpretation of the other two cases of major influence is open to question. As to the less important of the two, Congress is said to have had major influence on the Vandenberg Resolution of 1948, which "provided the legitimation for the origins of United States participation in the development of the North Atlantic Treaty."[48] However, the idea was initiated by Secretary of State Marshall and Undersecretary of State Lovett, and it was written in close collaboration by Lovett and Vandenberg. Vandenberg is considered by Robinson to be the "predominant influence" because he suggested that sev-

45. James A. Robinson, *Congress and Foreign Policy-Making* (Homewood, Illinois: Dorsey Press, Inc., 1962), p. v.

46. Roger Hilsman, "Congressional-Executive Relations and the Foreign Policy Consensus" (*American Political Science Review,* September, 1958); H. Field Haviland, Jr., "Foreign Aid and the Policy Process: 1957" (*American Political Science Review,* September, 1958).

47. Robinson, *op. cit.,* p. 62.

48. *Ibid.,* pp. 45–46.

eral Senate-initiated concerns about the United Nations be included in the resolution.

The most important issue where Congress supposedly had a major influence concerned the problem of whether or not to aid the French at Dienbienphu in 1954. According to the conventional account, Secretary of State Dulles had been urging President Eisenhower to provide the French with air support, as had the Chairman of the Joint Chiefs of Staff, Admiral Arthur W. Radford. To prepare for this possibility, Eisenhower asked Dulles and Radford to call together eight key congressional leaders for the purpose of discussing a joint resolution on the part of Congress which would express support of the action. When the congressmen learned that the British were reluctant to join such a venture and that other military advisers were opposed, the congressmen made their support conditional on British acceptance of the plan and certain concessions by the French. Dulles then tried to bring the British and French into the agreement, but in the end had to acquiesce in their plan to negotiate a truce and divide the country. This conventional summary of the decision-making process is then interpreted as an example of congressional veto power, often with a reference to Chalmers Roberts' account in *The Reporter*.

Surprisingly enough, a close reading of Roberts' article leads to quite a different conclusion, for he states unequivocally that the pivotal role was played by the National Security Council. His account, based upon confidential talks with insiders, and never questioned as to its reliability, tells how the crucial decision was reached long before the congressional leaders were finally approached:

> It is my understanding, although I cannot produce the top-secret NSC paper to prove it, that some time between Ely's arrival on March 20 [with the news that the French could not hold out much longer] and the Dulles-Radford approach to the Congressional leaders on April 3, the NSC had taken

a firm position that the United States could not afford the loss of Indo-China to the Communists, and that if it were necessary to prevent that loss, the United States would intervene in the war—*provided* the intervention was an allied venture and *provided* the French would give Indo-China a real grant of independence so as to eliminate the colonialism issue. The decision may have been taken at the March 25 meeting. It is also my understanding that this NSC paper has on it the approving initials "D.D.E."[49]

Roberts goes on to say that Dulles then made a March 29 speech in New York calling for a "united action" of the major powers. Roberts implies that it is neither surprising nor particularly obstructive that the legislators should repeat this demand a few days later:

The newspapers were still full of reactions to this speech when the Congressional leaders, at the April 3 secret meeting with Dulles and Radford, insisted that Dulles should line up allies for "united action" before trying to get a joint resolution of Congress that would commit the nation to war.[50]

As it turned out, Dulles could not get the British and French to go along with the American plan. They already had other plans, and the French continued to be as obstinate as they had been during the previous five years about granting any of the concessions to Vietnam that the US had been demanding as completely necessary. (The French feared an "American takeover" and wanted to keep the area as one of trade and cultural influence if they lost the war.)[51] The one question that thus remains is whether or not Congress could have shown independent power by refusing to grant the President's request to take part in a "united action." "This point," says Chalmers Roberts, "is worth a final word":

49. Chalmers Roberts, "The Day We Didn't Go To War" (*The Reporter*, September 14, 1954), pp. 32, 34. Even the italics are Roberts'.
50. *Ibid.*, p. 34.
51. Melvin Gurtov, *The First Vietnam Crisis* (New York: Columbia University Press, 1967), pp. 23–4, 42, 78, 84, 137–8.

On returning from Geneva in mid-May, I asked that question of numerous senators and representatives. Their replies made clear that Congress would, in the end, have done what Eisenhower asked, provided he had asked for it forcefully and explained the facts and their relation to the national interest of the United States.[52]

In short, on the basis of Roberts' account, there is not the slightest reason to believe that Congress had anything to do with the US decision to refrain from bombing Dienbienphu. The important decision was made in the National Security Council and would not have been resisted by Congress. What the outcome rather suggests is the limitations of American power over the British and French, along with the reluctance of a majority of the leading decision-makers within the NSC at that time to risk involvement in a major war in Asia.

If Congress exercises no decision-making power in the area of foreign policy, it does seem to have the power to harass certain initiatives by the executive branch due to its control of the purse strings. However, even this seeming veto power melts away or is neutralized when the power elite make a concerted effort. This can be demonstrated with two rather nice examples, the first concerning tariff policy, the second concerning foreign aid policy. As to the first, leading members of the power elite during the 1950's were advocating further reductions in tariffs, as they had been doing for some time. They had gone through the usual procedures—a special commission to study the matter (headed by former Inland Steel executive Clarence Randall) and a special committee of private individuals to influence opinion (The Committee for a National Trade Policy, headed by John Coleman of Burroughs Manufacturing, Charles Taft, Harry Bullis of General Mills, John J. McCloy of Chase Manhattan, and corporation lawyer George Ball). Their plans were resisted by Congress, and they re-

52. Roberts, *op. cit.,* p. 35.

ceived much less than they asked throughout the 1950's. Behind this congressional reluctance, however, were powerful business interests. In short, there was a conflict within the power elite. President Kennedy moved to remedy the situation when he took office. First, he appointed George Ball of the Committee for a National Trade Policy as Undersecretary of State for Economic Affairs, making him "the man who was personally responsible for the conduct of the nation's foreign economic policy."[53] Second, to help with his Trade Expansion Act, Kennedy appointed as his special aide Howard C. Petersen, president of the Fidelity-Philadelphia Trust and the head of a Committee for Economic Development committee on tariff policy.[54] As he had done previously as a CED spokesman, Petersen, along with others, met with leaders of the aggrieved industries, primarily chemicals and textiles, offering them special concessions. These maneuvers and changes "cut the protectionist coalition to shreds." The bill passed Congress: "It was the indirect effect of the administration's approach to and conversion of the textile lobby and to numerous other businessmen that indirectly affected Congress."[55]

This case is especially important because it is probably the most frequently cited evidence for "pluralism" in the making of foreign policy. However, the study has two major weaknesses. It is first of all vitiated by its failure to consider the role of the Council on Foreign Relations (which is never discussed) and the Committee for Economic Development in helping to bring big business thinking to a more favorable attitude in regard to low tariffs. There is no need for the authors' vagueness about this change. (Two of the authors, Bauer and Pool, actually served in a CFR study

53. Raymond A. Bauer, Ithiel de Sola Pool, and Lewis A. Dexter, *American Business and Public Policy* (New York: Atherton Press, 1963), p. 74.
54. *Ibid.*, p. 78; Schriftgiesser, *op. cit.*, pp. 181–7.
55. Bauer, et al., *op. cit.*, pp. 79, 422.

group on foreign tariff in the mid-fifties, a fact which is nowhere mentioned in the book.) It is also surprising that Pool, who wrote the chapter on Kennedy's Trade Expansion Act, did not identify Howard Petersen. Petersen, in charge of guiding the bill through Congress, is a banker and CED leader who had been involved in tariff policy discussions for some time. By leaving Petersen's CED work uncited, the ongoing role of members of the power elite is slighted. A second weakness of this study is that it does not make it clear enough that the pluralism it describes is within the big business community. As the previous quotes from this work make clear, the dispute is within the power elite. When business leaders reached an accommodation, the opposition in Congress was greatly weakened. Rather than saying the administration approached textile leaders, I would say that CED leaders compromised with their conservative brethren. The increasingly important "internationalist" wing of the big business community had to make some concessions to a diminishing "isolationist" wing which has been in retreat before the CFR-CED mentality since the mid-thirties. The seeming pluralism read into this book emerges because the authors have not explored the framework members of the power elite have developed for discussing, formulating and carrying out their wishes.

The second case study of Congress and foreign policy, which involves foreign aid, is equally complex. It highlights the major division within the power elite and shows the lengths to which members of the power elite often must go to have their way with a Congress that has many delaying powers. Many members of Congress in the mid-fifties were growing restive with the foreign aid program. Several wished to reassess the entire program. Almost totally lacking in the expertise to conduct the necessary inquiry, several reports were contracted for with a variety of "independent" research organizations. According to a scholarly account by H. Field Haviland, Jr., of The Brookings Institution, the most important of these reports was done by Max Milliken and Walt Rostow of the Center for International Studies at MIT.[56] This organization is supported by both the CIA and major foundations, and is thus sponsored by the same group of men who are heavily represented in the executive branch of the government. Haviland also claims that "the other reports were in harmony with the Milliken-Rostow thesis."[57] This is perhaps to be expected. They were done by, among others, The Brookings Institution and the National Planning Association (NPA), the latter of which in 1958 had ten of its forty-three directors in common with CFR and eight with CED. Four NPA officers were in both CFR and CED.

Despite the relative unanimity of the reports, there was still resistance to the program within Congress. Once again, however, it is likely that this reflected an ongoing struggle within the power elite, who are by no means unanimous on the amount and conditions for granting foreign aid. As it did in the case of tariffs, this seeming congressional veto power (which amounts to reducing aid requests) would diminish, I believe, if the power elite could make up their collective mind. The disagreement in this instance manifested itself in terms of two reports by power elite groups. The first, by yet another specially appointed committee of the President, was known as the Fairless Report, after its chairman, Benjamin Fairless of United States Steel. The second report was by an official government agency called the International Development Advisory Board, created in 1950 as "the chief public advisory group associated with the economic assistance program."[58] Its head at that time was corporate leader Eric Johnston, one of CED's founders and a former president of the US Chamber of Commerce. The differences in the two reports reflect a long-standing

56. Haviland, *op. cit.*, pp. 691–92.
57. *Ibid.*, p. 692.
58. *Ibid.*, p. 694.

disagreement within the power elite that has been drawn out by political scientists David McLellan and Charles Woodhouse.[59] Sitting on the more conservative committee along with Fairless and labor leader John L. Lewis were five prominent members of the power elite:

> Colgate W. Darden, Jr., married to the daughter of Irenee duPont, president of the University of Virginia, and a director of DuPont, US Rubber, and the Life Insurance Company of Virginia
>
> Richard R. Deupree, chairman of the board of Procter and Gamble
>
> Whitelaw Reid, chairman of the board of the *New York Herald Tribune*
>
> Walter Bedell Smith, vice chairman of the board, American Machine and Foundry Company, former military officer, and former director of the CIA
>
> Jesse W. Tapp, chairman of the board of the Bank of America

The second committee was more diversified sociologically. In addition to Johnston and five other corporate leaders, it included two college deans, two labor union leaders, one farm organization representative, a member of the US Committee for UNICEF and the president of Virginia State College.

After tracing the aid bill for 1957 through the conflict over these two reports and the usual nightmarish tangle within Congress, Haviland concludes his case study as follows:

59. David S. McLellan and Charles E. Woodhouse, "The Business Elite and Foreign Policy" (*Western Political Quarterly*, March, 1960); Charles E. Woodhouse and David S. McLellan, "American Business Leaders and Foreign Policy: A Study in Perspectives" (*The American Journal of Economics and Sociology*, July, 1966).

. . . this case study highlights the conclusion that, despite the powerful "veto" function of the Congress, as well as the stimulating effect of the special legislative studies, the executive branch had the advantage of the initiative, supported by tremendous staff and intelligence resources. Behind the facade of the "administration position," however, were important and continuing differences within and among the principal departments and agencies concerned, usually related to vested institutional interests and closely tied parallel differences within the Congress and the general public.[60]

If Congress is no mere rubber stamp that immediately jumps every time the power elite snap their fingers, it is for all its complaining, delaying, and threatening a rather impotent body when compared with the executive branch, which can get its way with Congress on foreign affairs any time it wants to with patience, tact, research, and vigorous leadership by the President. And when Congress seems most resistant, a closer look often reveals disagreement within the power elite between its internationalist and isolationist tendencies.

## PUBLIC OPINION
## AND FOREIGN POLICY

Public opinion used to be considered by some scholars as an important factor in determining foreign policy, but studies over the past decade have by and large failed to support this hypothesis. Today it is usually put forth by journalists caught up in the rush of day-to-day events and by politicians wishing to cater to the voters or disguise their real motives. The most comprehensive overall schema on

60. Haviland, *op. cit.*, p. 717. The reference to differences within the government concerns, among other things, the fact that Eisenhower appointed a fiscal conservative, George Humphrey, of M. A. Hanna Company, to head the Treasury, and an isolationist, John Hollister of the Taft law firm in Cincinnati, to head the International Cooperative Administration.

this problem is provided by James N. Rosenau in his *Public Opinion and Foreign Policy*.[61] He divides the population into three groups on the basis of empirical research by himself and others: the mass public, the attentive public, and the opinion-leaders. The overwhelming majority of the people are in the first group. They seldom are aware of foreign policy issues, read little about them, get what opinions they have from mass media, and react emotionally to slogans and crises. The second group, making up at best a few percent of the population, are slightly better educated than the mass public, have a little more money, and read more on foreign affairs. They tend to acquire their opinions from the "quality media" such as *The New York Times, Harper's Magazine,* and *The Reporter.* On the few occasions they have been studied in any detail, it is found they are businessmen, lawyers and professional people, and, as we will see, they are the people who join discussion groups and associations concerned with foreign policy.[62] They actually provide the public which the opinion-leaders use as their sounding board. The third group, opinion-leaders, are those who shape public opinion. In theory, according to Rosenau, opinion-leaders may or may not be the same persons who are decision-makers. However, he concludes that on foreign policy the opinion-leaders tend to be the same persons who are the decision-makers within the federal government.[63] In short, on the issue of foreign policy at least, the power elite are also a major factor in shaping public opinion.

Huntington comes to similar conclusions from decision-making analyses of military and defense policies. He finds the public opinion poll evidence against any determinative force by public opinion so "overwhelming" that "even a wide margin of error would not invalidate the conclusions

61. (New York: Random House, 1961).
62. Kenneth P. Adler and David Brobrow, "Interest and Influence in Foreign Affairs" (*Public Opinion Quarterly,* Spring, 1956).
63. Rosenau, *op. cit.,* p. 60.

drawn from them."[64] Reviewing this evidence, he finds that public opinion was never important, often in conflict with what the adminstration was doing, and often changed after the administration took its action. By juxtaposing quotes from corporate leaders with opinion poll data, he shows that their claims of responding to popular demand can be no more than an illusion or rationalization. In 1953, when Budget Director Joseph Dodge of The Detroit Bank said there would be cuts in military expenditures to "meet public demand," a Gallup poll found only 19% of the people thought the United States was spending too much for defense. In early 1957, shortly after Secretary of Defense Charles Wilson (formerly of General Motors) said that "the people in the country are in no mood to spend more dollars," a Gallup poll showed that only 9% thought defense spending should be cut. Sixty percent thought it should stay about the same; 22% thought it ought to be increased.[65]

On the basis of the work by Rosenau, Huntington and others, it is possible to suggest that public opinion is actually shaped by the foreign policies pursued by the power elite rather than the other way around. This may not be the case with domestic policy, where people have their own observations and personal contacts to aid their understanding, but it is the reality with foreign affairs, where people have to rely upon what the power elite tell them through the executive branch, foreign policy discussion associations, and the mass media. By far the most important factor in this shaping is the attitude of the President, who surrounds himself with members of the power elite as department heads, advisers, diplomats, and special emissaries. Samuel Lubell has documented the President's leading role by means of interviews with a great many people at the time the Russian Sputnik was launched:

64. Huntington, *op. cit.*, p. 235.
65. *Ibid.*, pp. 238–9.

. . . especially striking was how closely the public's reactions corresponded to the explanatory "line" which was coming from the White House. . . . In talking about Sputnik, most people tended to paraphrase what Eisenhower himself had said. . . . In no community did I find any tendency on the part of the public to look for leadership to anyone else—to their newspapers, or radio commentators, to Congressmen, or to men of science. Nor, with some exception, could people be said to be in advance of the President, or to be demanding more action than he was.[66]

The Presidency and the executive branch in general are not the only means by which the power elite influence public opinion on foreign policy. They also do so through certain associations and through the creation of special citizens' committees designed to influence opinion on a single issue. As to the associations, the most important are the tightly interlocked Council on Foreign Relations, the Foreign Policy Association and the National Advertising Council. Most FPA directors are CFR members as well as business leaders, while the corporation-financed NAC has representatives from CFR, FPA and CED among its directors. Except for its books, the CFR works primarily with opinion within the power elite. It is the FPA which deals with public opinion within the "attentive public." This group sponsors World Affairs Councils, discussion groups, and speakers. The FPA is "nonpartisan," but the important fact remains, as Rosenau notes, that an organization such as FPA "establishes the width, depth, and direction of the channel" of communication.[67] And, as Bernard C. Cohen concludes in a study of groups such as FPA (which summarizes evidence showing that the members are better educated and have higher incomes than the general population), they seldom seriously discuss political policies at all, let alone

66. Samuel Lubell, "Sputnik and American Public Opinion" (*Columbia University Forum,* Winter, 1957), p. 18.
67. Rosenau, *op. cit.,* p. 95.

alternative policies. They tend to keep discussions apolitical, emphasizing social, economic, cultural and historical aspects of foreign affairs. They also provide a great deal of positive information on the nature and role of the United Nations, which has gotten them a bad name in some circles.[68]

The National Advertising Council is probably less important than the CFR and FPA. It merely places corporate-financed advertising in the mass media. These advertisements advocate general propositions such as "support the United Nations" or "give money to Radio Free Europe." Perhaps these communications have a "sleeper effect" or create general ideological acceptance of international involvement, but such effects are difficult to measure or prove. Perhaps what we should say in the case of the NAC is that the power elite utilize all avenues to reach the general public.

As noted, the power elite also try to influence public opinion through the formation of publicity committees composed of prominent private citizens. The origins of one such committee have been studied in considerable detail by James N. Rosenau in *Foreign Policy and National Leadership*.[69] In early 1958, President Eisenhower asked corporate executive Eric Johnston, aforementioned founder of CED and a former president of the US Chamber of Commerce, to head a special White House meeting to convey information to the public on foreign policy aspects of national security. Johnston and his staff invited over 1,000 corporate, organizational, community and labor leaders to a one-day conference of meetings and speeches. Out of the conference came a new citizens' committee, the Committee for International Economic Growth (CIEG), charged with the responsibility of carrying the conference's message

68. Bernard C. Cohen, *Citizen Education in World Affairs* (Princeton: Center of International Studies, Princeton University, 1953), pp. 117–25.
69. (Princeton: Princeton University Press, 1963). Rosenau did not find the effort successful, but it is nonetheless instructive.

to the entire populace. Its original members in addition to Johnston were General and corporate director Lucius Clay, Milton Eisenhower (president of Johns Hopkins), Barney Balaban (a motion picture theater owner and president of Paramount Pictures), General Alfred Gruenther, Mrs. Eleanor Roosevelt, Mrs. Helen R. Reid (her husband was a wealthy businessman, her sons are Whitelaw and Ogden Reid) and George Meany (labor leader).

There are numerous other such committees that have been formed, but no other has been studied in any detail. One of the most important of these committees purportedly helped to convince the country of the need for the Marshall Plan:

> When the Committee for the Marshall Plan was formed, Stimson [Wall Street lawyer, CFR director, former Secretary of State and Secretary of War] agreed to serve as national chairman. Former Secretary of War Robert P. Patterson became chairman of an executive committee. . . . The executive committee included Dean Acheson (then in private life), Winthrop W. Aldrich, James B. Carey, David Dubinsky, Herbert H. Lehman, Philip Reed, and Herbert Bayard Swope. Its membership consisted of more than three hundred prominent citizens in different parts of the country. . . . Regional committees were promptly organized, the cooperation of national organizations enlisted, and relevant publications given wide circulation. The committee promoted broad news and editorial coverage in metropolitan newspapers, set up a speakers' bureau, and employed a news agency which arranged for press releases, a special mat service for small town and country newspapers, and national and local radio broadcasts.[70]

70. Harvey B. Price, *The Marshall Plan and Its Meaning* (Ithaca, New York: Cornell University Press, 1955), p. 56. Winthrop Aldrich is a banker and an uncle of the Rockefeller brothers; James B. Carey is a labor leader; Herbert Lehman was of the Lehman Brothers investment firm; Philip Reed is an executive with General Electric; Herbert Bayard Swope is a former New York newspaper editor and the brother of a former president of General Electric; and David Dubinsky is a labor leader.

CONCLUSION

In this essay I have tried to show who dominates the all-important issue-area of foreign policy, namely, a power elite which is rooted in the dividends and salaries of large corporation and financial institutions. I have attempted this in two different ways, one positive, one negative. The positive way was to show that the key persons and institutions in and out of government which determine foreign policy are part of a power elite which is the operating arm of the social upper class. The negative way was a process of elimination. I summarized evidence which suggests that other possible candidates for control of foreign policy— the military, Congress, public opinion—are of very minor importance for this issue-area. They may be important on some issues, but not foreign policy.

In addition to showing *who* makes foreign policy, this essay has shown *how* they do it—through participation in key government positions, through serving on specially appointed committees and task forces, and through financing and leading major non-governmental policy-planning, opinion-forming, and opinion-disseminating organizations. The role of these consensus-seeking policy organizations is seen as the missing link social scientists have demanded of a governing-class theory.

It is also important to note what has not been demonstrated. The essay has not proven that the power elite act only or primarily in terms of the interests of the corporations which are their ultimate base of power. It has not shown *why* they do what they do. However, it is certainly possible to make the beginnings of a case on this matter on the basis of the economists' assumption that people tend to act in their self-interest and on the psychologists' and sociologists' finding that people perceive and interpret the world in terms of their individual upbringing, cultural background and occupational roles. I would consider the following facts significant: The power elite are by and large part of an upper class which owns an overwhelming amount of corporate stock and has a set of educational and social institutions that are distinctive to this small group. Most of the power elite's members also receive non-dividend income and other "higher emoluments" from the corporations and their closely related charitable foundations. When these considerations are put alongside the very great importance of overseas operations for the health of many large American businesses, it is really hard to believe that we don't know why the power elite are so concerned with matters of foreign policy.

# CHAPTER SIX

# *How the Power Elite Shape Social Legislation*[*]

Impressive as the evidence may be for power elite control of foreign policy, critics of a governing-class theory are not necessarily swayed toward my view of the power structure by it, for many readily concede elite control of that particular issue-area. To demonstrate a governing-class theory, they continue, it is necessary to show that the hypothetical

[*] This paper would not have been possible without the previous excellent work of James Weinstein and David Eakins, with whom I have discussed social legislation at some length. Weinstein's *The Decline of American Socialism, 1912–1925* (New York: Monthly Review Press, 1967) and *The Corporate Ideal in the Liberal State* (Boston: Beacon Press, 1968), and Eakins' "The Development of Corporate Liberal Policy Research in the United States, 1885–1965" (Unpublished Ph.D. dissertation, University of Wisconsin, 1966) are essential reading in this area. Fortunately, Eakins' work will be available soon to a wider audience in book form.

ruling group dominates a wide variety of issue-areas. Foreign policy is not enough. What about social policy, for example, where on the face of it—workmen's compensation, social security, collective bargaining—there seems to be considerable evidence for the pressure of other social groups? Some authors actually claim that all of these innovations were made in spite of the opposition of the business community. Consider this sweeping statement from the *Harvard Business Review:* "Business has not really won or had its way in connection with even a single piece of proposed regulatory or social legislation in the last three-quarters of a century."[1]

There are two basic parts to this essay. In the first, which will parallel the outline utilized by Eakins, I will show the institutions through which the power elite have shaped social legislation.[2] It will be shown that the research associations and institutes sometimes called "middle class" were initiated, directed, and/or financed by members of the upper class. Further, it will be shown that these groups are tightly interlocked and work closely with one another. Evidence will be presented to show how important they were in providing the context, ideas and shape for various pieces of social legislation. In all of these points the essay is similar to the previous one. However, a further step will be taken in the second half of the essay, where the general framework will be applied to four important areas of social legislation: protective labor legislation, the regulation of business, social security and the recognition of labor unions. The detailing of these particular decisions reveals a surprising story. In short, it is no coincidence that the upper class' share of the wealth remains undisturbed and that members of the upper class retain their control of the

1. Theodore Levitt, "Why Business Always Loses" (*Harvard Business Review*, March-April, 1968), p. 82.
2. David W. Eakins, "The Development of Corporate Liberal Policy Research in the United States, 1885–1965" (Unpublished Ph.D. dissertation, University of Wisconsin, 1966).

important economic and political decisions in the United States, for most leaders within the power elite agree with utilities magnate Samuel Insull that it is better to "help *shape* the *right* kind of regulation than to have the *wrong* kind forced upon [you]."[3] Or, as banker Charles G. Dawes put it, the problems of the "great combinations and corporations" must be "settled by conservative men" so that the solutions "will not prove a barrier in the path of commercial and national progress . . ."[4]

## EARLY BEGINNINGS OF SOCIAL WELFARE LEGISLATION

The story of power elite involvement in the domestic arena begins in Bismarck's nineteenth-century Germany. It begins there because many American intellectuals who visited or trained in Germany were impressed with the social welfare state begun at that time with the help of liberal and socialist professors. These young American academics returned to the United States full of enthusiasm for much of what they had seen, advocating changes that would solve America's growing socioeconomic problems. Among these enthusiasts were Richard Ely, Edmund J. James, E. R. A. Seligman, Henry C. Adams, Henry Farnam, Simon Patten, and John Bates Clark, later to be the founders, in 1885, of the American Economic Association.[5]

3. James Weinstein, *The Corporate Ideal in the Liberal State* (Boston: Beacon Press, 1968), p. 87. My italics. This quote symbolizes the moderate view within the upper class on all social legislation.

4. Gordon M. Jensen, "The National Civic Federation: American Business in an Age of Social Change and Social Reform, 1900–1910" (Unpublished Ph.D. dissertation, Princeton University, 1956), pp. 268–9.

5. At least two members of this group, Seligman and Farnam, were members of the upper class. Seligman came from the famous banking family. His son Eustace is presently a partner in Sullivan and Cromwell and is a former president of the Foreign Policy Association. E.R.A.'s brother Isaac followed in their father's footsteps as a banker. Ely, while not rich himself, came from a prominent family tree and had assistance from several rich relatives. Some of these men will be important figures throughout this essay.

The changes these men advocated were in good part based upon the German example, although upper-class fondness for the British aristocracy also made the British experience with domestic problems a useful model. These changes included plans for tax reform, social insurance, welfare measures, and protective labor legislation. In short, the new economists believed that the state had a role to play in the economy. Intellectually, they criticized the English economic tradition which dominated American academia as being too hypothetical and for abandoning historically based studies of actual socioeconomic problems. Most importantly, they criticized the doctrine of laissez-faire individualism. They demanded an economics that placed man—not wealth—in the foreground, and gave proper attention to the "social factor" in his nature.

These German-oriented intellectuals broke away from the traditional American economists—whom they found restrictive—to form the American Economic Association. The key figure in founding the organization was Richard Ely. He had the help of another German-influenced scholar, Herbert Adams, "who had been instrumental in organizing the American Historical Association the year before."[6] The association did not go as far in its principles as some of its founders would have liked. The program was toned down—excluding any strong emphasis on government intervention—in the interest of attracting a larger membership. Nor was all of the toning down due to ideological antipathy to the idea of government responsibility and social welfare; some of it was based upon a very real fear of the growing regimentation and loss of individuality in Germany. The American reformers were not uncritical admirers of the German experience.

Nor were the upstarts entirely alone. They were encouraged in particular by three other scholars: Francis Amasa Walker, Carroll D. Wright, and Arthur T. Hadley.[7] Hadley

6. Eakins, *op. cit.*, p. 15.
7. *Ibid.*, p. 8.

was a member of the upper class who later became president of Yale University (1899–1921); his sons Morris and Hamilton both graduated from Groton and Yale, and went on to become leading Wall Street lawyers. Wright, the son of a minister, was United States Commissioner of Labor (1885–1903), while Walker, who had become a General during the Civil War, was one of the most admired scholars of his time, and the president of MIT from 1881 to 1897. Another important sympathizer and supporter was Andrew D. White, the first president of Cornell University (1867–1885) and the first president of the American Historical Association.[8] White was a member of the upper class; his father's fortune had been made in the early days of railroads. He gave several hundred thousand dollars to Cornell as well as giving minor support to other causes.

The new economic association stressed empirical, fact-gathering research into practical problems. Among the first reports requested of standing committees were those on the Normal Working Day, Factory Employment of Women, and a National Railroad Commission. In short, the AEA was preparing to provide the economic expertise that was to be essential in the later efforts of big businessmen to rationalize the socioeconomic system. The role of such economists was to be a central one.

Although the AEA developed in the "right" (practical, pragmatic) direction in its early years, it was a little too cautious and scholarly for some of its more enthusiastic and ambitious members. They turned to several other organizations in the 1890's as an outlet and vehicle for their reformist ideas. For example, a few became socialists, while others turned to the Episcopal-led Church Social Union (Ely was its secretary) and CAIL (Church Association for the Advancement of the Interests of Labor). CAIL is especially interesting as an upper-class precursor to certain

8. *Ibid.*, pp. 15–16.

business-dominated reformist organizations of the early twentieth century. The idea of labor arbitration by a tripartite board of business, labor, and "public" members, which was later to be an important part of the National Civic Federation program, was used by this group. Indeed, several of the same leaders, in particular a very important man named Seth Low, were involved in both CAIL and the NCF.[9] These Episcopal organizations were an important bridge between the British and American upper classes. According to E. Digby Baltzell, Episcopal bishops in this country were greatly influenced by their British counterparts and became the moral spokesmen of the American upper class. The Episcopal Church was the first protestant church in America to recognize the right of labor to organize.[10] Perhaps religious convictions, and the belief in *noblesse oblige,* helped to moderate any temptation on the part of the rich to take a purely "economic" view of social welfare.

Despite their energetic efforts, the academic reformers were having little noticeable impact. However, as the new century began, they became involved in economic research in cooperation with the most powerful and forward-looking segment of the corporate community. In essence, they became "conservative," if they were not already. Ely, for example, complained in 1910 that he and some of his friends who had been called "radical" had been misunderstood. Although their method seemed "radical in theory," Ely added that "now everyone, of course, knows that it leads to essentially conservative conclusions in practice."[11]

Among the new economists who became involved with

9. Spencer Miller and Joseph Fletcher, *The Church and Industry* (New York: Longmans, Green & Co., 1930), pp. 59–60.

10. E. Digby Baltzell, *Philadelphia Gentlemen: The Making of a National Upper Class* (Glencoe, Illinois: The Free Press, 1958), pp. 233–5.

11. Eakins, *op. cit.,* pp. 42–3. Ernest Gruening, *The Public Pays: A Study of Power Propaganda* (New York: The Vanguard Press, 1964), pp. 94–8, discusses the role of Ely in aiding the private utilities during the 1920's.

corporate leaders were George Bemis and John R. Commons, who in 1899, in conjunction with wealthy Democrat George H. Shibley, founded their own Bureau of Economic Research. While the venture lasted for only two years, it was an important prototype for several later groups and an important platform for the two economists involved. Bemis went to work for Cleveland reform mayor Tom Johnson, and, more importantly, Commons was asked to take charge of the New York office of the newly-formed National Civic Federation, with the task of "gathering data on 'questions of taxation and arbitration of labor disputes.' "[12] About the same time he also received a "very good contract" to work for United States Labor Commissioner Carroll Wright—one of the aforementioned sympathizers with the new economists among the older generation. Commons, a student of Ely at Johns Hopkins who was eventually to follow Ely to the University of Wisconsin, is a central figure in many of the events to be discussed in this essay. It is therefore important to emphasize how crucial he found his "big years" with the NCF and how many of the ideas credited to him were worked out in conjunction with that group.[13] Then too, the fact that Commons was working for both the National Civic Federation and the Labor Commissioner points up another important development: scholars, especially economists, were becoming important to the smooth functioning of the socioeconomic system. Their advice on how to run the system was more and more sought by the power elite. This symbiosis now has grown to the point where some believe that the experts have taken over the system. However, before developing that strand of the story, it is necessary to consider the National Civic Federation, for it is crucial

12. Eakins, *op. cit.* p. 41.
13. John R. Commons, *Myself* (New York: Macmillan, 1934); Marguerite Green, *The National Civic Federation and the American Labor Movement, 1900–1925* (Washington, D.C.: Catholic University of America Press, 1956), pp. 54–5, 67–8, 129–30.

to an understanding of how the power elite shaped social legislation in the twentieth century.

## THE NATIONAL
## CIVIC FEDERATION

It was not only intellectuals who were observing the German welfare state and growing apprehensive about the social unrest at the lower levels of American society. Big businessmen were also traveling all over Europe for business and pleasure, and they too were groping for solutions to the problems they saw at home. One of the first self-conscious, nationwide responses by big businessmen as a group to domestic unrest was the National Civic Federation, which was formed in 1900. By 1903, it included among its members one or more persons from almost one-third of the then largest 300 corporations, excluding railroads. Of 190 big businessmen from that era studied in detail by historian William Miller, forty-three were in the NCF.[14] Its first president was Senator Mark Hanna, coal and steel magnate, and leader of the Republican Party. Its second was August Belmont—banker, traction magnate, and a leader of the Democratic Party (as was his father, its chairman from 1860–1872, before him). The third president, Seth Low, who presided from 1908 to 1915, is less known today, but his role during the Progressive Era would be hard to overestimate. Big businessman, university president, reform mayor of New York, Episcopal leader, Republican, this son of an old New York family was one of the best-known and most respected members of the upper class in that era.

The NCF had a short but important history as the lead-

14. Jensen, *op. cit.*, pp. 57–9, p. 344, for this and other evidence that the leaders of the NCF were big businessmen of great wealth. The "Morgan interests" were well represented and the only conspicuous absence is the "Rockefeller interests."

ing organization of the power elite. Its major importance was in resolving key labor disputes in the first years of the century, and in the process developing a *modus vivendi* with the labor leaders it invited to be among its members. However, it also pioneered in convincing its fellow businessmen to undercut the unions by developing welfare programs that made unions unnecessary. Finally, it championed protective labor legislation and the "right" kind of business regulation. As will be shown when we consider the Federal Trade Commission Act of 1914, the NCF developed the major principles embodied in the act. In addition to the prestige and power of its business members, this NCF role was made possible by its respected research reports and commissions on crucial subjects, which is where middleclass economists such as Commons fit into the picture. "Model" legislation and the advocacy of "regulatory" commissions, based upon the best information it could buy, were second in importance only to its educational efforts among big businessmen.

The NCF did not develop suddenly in 1900. Its history goes back to the Chicago Civic Federation, which was formed in 1894 due to the growing discontent with corruption, vice, and mismangement in that city, and the shock over the recent assassination of its wealthy mayor, Carter Harrison, Sr.[15] The CCF was conceived as a nonsectarian, nonpolitical group working "to advance Chicago's municipal, philanthropic, industrial and moral interests."[16] The CCF, in turn, had its antecedents in other big business groups that had been formed in Chicago over the last quarter of the century in order to deal with the problems of its burgeoning growth. Most of the same business leaders who had led previous business reform groups were im-

15. Sidney I. Roberts, "Businessmen in Revolt: Chicago 1874–1900" (Unpublished Ph.D. dissertation, University of Chicago, 1960), pp. 115*ff*.
16. Eakins, *op. cit.*, p. 61.

portant in the CCF.[17] The first president of the organization was Lyman Gage, president of the First National Bank of Chicago, later to be Secretary of the Treasury under President McKinley. Other posts in the organization also were filled by leading businessmen, although a few women (including reformer Jane Addams), a labor official, and a few University of Chicago professors were among the leaders. As all accounts make clear, it was an organization of the big businessmen of Chicago.

The CCF appears to have been very successful in its efforts. It set up several standing committees which immediately went into action, offering and electing reform candidates to city council, exposing election frauds, urging civil service reforms, and arguing for primary elections.[18] However, the interests of some of its members went beyond Chicago. By 1899 the CCF had organized four national conferences: on labor arbitration in 1894, on primary elections in 1898, on foreign policy in 1898 and on trusts in 1899. This last meeting was perhaps the most important. The CCF secretary, Ralph Easley, traveled around the country inviting carefully selected delegates and inducing various governmental bodies to send delegations. It was after this conference that Easley and some members of the CCF began planning for a National Civic Federation. At this point the CCF lapsed from national prominence and the NCF came to the fore. The later years of the CCF were to be confined to narrow city issues, and it took an increasingly conservative view once it had helped install inexpensive and efficient city government.[19]

Secretary Easley was a prime mover in the development of the new federation. He was not an idea man, but a tireless and devoted worker whose goal as a self-styled con-

17. Roberts, *op. cit.*, p. 120.
18. Eakins, *op. cit.*, pp. 61–2.
19. Daniel Levine, "The Civic Federation of Chicago," *Varieties of Reform Thought* (Madison: The State Historical Society of Wisconsin, 1964).

servative was to bring about a better understanding between big business and organized labor. With an advisory committee that included "only representative, conservative, practical men of affairs, Republicans and Democrats," Easley began to seek memberships.[20] Although government office holders, professional politicians, "cranks," and "revolutionists" were excluded from the founding committee, a great many NCF members were cabinet officers and other important government appointees from the social upper class.[21] Among the members were some of the "new" economists, such as E. R. A. Seligman, who headed the Taxation Department. Ely was a member of the founding committee, along with former students of his such as Bemis and Commons. Labor leaders, notably Samuel Gompers of the American Federation of Labor and John Mitchell of the United Mine Workers, were invited into the association.

The NCF was immediately involved in important issues. During its first few years its members were instrumental in mediating several labor disputes. According to Jensen, NCF members were to have this field "very nearly to themselves" because other Progressive Era groups had little to say about relations between labor and capital.[22] Around 1905, however, this phase of its work declined in importance, and the "welfare department" came to the fore, providing a program of reforms that would make labor unions unnecessary or less powerful. The NCF sent pamphlets and representatives to businesmen all over the country, advising them on welfare measures for the workers. It helped as many as fifty companies a year in developing such programs.[23] One of the main backers of this welfare work, which excluded labor leaders, was Edward A. Filene, a department store owner who was an important business leader into the New Deal years.

20. Eakins, *op. cit.*, p. 67.
21. *Ibid.*, p. 67; Jensen, *op. cit.*, pp. 50–1, 60–2.
22. *Ibid.*, p. iii.
23. *Ibid.* p. 157.

It is impossible to capture the flavor of the greatest achievement of the NCF membership in a few summary words. This concerns their development of a moderate position on industrial conflict that enabled them to bring important American Federation of Labor leaders into ideological agreement with them. The NCF, in short, tried to conciliate the menacing gulf between capital and labor. It sought a third way between the smashing of unions—the solution of many employers, best symbolized by the National Association of Manufacturers—and the smashing of capital—the solution of the socialists. In the words of Secretary Easley, NCF's greatest concern was "reconciling the conflict between employers and employees" despite the "socialists in the wage-earners' camp and the anarchists in the employers' camp."[24] On the one hand, the NCF feared strong unions and the possibility of socialism, which was a growing movement in the early twentieth century and a strong minority force within the AF of L itself. On the other, they did not like the "anarchism" of the small businessmen and of the National Association of Manufacturers; "responsibility," "cooperation," and "efficiency" were words they preferred to the nineteenth-century laissez-faire shibboleths. Despite their distaste for powerful unions, and their use of all possible methods, including violence, to keep them impotent, most members of the NCF did not want to come to open warfare with "our workmen."

It is Weinstein's belief, as the foremost expert on the NCF and its role, that this group of corporate managers developed the assumptions and ideology that have steered the moderate corporate leaders throughout the century. They transcended "interest consciousness" to become "class conscious" and "system conscious," as is made abundantly clear in their voluminous correspondence that is now available to historians.[25] When the history and role of the NCF is better known, a whole new perspective on twentieth-cen-

24. Eakins, *op. cit.,* p. 58.
25. Weinstein, *op. cit.,* Chapter 1; Jensen, *op. cit.,* pp. 81–4.

tury America will be developed. Identifying the "business community" with the National Association of Manufacturers, as so many scholars are wont to do, has led to the assumption that the types of programs advocated by the NCF in the first years of the century were "liberal" movements against the power of big business. The work of Eakins, Jensen, and Weinstein suggests the reality is something else. That Samuel Gompers was friends with August Belmont and went hunting with Ralph Easley, that NCF leaders and members of their Women's Department (such as Mrs. Borden Harriman) invited labor leaders to their homes, and that labor leader John Mitchell got personal investment advice from his NCF friends—all of these will be seen as symptoms of the way things were to develop between big business and big labor in the twentieth century.

## THE DECLINE OF THE NCF

The role of the NCF between 1900 and World War I was indeed a major one in shaping domestic policy, but after that time its main ideological tenets were to be carried for the power elite by other organizations. There were several reasons for its demise. First, following certain of the reforms of the Wilson Administration, NCF leaders had gone just about as far as they were willing to go with organized labor. From that point on many felt constrained in an organization which could make pronouncements as a group only when labor and business members agreed; they wanted to pursue certain interests within groups that were made up exclusively of businessmen, and several such groups were developed. Secondly, the research role of the NCF was taken over by several specialized groups, to be discussed shortly, which were better equipped to fulfill this important function. Thirdly, the NCF developed a partisan identification. Secretary Easley and AF of L leader

Gompers became vehement in their denunciation of "radicals," especially during the war. This activity tarnished the
high-minded, nonpartisan image that is so essential for
such a group:

> When it was reactivated at the end of the war, it ·[the NCF]
> was a greatly changed institution. Where formerly it had been
> concerned with reform, now it was concerned with protecting
> American institutions from a wide variety of foreign radicals,
> such as socialists, bolsheviks, or German sympathizers.[26]

During the 1920's the NCF was only useful as a place to
meet with labor leaders. Important lawyers and businessmen such as Elihu Root, Otto Kahn, William H. Taft,
Owen D. Young and Franklin Roosevelt continued to belong.[27] However, Easley and Gompers also spent time
fighting any initiatives to recognize Soviet Russia. By the
late twenties even its limited usefulness in dealing with labor
was ended, and the organization drifted further into right-
wing hysteria and anti-communism. It was a mere shell
of what it had been, its early importance drowned out by its
irrelevance and redbaiting. Although Easley approved of
the National Recovery Administration (NRA) and criticized
the Work Project Administration (WPA), there is no
evidence that the NCF had any effect on events in the
1930's. When Easley claimed that the WPA supervisors
were "reds" and that projects were handled wastefully and
inefficiently, he was answered by Colonel Brehon Somervell, who was to be in charge of supplies during World
War II and president of the Koppers Company after the
war. Somervell called Easley's charge "fatuous, absurd,

---

26. Jensen, *op. cit.*, p. 333.
27. Eakins, *op. cit.*, p. 80. Roosevelt also had contact with labor leaders
as Assistant Secretary of the Navy during World War I, and through
his wife's involvement in the National Consumers' League and the
Women's Trade Union League. In 1925 Mrs. Roosevelt served in an
NCF "political education" department (*The New York Times*, December 14, 1925), p. 16.

illogical, and unreasonable twaddle."[28] The NCF disappeared in 1939 when Easley died. The energetic organizer and admirer of big businessmen had been unable to keep up with the pressure of events, a fate that also befell some of his corporate friends.

## THE AMERICAN ASSOCIATION
## FOR LABOR LEGISLATION

Closely related at its outset to the National Civic Federation in spirit, practice, financing and membership was the American Association for Labor Legislation (AALL). It was founded in 1906 by Richard Ely (its first president) and other political economists of the American Economic Association. There was a considerable overlap of its leadership and financing with the NCF. Seth Low, V. Everitt Macy, publisher Hamilton Holt, and banker Isaac Seligman were among those who were leaders in both groups. Indeed, one of its organizers, statistician Adna Weber, wrote that "It seems clear to my mind that the work of an Association for Labor Legislation would appeal not only to economists and to members of the American Political Science Association, but also to the men of affairs who belong to the Civic Federation."[29] However, in addition to economists and NCF members, the AALL also included many liberal-minded reformers and even a few socialists. In particular, the feminine influence was important, and upper-class women from the National Consumers' League, Women's Trade Union League, and the settlement house movement were on its advisory council. The goal of the AALL was to promote "uniform progressive state and local labor laws and, where

28. Easley Obituary (*The New York Times,* September 8, 1939), p. 23.
29. Richard M. Lyon, "The American Association for Labor Legislation and the Fight for Workmen's Compensation, 1906–1942" (Unpublished Master's thesis, Cornell University, 1952), pp. 40–1.

possible, national labor legislation."[30] Its early motto was "Conservation of Human Resources," but it later added "Social Justice is the Best Insurance Against Labor Unrest."[31] Unlike the NCF, the AALL remained nonpartisan, and unlike the NCF it did not lose its usefulness throughout its thirty-nine-year existence. Perhaps this is because it never concerned itself with the problems of radicalism and labor unions, although some members were very important in gaining recognition for unions through their individual efforts. This caution, and its persistence, are probably the reasons why "the program of the association was remarkably similar to the social security measures of the New Deal. . . ."[32]

As noted, several economists and other scholars were instrumental in founding the AALL. Besides Ely, there was Henry Farnam of Yale University, who was also one of the organization's most important financial backers in its early years. Also involved was economist Frank Taussig of Harvard, then president of the American Economic Association. Taussig was a member of the social upper class, from a wealthy St. Louis family. Two scholars from Columbia University, Henry R. Seager and Joseph Chamberlain (*Social Register,* New York), were of great importance to the AALL. Seager was important in formulating many of the early programs, while Chamberlain founded a bill-drafting institute at Columbia which drew up several model labor laws that were used in states all over the nation. Chamberlain, a Republican, was president of the AALL in 1930 and from 1935 to its end in 1945.

The AALL was governed by a general administration council, made up of from twenty-five to one hundred members, which in turn appointed an executive committee from among its members to set bylaws, choose delegates, conduct

30. Eakins, *op. cit.*, p. 59.
31. *Ibid.*, p. 97.
32. *Ibid.*, p. 59.

the business of the association, and direct expenditures. The executive committee then hired a secretary to carry out its instructions. The first secretary was Adna Weber (1906–07), and the second was John R. Commons (1907–09), who had just left the National Civic Federation to teach at the University of Wisconsin, where half of his salary was being paid in a special arrangement by two corporate leaders.[33] Commons wanted to resign his AALL post as soon as things were functioning, but Farnam asked him to stay on in theory because "we need your name very much."[34] In practice, however, Commons soon turned over the work to a student that he and Ely had trained, John B. Andrews. Andrews officially became secretary in 1909. An effective speaker, good organizer, and tireless worker, he then carried on the work of the organization until his death in 1943.

As a "middle-class" and "academic" reformer, Andrews deserves much credit for the accomplishments of the AALL, but it is also important to realize that he carried out his work as the representative of an organization backed by prominent members of the upper class. Among those who served on the Council at one time or another were Louis Brandeis (a wealthy Jewish corporation lawyer with a reformist bent), Woodrow Wilson, Bernard Baruch, Eustace Seligman, Gerard Swope, John G. Winant, Robert Amory, Edward A. Filene, Alice Hamilton, and Mrs. Thomas Lamont. Further, almost all of its financial support came from a few wealthy backers and a handful of foundations. Among these were John D. Rockefeller, Charles M. Cabot, Elbert Gary of United States Steel, William C. Redfield (President Wilson's Secretary of Commerce), Mrs. Madeline Astor, Anne Morgan (daughter of J. P. Morgan), Felix Warburg,

33. Commons, *op. cit.*, p. 133.
34. Lloyd F. Pierce, "The Activities of the American Association for Labor Legislation in Behalf of Social Security and Protective Labor Legislation" (Unpublished Ph.D. dissertation, University of Wisconsin, 1953), p. 13.

the Seligmans, Adolph and Sam Lewisohn and Mrs. L. K. Elmhirst.[35] Foundation gifts came from Carnegie, Milbank and Russell Sage.

The AALL was effective because it had a minimum program which stressed justice and efficiency. It tried to suggest programs that would aid business as well as improve the working conditions of the labor force. Particularly important as part of its program was the stress on uniform state laws so that employers in one state would not have any competitive advantages over those in states that adopted potentially costly protective legislation. Beyond the emphasis on uniform state laws, a concern it shared with the NCF and then-President Taft, the AALL assumed (1) that research on existing institutions was essential to the development of sound legislation, and (2) that the state was to be a major mechanism for effecting needed reforms.

The first function of the AALL was investigation. It undertook and encouraged research as the necessary basis for any reform. Students of the organization agree that it did its homework well and that its expertise was an important factor in its considerable success. As Pierce notes in relation to one of its programs, "Representatives from all levels of government throughout the nation continuously sought the advice of the association on various aspects of their administrative problems."[36] The second major function of the association was education. This was accomplished through public speeches, special conferences on specific topics, appearances before legislatures and commissions, publications and a press service that provided articles to newspapers. Judging by the AALL's newspaper clipping file, it "received

---

35. These names were collected from a variety of sources, including several volumes of the association's *American Labor Legislation Review*. For an account of the AALL's income for the year 1912 which makes the point very clearly, see Irving Yellowitz, *Labor and the Progressive Movement in New York State, 1897–1916* (Ithaca, New York: Cornell University Press, 1965), pp. 72–3.
36. Pierce, *op. cit.*, p. 414.

an enormous amount of publicity for its program through this medium [its press service]."[37] AALL conferences are too numerous to mention here, but they were often the first ever held in the United States on the problems of concern to the organization. While its publications included a great many pamphlets that were widely circulated, the AALL also was responsible for the quarterly *American Labor Legislation Review,* which provides a detailed account of the protective labor legislation movement. The third function of the AALL was the promotion of uniform labor legislation. It drafted model bills, often with the help of the Columbia University Legislative Drafting Research Fund, and then lobbied vigorously for them.

The AALL fought on five major fronts: industrial disease, industrial accident (workmen's compensation), unemployment, old age pensions, and health insurance. All accounts agree that the AALL was central in the successes, however limited, of the first four programs. The only failure was on health insurance, where moderate forces within the power elite had to do battle with the insurance companies and the American Medical Association in addition to their usual protagonists, best symbolized by the National Association of Manufacturers. Because the AALL was only one of several power elite organizations pushing such legislation, it is difficult to say it was "the" force behind the considerable changes that took place in the thirty years following its founding. However, Pierce's detailed study of the organization judges its importance as follows in its areas of concern:

*Industrial Disease Legislation*

1. Drafted and was largely responsible for the adoption of industrial disease reporting legislation in the leading industrial states.

2. Drafted and secured adoption of the "phossy jaw" bill, the only federal bill which has been enacted to prohibit

the use of an industrial substance to protect the health of industrial workers.

3. Prepared model bills to regulate the conditions of work in such a way as to prevent or minimize lead poisoning and compressed air illness. State legislation based on these bills was enacted in a number of states and, in addition, they were used extensively by the Industrial Commissions in formulating rules to make the conditions of work "safe" in these occupations.

4. Agitated, with partial success, for extension of workmen's compensation legislation to the victims of industrial diseases.

## Industrial Accident Legislation

1. Initiated and provided the chief impetus for accident reporting legislation in the United States between 1911–1915. During this period the Association's model law was adopted in whole or in part by states containing more than one-half of the manufacturing population of the nation.

2. Aroused sufficient interest in preventing coal mine explosions to secure legislation requiring rock dusting in some states and voluntary installation by many coal mine owners in others.

3. Played a major role in securing the adoption of workmen's compensation legislation by all of the states except Mississippi.

4. Drafted and was primarily responsible for securing enactment of workmen's compensation for the following workers under federal jurisdiction: the federal employees in 1916; the Longshoremen in 1929; and the private employees in the District of Columbia in 1928.

5. Played a key role in the campaign which resulted in the passage of a bill which provided for the creation of a federal–state system of vocational rehabilitation for eligible industrial cripples.

## Health Insurance

Largely responsible for the first health insurance movement in America. Drafted the first American health insurance bill, but failed to secure its passage by national and state legislatures.

## Unemployment

1. Helped to secure state legislation designed to regulate the activities of fee-charging employment agencies.

2. Participated in the movement which resulted in the passage of an act by Congress in 1933 which authorized the establishment of a system of federal–state employment offices.

3. Sponsored the campaigns which resulted in the enactment of advance-planning legislation by Congress in 1931.

4. Initiated and maintained interest in unemployment insurance legislation until a bill providing for a federal–state system of compensation was passed by Congress in 1935.

## Miscellaneous Legislation

1. Contributed to the educational campaigns which resulted in the passage of legislation promoting maternity care and limiting the hours and establishing minimum wages for working women.

2. Led the movement which resulted in passage of one-day-of-rest-in-seven legislation in a small number of states.

3. Participated in the movement which led to the passage of old age benefit legislation, first by the states and then by the federal government.

4. Contributed significantly to the improvement of labor law administration in America.[38]

I do not want to overstate the role of the AALL. No one organization was the real power. Rather, along with its many achievements, the existence of the AALL was symptomatic of the outlook of the many elite-sponsored organizations which dominated social reforms in the early

38. *Ibid.*, pp. 33–4.

twentieth century. Nor were the relationships among these organizations merely symbolic or ideological. There were many concrete links among them, and they were continually holding joint conferences. Josephine Goldmark, a member of the National Consumers' League and a sister-in-law of Louis D. Brandeis, tells of the day a friendly magazine editor walked into the Charities Building in New York where many of these groups had their headquarters and asked, "What's this bunch calling itself today?"[39] In fact, it was a meeting of the AALL, but most of the people present were leaders of child labor committees, charity organizations, and consumer leagues. Aside from interlocks with NCF, the National Consumers' League, the Women's Trade Union League, and the Russell Sage Foundation, the AALL had among its advisers the first president of the National Industrial Conference Board, a co-founder of the National Bureau of Economic Research, and the founder of the Twentieth Century Fund. Clearly, one segment of the power elite was involved with the middle-class reformers who did much of the day-to-day work in the battle against the "conservative" NAM mentality within the governing class.

There is only one group that did not play a key role in the fight for protective labor legislation, and that is organized labor itself. Several accounts make this clear, even if the one by Brandeis' daughter calls the AALL "middle class" in making its point.[40] Labor was not in the forefront in these fights because it had considerable suspicion of reformers, because it feared that such paternalistic measures would weaken the union movement, and because it feared the use of the state as the instrument of such reform. Organized labor had to be convinced by the AALL and simi-

39. Josephine Goldmark, *The Impatient Crusader* (Urbana: University of Illinois Press, 1953), pp. 68–9.
40. Elizabeth Brandeis, "Organized Labor and Protective Labor Legislation," in Milton Deber and Edwin Young, eds., *Labor and the New Deal* (Madison: University of Wisconsin Press, 1961), pp. 196–7.

lar groups to go along with many of the reforms. When the AALL drafted a bill in 1915 to create a state industrial commission for New York (it passed without hearings), Gompers was so angry that he resigned from the association, calling it an association for the assassination of labor.[41] "Conditions," and the fear of future trouble, not the pressure of organized labor, led to the reforms in which the AALL took a leading role. When it is added that AALL research often showed businessmen that certain reforms were actually less expensive than the conditions that produced them, it can be seen that protective labor legislation was just good business.

## THE TWILIGHT OF THE AALL

There were several reasons for the decline in importance of the AALL which began in the 1930's. First, it was a victim of its own success. With the passage of the Social Security Act in 1935 all of its major objectives except health insurance had been achieved. Then too, many of its key members were more than ever involved in the government, serving as consultants and advisers in New Deal agencies and committees. Thirdly, the AALL was weakened by the disagreement among its members over details as to the financing of the Social Security Act. While many men continued to be in both the AALL and a rival association that developed in the early 1930's, much of the zest had gone out of the former.

Little was done by the AALL in the late 1930's after the passage of social security, and the association could not survive the loss of interest in it with the coming of World War II in 1942 and the death of Dr. Andrews in 1943. It

41. Eakins, *op. cit.*, p. 95; Pierce, *op. cit.*, p. 395.

was formally disbanded in 1945 after being inoperative for two years, another important power elite organization that is all but forgotten.

## THREE POLICY RESEARCH ORGANIZATIONS, 1916–1920

As the NCF and Easley lost their usefulness, and with the AALL focusing its attention on labor legislation, leading members of the power elite turned to new forms of organization between 1916 and 1920 to meet their other needs for an efficient, productive, and stable corporate society. To this end businessmen active in the NCF and AALL founded three policy-oriented research organizations: the Institute for Government Research, the National Bureau of Economic Research, and the Twentieth Century Fund. Each has played an important role in the development of corporate economic and welfare policies.

The Institute for Government Research was founded in 1916 with the generous financial support of a wealthy St. Louis merchant, Robert Brookings. Eleven years later it was to be one of three organizations that were merged to form a larger corporate research organization, The Brookings Institution. The aim of the Institute for Government Research was to create a sound and efficient government through practical research. Among the first trustees of the Institute were banker and railroad executive Frederic H. Delano, uncle of Franklin D. Roosevelt and a member of the first Federal Reserve Board; James F. Curtis, banker, Assistant Secretary of the Treasury under President Taft, and deputy governor of the New York Federal Reserve Board under President Wilson; Arthur T. Hadley, president of Yale University; Herbert Hoover, self-made millionaire and engineer; and Felix Frankfurter, Harvard law professor, later confidant of President Franklin Roosevelt. The first director of research was William F. Willoughby, a

Princeton professor who had served as president of the AALL in 1912–13, as an assistant director of the United States Bureau of the Census, and as a member of President Taft's Commission on Economy and Efficiency.

Perhaps the institute's most important early success was in the development of the Bureau of the Budget, a policy proposal that was instituted in 1921. Many of the institute's leaders had become involved in budgeting problems as members of President Taft's Commission on Economy and Efficiency. When Congress ignored their recommendations, "the leaders of the commission decided to create a private research organization to bring about the proposed reforms."[42] Turning their attention to other problems during the war, the institute leaders returned to the budget proposal in the early 1920's. Research director Willoughby helped to draft the bill that brought the bureau into existence, and President Harding then asked the institute "to play the major technical role in bringing the budget system into sound and vigorous operation."[43]

The first world war brought big businessmen and scholars into closer relationship as they worked together in various agencies and boards of the federal government. Among the academic talent brought into the government at this time were economist Edwin F. Gay of the Harvard Business School and economist Wesley C. Mitchell of Columbia University. They worked with the liberal big businessman Henry S. Dennison, later to be co-founder of the Twentieth Century Fund, in organizing statistical work for the War Industries Board. Despite pleas by Mitchell, the government did not choose to continue this bureau for planning and statistics after the war ended. Thus, Mitchell, along with Gay and other scholars, was forced to develop a new private organization. Incorporated in 1920, it was called the National Bureau of Economic Research, and it is often

42. Eakins, *op. cit.*, p. 135.
43. *Ibid.*, p. 139, quoting a Brookings Institution pamphlet.

assumed by the general public to be a government agency. At first glance, the NBER was the least "corporate" of the research organizations. None of its early directors was a leading figure in the business community, although one of its founders, Malcolm Rorty, was the chief statistician with AT&T (having previously served as an assistant vice president of Western Union for two years). However, its main source of funds was the Carnegie Corporation. Among foundations the Commonwealth Fund and the Laura Spelman Rockefeller Memorial were also important backers. The NBER also received government contracts, as well as support from the National Research Council, a government body made up of the most important businessmen in the country and in large part financed by big business and foundations.[44] By 1923 Thomas Lamont of J. P. Morgan & Company was chairman of the board of trustees, with Owen Young of General Electric and E. R. A. Seligman also serving on the Board.

The NBER avoided ideological and partisan disputes. It stressed fact-gathering, assuming that such facts would show the way to necessary reforms within the system. This orientation was in large part a reflection of the philosophy of Mitchell, who was its research director from 1920 to 1948. Mitchell, one of the earliest and most consistent practitioners of a value-free social science that studies what is rather than questioning the assumptions of the system, believed that a rationalized capitalism could lead to satisfaction for all groups within the country.[45] The son of a physician, he married into the upper class when he married Lucy Sprague, daughter of a very wealthy Chicago merchant.[46] Mitchell's successor as research director of the NBER was Arthur Burns, who later became well known as President

44. *Ibid.*, pp. 121–3, 129.
45. *Ibid.*, pp. 129–32.
46. Lucy Sprague Mitchell, *Two Lives* (New York: Random House, 1957), Chapters 1–3.

Eisenhower's chief economic adviser. For a short time, Burns used the NBER as his unofficial staff in preparing reports for the Council of Economic Advisors.[47] This was not unusual, for one of the NBER's major functions from its very beginning was providing expert economic advice to governmental agencies. Herbert Hoover, as Secretary of Commerce and as President, called on it several times during the 1920's.

The Twentieth Century Fund was founded in 1919 by NCF and AALL member Edward A. Filene, who remained the new organization's leader until his death in 1937. At first it merely awarded money for research projects, but later it organized its own research groups on questions concerning labor relations and other pressing socioeconomic problems. Joining Filene as a benefactor of the TCF was industrialist Henry S. Dennison. Among the early directors were three who also held positions in the Foreign Policy Association. Among those who joined the board of directors in the thirties were such important New Dealers as corporation lawyers A. A. Berle, Jr. and Francis Biddle, and businessmen Morris Leeds and Charles P. Taft (son of the former President and the moderate brother of conservative Ohio senator Robert Taft). In the 1940's it emphasized studies on postwar economic planning as well as turning its attention to foreign trade and foreign investments.

## THE BROOKINGS INSTITUTION

The final research organization founded by members of the power elite in the years before the Depression was The Brookings Institution. It was created in 1927 by merging three existing organizations: the Institute of Government Research, the Institute of Economic Research, and the

47. Eakins, *op. cit.*, p. 473.

Robert Brookings Graduate School of Economics and Government. As already noted, the Institute of Government Research had been founded in 1916 with a large grant from big businessman Robert Brookings, chairman of the price-fixing committee of the War Production Board. The realization that many of that institute's concerns were really economic questions had led to the founding of a second institute, the Institute of Economics, in 1922. Although the president was Robert Brookings, the money for this enterprise came primarily from the Carnegie Corporation, 1.65 million dollars over the first ten years. One year later, in 1923, Brookings founded the Robert Brookings Graduate School for Economics and Government, which was to teach the art of handling practical problems to students with at least one year of graduate work in economics or politics. In this school Brookings wanted to "turn out craftsmen who [could] make contributions toward an intelligent direction of social change."[48] Many of its students later held positions in New Deal agencies and in corporate research organizations.

When the three organizations were brought together in Washington, D.C. as The Brookings Institution in 1927, they received another large gift from Robert Brookings, as well as donations from the Carnegie, Rockefeller, and George Eastman foundations. Its trustees were among the leading businessmen and corporation lawyers of the day. Also included were university presidents such as Arthur T. Hadley of Yale and Frank Goodnow of Johns Hopkins, and scholars such as William Willoughby and Leo Rowe. One of its best-known trustees was corporation lawyer Dean Acheson who joined the board in 1937 and remained on it until 1947, when he became Secretary of State. From its founding the institution provided a great deal of expertise and advice to the federal government. It became

48. *Ibid.*, p. 182.

more and more conservative throughout the thirties and forties, except on foreign policy, where its views were very similar to those of the other corporate research groups.

## A GENERAL LOOK AT THE EARLY CORPORATE POLICY ORGANIZATIONS

This essay has not gone into great detail about any one policy organization and its accomplishments. However, taking into account what has been presented, and considering that there is massive detail in the sources that have been cited, the following general points emerge about early planning organizations such as the National Civic Federation, the American Association for Labor Legislation, The Brookings Institution, the National Bureau of Economic Research, and the Twentieth Century Fund:

1. All the groups were intertwined with members of the upper class and their corporations in a variety of ways. They are organizations of the power elite.

2. Private foundations controlled by members of the power elite, particularly those of Carnegie and Rockefeller, were involved in one way or another in the financing of many of these groups. It was philanthropic money that enabled several of them to exist. Further, foundation officials were in on the founding of some of them, and sat on many of the directing boards. As one small example of this link, it was Secretary of Commerce Herbert Hoover who gave a large boost to the NBER in the mid-twenties by securing funds for it from the Carnegie Corporation.[49]

49. *Ibid.*, p. 145. Hoover was actually a rather progressive businessman, and it is an exaggeration to stress the contrast between his policies and those of the early New Deal. The important point is the gradual, halting development throughout the century of the corporate acceptance of

3. Some of the planning organizations were more "progressive" than others, with what was considered as going too far something that varied from issue to issue and decade to decade. The differences among the organizations were most pronounced during the 1930's when there were serious disagreements about how to deal with the continuing Depression. It is the differences among these corporate organizations that are sometimes used as examples of the pluralism and diversity of our society. That these disputes were very real, and could have led to greater hardship for the underlying population if resolved more conservatively than they were, is not to be denied. However, from a larger perspective, looking down at the foci of power within the overall system, these differences were primarily technical conflicts within the power elite over means to agreed ends, those ends being the maintenance of the wealth distribution and a private property system in which a very small percentage of the population enjoys great prestige, privilege and authority.

4. It was within these power elite groups that most of the debate on the shape of twentieth-century America took place. Corporate leaders, interacting with economists (and to a lesser extent law professors and political scientists), defined the questions, set the limits on what were considered acceptable alternatives and provided most of the information with which decisions had to be made.

5. It is clear that these groups were involved in the shaping of certain domestic legislation. Leaders and employees of these groups functioned as lobbyists,

---

government as a means for solving economic problems. Not all members of the power elite could make the ideological adjustment to this need, which in some measure accounts for differences of opinion within the corporate community.

educators, and members of special government committees and fact-finding commissions. The work of Eakins, Jensen, Lyons, Pierce, and Weinstein demonstrates their involvement in considerable detail.

6. Many men from the corporate planning groups worked in and with the executive branch of the government in many different ways. The corporate merger with an expanding executive branch was well underway in the first two decades of this century. The line between government-financed and business-financed research organizations became hazy, with public financing of private groups through contracts, private financing of public agencies through foundations, and a constant shuttling back and forth of men, reports and information. It is not surprising that many people would assume that the NBER is a governmental agency.

7. Radicals on the one hand and small businessmen and farmers on the other, were by and large absent from these groups. Nor was organized labor a significant factor in them. However, AF of L leaders were invited into the councils of some of them on the ideological terms set by the corporate leaders. As will be shown in the final section, labor leaders were more than willing to accept these terms.

## THE NPA AND THE CED

Two power elite planning organizations which are very important at the present time had their origins in the early 1940's. Their primary concern in their first years was postwar planning that would diminish the possibilities of another Depression. Indeed, as Eakins shows, all corporate planning organizations had this concern in the early forties, and all came to the conclusion that expansion of foreign trade and foreign investments were essential aspects to the answer to this very real problem.[50]

The first of these new organizations was the National Planning Association, which was organized in 1941 out of the older (1933) National Economic and Social Planning Association. NESPA had grown out of a discussion group that met in Washington during the early New Deal; most of its members were social science experts who worked for labor organizations and corporate research groups. NESPA was decidedly avant-garde in many eyes because it was concerned with the problem of "planning," a red flag word to followers of laissez-faire. However, few of its members advocated socialist planning, but rather government and business planning. At any rate, only George Soule, a labor economist close to Sidney Hillman of the CIO, and A. F. Hinrichs, another young economist, remained on the board of directors when NESPA was reorganized into the National Planning Association. E. J. Coil, an economist who had served in New Deal agencies, remained as research director.

The chairman of the new organization was William L. Batt, president of SKF Industries, and soon to be an important figure in the industrial mobilization for World War II. When Batt's government duties became too pressing, he relinquished his NPA post to Charles E. Wilson of General Electric. However, when Wilson moved from vice chairman to chairman of the government's War Production Board, Batt returned to the chairmanship. During this time an AF of L official was NPA vice chairman, and a CIO leader was secretary. The new board of trustees reflected the fact that this organization welcomed the presence of noncorporate leaders. In addition to the many businessmen

50. *Ibid.*, p. 296*ff.* It is here, along with Council on Foreign Relations publications and reports, that the evidence for the expansionist nature of American postwar foreign policy can be found. See also David W. Eakins, "Business Planners and America's Postwar Expansion," in *Corporations and the Cold War,* David Horowitz, ed., (New York: Monthly Review Press, 1969).

on the board, there were several labor officials, farm organization leaders, and academic experts. Needless to add, the organization interlocked with the other corporate groups. To demonstrate this with one concrete example, NPA trustee Charles Taussig, president of his family's American Molasses Company, was a close friend of A. A. Berle, Jr. of the Twentieth Century Fund. Berle was Taussig's lawyer, and served on the board of his sugar company when not in government service.

The NPA has done a great many studies, especially on foreign economic opportunities and foreign policy problems, but one of its most important domestic contributions concerns its effort in behalf of the Employment Act of 1946. The importance of this act, which created the Council of Economic Advisors, an annual economic report by the President, and a Joint Congressional Committee on the Economic Report, should not be overemphasized, but it did put the government on record as being concerned with the maintenance of employment. While Stephen Bailey, who studied the origins of the act as a case study in how Congress makes a law, agrees that NPA members "loom large" in its history, Eakins suggests that he does not give full due to the NPA effort.[51] Eakins' view is perhaps supported by the personal recollections of one of the participants, economist Gerhard Colm, then with the Bureau of the Budget, until his death the chief economist of the NPA:

> As a result of these discussions among the Trustees, NPA initiated several study groups dealing with postwar adjustment problems. One of these was under the chairmanship of Robert Nathan and considered policies which would prevent recurrence of a depression. This study group worked in close cooperation with staff members of the Budget Bureau (with the approval of Budget Director Smith, I and my assistant,

51. Stephen Bailey, *Congress Makes A Law* (New York: Columbia University Press, 1950), p. 21; Eakins, "The Development of Corporate Liberal Policy Research in the United States, 1885–1965," *op. cit.*, p. 394*ff*.

Grover Ensely, were active members of this group) and with staff members of the Board of Governors of the Federal Reserve System. An NPA staff member, Sam Thompson, acted as rapporteur for the group. Mr. Sonne [Christian H. Sonne, a big businessman who had taken over as chairman of NPA] kept in close contact with this work. This resulted in a pamphlet on National Budgets for Full Employment, which was circulated in preliminary form in 1944 and published in 1945. This document was designed to show that through alternative economic projections various approaches to maintaining full employment could be explored. The work of this group had considerable impact both on a Congressional working group (under the chairmanship of Bertram Gross) and on the work in the Executive branch, because it clarified basic concepts such as the full-employment objective and alternative policy instruments which could be used to achieve the objective.[52]

The second major corporate organization to be formed in the early forties was the Committee for Economic Development. The importance of this organization, on both domestic and foreign policy, probably cannot be overestimated. It was the outgrowth of a realization on the part of many big businessmen that serious planning would have to take place if future depressions were to be averted, particularly in the light of the industrial expansion necessary to prosecute World War II. Credit for the founding of the organization is usually given to multimillionaires Paul Hoffman and William Benton, but such an organization had been in the minds of other leaders, including the big businessmen running the Department of Commerce in the early 1940's. Thus, the Hoffman-Benton suggestion met with immediate sympathy, and the Committee for Economic Development was born in 1942.

Except in its functioning, it is almost impossible to separate CED from another big business organization, the Business Advisory Council. Founded in 1933 to advise the

52. Gerhard Colm, personal communication, August 29, 1968.

Department of Commerce, the BAC was essentially a discussion committee of thirty to sixty leading businessmen who were sympathetic to the attempts being made by President Roosevelt to deal with the Depression. It also provided business appointments to the government; corporate leader Thomas McCabe estimated in 1949 that the BAC had sent "almost a hundred men from industry to government since 1933."[53] However, the BAC was not equipped to educate its members or to carry out extensive research, and the CED was formed to fill this need. With but two exceptions the early members of the CED were BAC members. The CED immediately developed discussion groups in which business leaders talked about major economic problems among themselves and with hired economists. Their care ·in choosing these economists is clearly expressed by the CED historian, Karl Schriftgiesser.[54] Among the economists helping the CED in its early years were Summer Slichter of Harvard (two of his brothers were corporate directors in their native Wisconsin), Robert Calkins of Columbia, Calvin Hoover of Duke, Gardner Means, and Theodore Yntema. Yntema later became a Ford Motor vice president, while Calkins went on to become the director of The Brookings Institution.

The first CED task was to determine productive capacity and potential employment after the war. CED estimates were among the most accurate, inspiring confidence in the organization.[55] Following the war the CED played an important role in the development and staffing of the Marshall Plan, a role that was referred to in the context of the previous essay. It also took an extensive look at the func-

---

53. Eakins, *op. cit.*, p. 342.
54. Karl Schriftgiesser, *Business Comes of Age* (New York: Harper & Row, 1960), p. 61.
55. *Ibid.*, p. 42*ff.*; Arthur Prager, "With Insight and Inducement" (*Saturday Review*, January 13, 1968), p. 79.

tioning of the Federal Reserve System, which is interesting in light of the fact that President Truman appointed CED leader Thomas McCabe to head the Federal Reserve Board in 1948.

According to Eakins and Schriftgiesser, the CED also played a crucial role in bringing forth the moderate suggestions that salvaged the Employment Act of 1946 from its conservative NAM opponents.[56] While Bailey is also well aware of CED's important involvement in that bill, he does not impress upon the reader that the CED is at least as representative of powerful business interests as the NAM, which he tends to identify with the business community.[57] In short, Bailey's book, a favorite among pluralists, is an excellent account of a conflict between the NAM and CED-NPA wings of the power elite.

## THE POLICY GROUPS TODAY

If the policy groups had some differences during the thirties and forties, they drew together during the fifties and sixties. The conservative groups became more moderate, and the liberal groups were seen to be more moderate than some had thought. Starting on the right, the National Industrial Conference Board, an economic research group closely related to the National Association of Manufacturers, gradually moved back into the mainstream after its longtime director, economist Virgil Jordan, resigned in 1949. Jordan did not keep pace with developments in the late thirties and forties, and was constantly claiming that big businessmen in

56. Eakins, *op. cit.*, pp. 396–400; Schriftgiesser, *op. cit.*, pp. 88–99; Karl Schriftgiesser, *Business and Public Policy: The Role of the Committee for Economic Development, 1942–1967* (Englewood Cliffs: Prentice-Hall, 1967), pp. 20–4.
57. Bailey, *op. cit.*, pp. 10, 132, 138, 166, 169, 238.

the NPA and CED were being tricked and duped by their slick academic experts. At Brookings, a director who had become almost as conservative, Harold Moulton, was replaced in 1952 by Robert Calkins, who guided Brookings into the general corporate consensus on all issues. By the mid-fifties Brookings had four CED members among its big business trustees. With the help of the Carnegie, Rockefeller, and Ford foundations, it expanded its services greatly during this period, developing its seminar program for business and government leaders, providing more research space and money for scholars, and undertaking overseas projects at the behest of the federal government.[58] The National Bureau of Economic Research remained the moderate organization it always had been. Perhaps it had a slightly more conservative tinge, for among the economists it hired for one project or another were three who became advisers to Barry Goldwater in 1964. However, it also numbered a CED research director and other CED officials among its directors.

The NPA and the CED actually discussed a merger during 1957, but NPA leaders decided they wanted to maintain their open and frank discussions with labor and farm leaders, which would not be possible in the businessmen-only atmosphere of the CED. CED, on the other hand, did not want to risk losing the support of those businessmen who would object to taking labor and farm leaders into the group. However, the relationship between the two groups was very close, with the top four NPA officials also being members of the CED and, incidentally, the Council on Foreign Relations. Six of the ten members of the NPA executive committee in 1955 were also trustees or officers of the CED.

NPA also maintained close relationships with the major foundations. In 1953, for example, it received $440,000

58. Eakins, *op. cit.*, pp. 483–9.

from the Ford Foundation to write a report on the future of American technical cooperation in Latin America. In 1956 NPA reaffirmed that its goal was "to maintain and strengthen private initiative and enterprise," and that "through effective private planning we can avoid a 'planned economy.' "⁵⁹ Emphasis was placed on studies of foreign business opportunities, and on case studies of ideal American overseas operations (Sears in Mexico, Creole Petroleum in Venezuela, Firestone in Liberia, and United Fruit in Guatemala).

As for the CED in recent years, it too has concerned itself in large measure with problems of foreign policy. However, it also has been involved with problems of fiscal policy and governmental budgeting. In 1958, with a 1.3 million dollar grant from the Ford Foundation, CED set up a Commission on Money and Credit to suggest policies which would "improve the structure, operation, regulation and control of our monetary and credit system."⁶⁰ Among the members were the heads of NPA and the Twentieth Century Fund, along with David Rockefeller, CED leaders and economists from the various power elite research groups. According to Eakins, there is every reason to believe that the suggestions of this commission received a serious hearing within the government in the 1960's. One of the government officials whom President Kennedy appointed to three interagency committees charged with the task of examining the commission report was economic adviser Walter Heller, a former CED consultant. Heller chaired one of the committees and sat on the other two. CED also took a leading role in bringing about a new method of governmental budgeting: "CED's campaign for the use of a more modern and more revealing budgetary system (begun, as we have said, in 1947) began to bear fruit in March, 1967, when President Johnson created a special Commission on Budget

59. *Ibid.*, p. 478.
60. *Ibid.*, p. 503.

Concepts."[61] Chaired by banker David M. Kennedy, a CED trustee, the sixteen-member commission of "businessmen, economists, Wall Streeters, and congressional leaders" included six men besides Kennedy who were closely identified with CED. The report of the commission was presented to President Johnson in October, 1967, and it was reported that "Johnson will use the new format and some of the specific changes in his fiscal 1968 budget, already being prepared for submission to Congress in January;" there is reason to believe that the new budget concept is "quite close" to the one urged by CED.[62] And when Richard M. Nixon became President in 1969, David Kennedy became Secretary of the Treasury, a position from which he can oversee the implementation of concepts he helped develop as a CED leader.

The Twentieth Century Fund, chaired by Berle after 1951, remained the most liberal of the power elite research groups. Its trustees in the 1950's included many well-known Democrats (some upper class, some middle-class) as well as the head of the National Planning Association and the former head of the CED. The presence of J. Robert Oppenheimer and Robert Lynd on its board, along with its sponsorship of several critical liberals, even led to an investigation of that group by an ultra-conservative congressional committee. The TCF still establishes some committees on a wide variety of problems, but has turned more and more to commissioned studies and reports by experts.

The financing, leadership, and activities of the major power elite research organizations of the present day—National Bureau of Economic Research, The Brookings Institution, Committee for Economic Development, National Planning Association, and Twentieth Century Fund—suggest certain conclusions about the shaping of social

61. Schriftgiesser, *Business and Public Policy, op. cit.*, p. 187.
62. "Johnson Gets Plans for New Budget Setup," Cleveland *Plain Dealer*, (October 18, 1967), p. 35; Schriftgiesser, *op. cit.*, p. 188.

legislation in this country. First, with the exception of the highly specialized Council on Foreign Relations, the same power elite organizations tend to be involved in the shaping of social legislation as we found to be involved in the planning of foreign policy. Second, aside from the added element of public pressure, the same mechanics seem to characterize the process for developing social policy as was found in the case of foreign policy. There are various policy-planning organizations which can be tied to the upper class and the corporations on the one hand and the federal government on the other. These organizations prepare reports and train men for government service. The government appoints committees and commissions to make reports and recommendations. The men who are appointed to these government groups are from the corporations and the policy-planning organizations. The recommendations of these research groups and governmental commissions are adopted by the executive branch or, if legislation is necessary, lobbied through an often resistant legislative branch where other groups in the population express themselves by means of pressure groups and elected representatives. Even in Congress, however, the most important force seems to be the NAM–United States Chamber of Commerce mentality, which is the conservative tendency within the power elite. In summary, there is a complex interrelationship among corporations, foundations, research and planning organizations, and the federal government. And all along the line, in positions of leadership, we find members of the social upper class and their top-level employees; that is, we find the power elite. If this is not in itself evidence for power elite dominance of social legislation, it does suggest power elite involvement in such problems. The rest of the essay will show how this power elite involvement shapes, channels, and moderates pressures from other groups who are seeking more radical changes in the socioeconomic system.

## PROTECTIVE LABOR LEGISLATION — WORKMEN'S COMPENSATION

Within the context provided by the previous sections of this essay, it is possible to see how the power elite are involved in the making of specific pieces of social legislation. I do not say it is possible to prove that *they* made the legislation down to its last detail because I believe it is virtually impossible to show who influenced whom in any definitive way in such complex situations. Contrary to those who confidently state conclusions after conducting interviews and reading old newspapers, I believe such studies only give us a rough picture of what actually happened. Indeed, by stressing the details of the process on one particular issue, perspective on the problem is often lost. A brief consideration of the groups behind the Taft-Hartley Act of 1947 may help to make this point about perspective and context more concrete. According to a detailed study of the NAM, that organization played a key role in formulating the policies in that act.[63] However, another source points out that a Brookings Institution draft bill of 1947 was very similar to the act, and we do know that Senator Taft thought very highly of The Brookings Institution.[64] But we also know that the Twentieth Century Fund advocated the definition of unfair labor practices, and that a CED pamphlet of 1947 "anticipated" many Taft-Hartley provisions.[65] Thus, while it might not be possible to unravel what happened exactly, we can say with some confidence that several interrelated power elite organizations and institutes were in accord that certain changes should be made in the Wagner Act. They all saw labor as getting a little too much power,

63. R. M. Gable, "NAM: Influential Lobby or Kiss of Death?" (*Journal of Politics*, May, 1953), p. 271.
64. Eakins, *op. cit.*, p. 414.
65. *Ibid.*, p. 417.

and various individuals and reports from NAM-Brookings-CED-TCF initiated a change that was readily accepted by a conservative Congress.

With the difficulties and limits of such studies before us, I am going to look in varying detail at how legislation apparently was developed on four important aspects of social policy often cited by pluralists as evidence that contradicts a power elite theory: protective labor legislation, the regulation of businessmen, social security, and the recognition of labor unions. I turn first to workmen's compensation as an important example of protective labor legislation. Contrary to what might be expected, workmen's compensation had to be forced upon organized labor by moderate members of the power elite. However, the moderates did not suggest this legislation out of the goodness of their hearts, and the story of how they came to favor it is a good example of how and why social legislation is enacted.

The National Civic Federation, as noted, supported unionism in principle, but did everything possible to impede its growth. It advocated a variety of paternalistic reforms, including recreational and educational facilities, Bible training, savings plans, and safety and health programs. However, despite this seeming benevolence, working conditions were an open scandal: "Not only were American working conditions worse and accidents more frequent than in European industry, but provisions for the injured worker were virtually nonexistent in the United States, while they were extensive in Europe."[66] While this situation had existed in the past, two factors led the big rich to correct it at this time. First, the AF of L had turned to politics following several critical court decisions and restrictive acts by Congress. Second, although employees usually lost in court

---

66. Weinstein, *op. cit.*, p. 41. This account primarily follows Weinstein's analysis of the problem in Chapter Two of his book. However, it follows Pierce, *op. cit.*, and Lyon, *op. cit.*, in emphasizing the role of the American Association for Labor Legislation as well as the NCF.

when they tried to claim damages from accidents, many members of the power elite were annoyed by the uncertainty of time-consuming litigations, which were potentially very costly. Some states were becoming more lenient toward labor in such cases, and the unions were hopeful for the future even if workers had been slighted in the past ("only an estimated fifteen percent of the injured employees ever recovered damages, even though seventy percent of industrial accidents were estimated to be the result of the nature of the work or of employer negligence").[67] One NCF expert on the matter expressed himself as follows: "We must make a move toward compensation soon. Otherwise we will continue, with ever increasing impetus, down the broad road of the employer liability laws, which leads to social destruction."[68] This statement may be overwrought, but as Weinstein notes, "such a development [state sympathy with employee demands for damages] would increase uncertainty for business and might substantially raise the cost of liability insurance."[69] To summarize, then, the NCF saw a number of reasons to champion workmen's compensation. First, there was a very bad situation in terms of accidents. Second, there was growing political unrest in the working class that might be partially undercut by such a measure. Third, there was the expense and uncertainty of court cases. For all of these reasons, moderate members of the power elite began to champion workmen's compensation administered by the state. Interestingly, one of their major opponents was organized labor, which both distrusted the state and had hopes for a better day in the courts. Even after being convinced to go along with regularized state compensation, labor still wanted the right to take cases to court. That the big businessmen vetoed such an option is another indication of their importance on this social reform.

67. *Ibid.*
68. *Ibid.*, p. 45.
69. *Ibid.*

The leaders in the movement were the closely related AALL and NCF. The AALL began to call for such legislation in 1907, and NCF became involved shortly thereafter. While Weinstein emphasizes the importance of NCF in convincing labor and business to support the compensation idea, the fact remains that the AALL, as well as the National Consumers' League, was very active in the details of the campaign. The AALL was especially important on the three major compensation laws passed on the federal level, which covered federal employees, maritime workers, and District of Columbia employees.[70] In 1910 the NCF-AALL clique was able to secure the support of the NAM, whose members overwhelmingly favored the idea when they were polled.[71] Gompers and the AF of L had capitulated in 1909. Both the AALL and the NCF drew up model bills which were sent to state legislatures around the country. The NCF bill had been discussed first by the Department on Compensation for Industrial Accidents and their Prevention, headed by August Belmont. Disagreements within NCF over the exact nature of the legislation (state versus private insurance, level of compensation, coverage, waiting periods) were worked out under the leadership of this "department" of the NCF. The German experience was drawn upon in the person of Major A. E. Piorkowski of the Krupp Company, the British experience by the presence of a member of Parliament.[72] The model bill was sent out by NCF in 1910 even though some members favored a more liberal measure. Twelve states passed compensation or accident insurance bills in 1911, and by 1920 all but six states in the South had workmen's compensation.

One potential problem blocked the NCF-AALL program—conservative courts. In 1911 the New York Court

---

70. Lyons, *op. cit.*, is devoted exclusively to the AALL role in securing workmen's compensation; Pierce, *op. cit.*, also devotes a number of pages to it, 190*ff.* on the three federal laws and 154*ff.* on the state laws.
71. Weinstein, *op. cit.*, p. 47.
72. *Ibid.*, pp. 50–1.

of Appeals declared that state's conservative compensation act to be unconstitutional, calling it "plainly revolutionary."[73] NCF members were angered. Corporate lawyers in the group submitted a brief to Congress in support of federal compensation. Ex-President Roosevelt, a member of NCF who often spoke before it, was extremely critical, and called for "laws permitting the recall of judicial decisions . . ."[74] More cautious millionaires developed a new law that could not be struck down by the courts. Courts in other states soon after upheld such acts in their respective states. From that point on there was no serious opposition to the principle of workmen's compensation.

Despite the fact that NCF corporate leaders such as George Perkins, August Belmont, P. Tecumseh Sherman, Elihu Root and Clark Firestone were the leaders of the drive for workmen's compensation, this does not mean they did not have to compromise on some aspects of the issue. The details of specific acts varied from state to state. Some insurance men among the power elite considered state insurance "socialistic," so the rest of the big businessmen often had to convince labor to withdraw its support for state insurance in exchange for higher payout rates. (The NCF also suggested that private versus state insurance could be placed at the option of the employer.) Then too, the pressures of the very active Socialist Party also helped to drive compensation rates above 50% of weekly pay, even though the businessmen favored 50% or less. The socialists had demanded 100%.

Compromises, then, were made, but they were made within the basic framework worked out by the moderate members of the power elite. If this is the essence of pluralism, then so be it. The important thing from my point of view is to see the way in which big businessmen responded to a set of closely related problems by developing legislation

73. *Ibid.*, p. 56.
74. *Ibid.*, p. 57.

that cost them very little and helped head off undue unrest. From their point of view, the result of the act was a more efficient and stable work force, and relief from the nuisance and potential costliness of court cases.

If the role of big business is clear from tracing the origins of the legislation, it is even clearer when *what is*, present-day reality, is compared with *what could be*. Instead of a fully humane working environment, we have one that constantly verges on the minimum acceptable standard. Consider the picture painted by an admirer of big business, syndicated business and financial columnist Sylvia Porter: 14,000 Americans were scheduled to lose their lives in job accidents in 1968; 2.5 million were to be disabled by job-related diseases and accidents; one thousand mine workers were due to die from lung cancer due to radiation exposure; 80% of the nation's bituminous coal miners have pneumonoconiosis, "a serious disease caused by coal dust."[75] Of 1,339 companies doing business with the government, 95% violated minimum safety and health standards: "Corporations, in general, are doing tragically little to protect employees."[76]

## THE REGULATION OF BUSINESS—THE FEDERAL TRADE COMMISSION ACT OF 1914

It is well understood by most social scientists that businessmen dominate the regulatory commissions that are supposed to regulate them. This has been documented time and time again. However, until the work of Gabriel Kolko it was not generally known that the big businessmen created the commissions, and until the work of Weinstein and

75. Sylvia Porter, "Accident Toll of Workers" (*San Francisco Chronicle*, July 30, 1968), p. 43.
76. *Ibid.*

Jensen it was not realized how organized and sophisticated they were in doing it.[77] This account will follow that of Weinstein, who begins by noting that it is popularly believed that the Federal Trade Commission Act of 1914, which is the object of this particular inquiry, was an anti-big business measure instituted by an anti-big business Wilson administration. He then shows that nothing could be much further from the reality.

As might be suspected by now, the major group behind the idea of the FTC was the National Civic Federation. The NCF had been concerned about the proper regulation of business from its earliest years. There were a number of reasons for this concern. First, there was the uncertain legal status of big corporations following the Sherman Act and various court interpretations. Second, there was the problem of dealing with cutthroat competition, that is, with regulating disputes within the big business community. Third, there was the problem of dealing with socialist and muckraking agitation. Finally, regulation varied from state to state, and the corporations were eager to see such functions taken over by the federal government, probably for reasons of simplicity, efficiency and ease of control.[78] The problem for the NCF, then, was to find a way to take care of all of these problems with as few concessions as possible. History suggests that it succeeded admirably. The legal status of the corporations is secure, competition is nicely regulated, and no one argues against the trusts.

The first NCF success in the area of regulation, which set the stage for later developments, came from its Commission on Public Ownership of Public Utilities, established in 1905. Its task was to head off the growing clamor for

77. Gabriel Kolko, *The Triumph of Conservatism: A Reinterpretation of American History, 1900–1916* (New York: Free Press of Glencoe, 1963); Gabriel Kolko, *Railroads and Regulation* (Cambridge: Harvard University Press, 1965); Weinstein, *op. cit.*, Chapter 3; Jensen, *op. cit.*, pp. 269–97.
78. Kolko, *The Triumph of Conservatism, op. cit.*, p. 132.

public ownership of public utilities, to "take the matter out of politics," as Easley wrote to Senator Nelson Aldrich.[79] Among its members were big businessmen and labor leaders as well as John R. Commons. According to Weinstein, the commission's report "established a general framework for regulatory laws. The Wisconsin public utilities law, for example, was drawn up on these principles by Commons [in 1907]."[80] Regulatory commissions designed to police public utilities soon made their appearances in other states.

The NCF just missed a bigger success in 1907 and 1908, a success which might have made the FTC unnecessary. However, it was defeated by the NAM and small businessmen within the Republican Party. This specific episode in the more general story leading up to the FTC can be begun with the federation-sponsored National Conference on Trusts and Combinations, held in Chicago in October, 1907. The recommendations of the conference were generally sympathetic with NCF objectives. One of them called for the establishment of a congressional commission to study the problem, and NCF leaders went to Washington to present their suggestion: "Much to the Federation's surprise, the congressmen suggested that instead of a commission, the NCF draw up a bill embodying its suggestions."[81] The NCF president, Seth Low, immediately appointed an informal committee that included E. H. Gary, chairman of United States Steel; Samuel Mather of Pickands, Mather; investment bankers Isaac Seligman and James Speyer; W. A. Clark, president of the United Verde Copper Company; August Belmont; and George W. Perkins of J. P. Morgan & Company. There were also six labor leaders who were NCF members. Then too, the Commissioner of Corpora-

79. Weinstein, *op. cit.*, p. 74. Easley also noted that such a "high class, representative commission" would give the Attorney General's office "good grounds" to "slack up a little on its prosecutions."
80. Weinstein, *op. cit.*, p. 25; for greater detail on NCF involvement in public utility regulation, see Jensen, *op. cit.*, Chapter 8.
81. Weinstein, *op. cit.*, p. 77.

tions at that time, Herbert Knox Smith, and the 1904 Democratic Presidential candidate, Alton B. Parker, were members. The bill that emerged from this NCF group, a bill which was drafted mostly by attorneys for J. P. Morgan & Company and the Atchison, Topeka and Santa Fe, included attempts to satisfy certain qualms of the NAM and a clause giving unions a way to avoid the clutches of the Sherman Act. It was introduced in 1908, but defeated by an all-out effort by the NAM, small businessmen, and middle-sized business associations. Some, such as Kolko, think it was the clause concerning labor unions that angered the smaller businessmen, while Robert H. Wiebe, another of the few historians to study the businessmen of this era, believes that "the crucial issue was the latitude promised to big business."[82] In any case, the NCF effort was thwarted.

"Reasonable" and "unreasonable" were the key words in the National Civic Federation proposal. This was similar to President Roosevelt's distinction between "good" and "bad" trusts: "It was clear to them that when Roosevelt denounced 'bad' trusts his main target was Rockefeller and his Standard Oil Company, rather than the Morgan and other corporations in the Civic Federation."[83] In any case, and without trying to trace the causality, a Supreme Court decision in 1911 in the Standard Oil case, which promulgated the "rule of reason" allowing "reasonable" trusts, changed the situation considerably, for it took much of the pressure off the big corporations. Some, such as President Taft, thought the Supreme Court decision made further legislative action unnecessary. However, Seth Low and several others in the NCF did not agree, and they continued work on a new bill that had been under discussion in an NCF committee since 1909. The new approach was

82. Kolko, *op. cit.*, p. 135; Wiebe is quoted in Weinstein, *op. cit.*, p. 80.
83. Weinstein, *op. cit.*, p. 71.

modeled on the already existent Interstate Commerce Commission that regulated railroads, and on the British Board of Trade.

Confusion and conflict over the meaning of the Sherman Act continued, and NCF members continued to press for a regulatory agency. When several different sources began to make the same suggestion in late 1911 and early 1912, the NCF group moved rapidly. United States Steel's Gary, a member of the earlier NCF committee that wrote the defeated amendments to the Sherman Act in 1908, "acting in his capacity as president of the American Iron and Steel Institute, assigned its counsel to work with the federation in drawing up a bill and to assist it 'in every possible way.' "[84] A federation subcommittee of Seth Low, Jeremiah W. Jenks (one of the new economists who had been with the NCF since its inception), John B. Clark (another of the new political economists of the 1880's), and Talcott Williams (a newspaper publisher) prepared a bill that met with the general approval of the federation. "That bill was then sent to Senator Newlands, to Representative Henry D. Clayton, to newly elected President Wilson's Commissioner of Corporations, Joseph E. Davies, and to the President himself."[85] About a month after receiving the bill, Newlands, an NCF member of great personal wealth, and Clayton introduced identical bills on the same day. The timing and the men involved suggest the importance of the NCF proposal.

Other such bills had been introduced, including one by Senator Albert B. Cummings, who had consulted with NCF's Perkins and corresponded with Easley on the matter, and one by progressive Republican Robert La Follette. Thus, it is impossible to say with certainty that the NCF was *the* force behind the bill. Even if the interviews that

84. *Ibid.*, p. 87.
85. *Ibid.*, p. 88.

pluralists are so fond of collecting were available, we could never be sure that all of the "actors" were accurate or honest in their reflections. However, we can compare the NCF bill with the final bill: "Low's bill was almost a model for the final legislation in every other respect."[86] The "other" refers to two minor divergencies. First, the commission had only five members instead of seven. Second, there were no federal licensing provisions for interstate business. If this correspondence between Low's bill and the final bill is not convincing in itself, leaving out as it does the admittedly complex process of negotiation that went on over a period of several months, it is nonetheless true that NCF members were very pleased by the outcome. For example, Talcott Williams, who had a hand in drafting the NCF bill, told the Federation's executive committee, as revealed in private minutes only much later available to historians, that the NCF had had a "profound effect" on Congress.[87]

Perhaps some skeptics will want more detail, and they can find it in the works and citations of Kolko and Weinstein. However, the shaping role of big businessmen is overwhelmingly obvious to me. That they were under pressure is freely acknowledged, and was so at the time by NCF leaders. What pleased them was the way in which they handled that pressure. The Federal Trade Commission solved a number of their problems by dealing with legal-, small business-, muckraker-, and socialist-generated uncertainties. They were now free to regulate themselves by means of a governmental agency that was safely removed from courts and politics. The law written, the businessmen concerned themselves with *who* was going to *interpret* it, which is where the standard studies of regulatory agencies pick up and demonstrate the story of their subordination to big business.

86. *Ibid.*, p. 89.
87. *Ibid.*, p. 90.

## THE PASSAGE OF THE
## SOCIAL SECURITY ACT, 1935*

If the earlier discussion of the American Association for Labor Legislation has established that it was financed and directed by leading moderates of the power elite, then little time need be spent in discussing all the details leading to the passage of social security legislation in 1935. According to Roy C. Lubove, who has made one of the most detailed studies of the historical background of this legislation: "The American Association for Labor Legislation (AALL) created and sustained the organized social insurance movement in the United States."[88] That said, however, the historical record once again shows that other groups were involved, and that growing discontent spurred the enactment of legislation; the AALL was unsuccessful until the 1930's when the situation was very nearly desperate for many people and the "extremist" Townsend Plan, calling for $200 a month for everyone over sixty, had caught the fancy of tens of millions of angry victims of the Depression. Then too, the enactment of social security is noteworthy as a case study in how the role of big businessmen and corporation lawyers is almost completely ignored by historians.

The AALL movement for social insurance—primarily unemployment compensation and old-age pensions—began in the years between 1910 and 1915. While AALL conferences and writings had little immediate effect, they did set the terms of the debate and supply much of the information

* This section has benefited from my discussions with Mark Goldowitz, who undertook a detailed research project of his own on social welfare legislation in conjunction with my work on domestic legislation.
88. Roy C. Lubove, *The Struggle for Social Security, 1900–1935* (Cambridge: Harvard University Press, 1968), p. 29. Lubove, however, then goes on to say that "the AALL testified to the emergence of the social scientist as an influence in social legislation and reform." Nowhere does he discuss the financing of this organization, its corporate directors, or its connections with other elite-led associations.

that was drawn upon in later discussions. The AALL campaign for old-age pensions was joined by a middle-class grass roots organization, the Fraternal Order of Eagles, in 1921. FOE leaders met with AALL leaders, and it was basically an AALL-drafted "standard" bill that the Eagles were able to sell to several state legislatures during the twenties.[89] Some state courts, however, declared these bills unconstitutional; other bills were never funded by the legislatures. One other organization came into the fray during the twenties. Called the American Association for Old Age Security, it was headed by Abraham Epstein, a former lobbyist for the FOE program who had long been active for social insurance programs in Pennsylvania. Epstein became disenchanted with FOE's willingness to compromise its program. He also believed that the AALL-type plan, which rewarded employers who kept unemployment low (by permitting them to pay less into the unemployment fund), was not adequate. The AALL plan, it should be noted, was based on the assumption that the unemployment problem was similar to the accident problem, and that by giving incentives to employers they would be motivated to regularize employment in the same way they had supposedly reduced accidents in order to reduce their workmen's compensation contributions. This view, championed by John R. Commons, became known as the American Plan or Wisconsin Plan, while Epstein's plan for social insurance became known as the Ohio Plan, after the state commission which first advocated its adoption.

Secretary Andrews of the AALL was upset by the founding of the rival organization, but there was little he could do about it. In any case, many people were leaders in both organizations, and the level of the debate concerning the merits of the two plans was generally a high one.[90] The matter was to be decided by the overwhelming unemployment of the Depression, which was clearly beyond the

89. Lubove, *op. cit.*, pp. 138–9; Pearce, *op. cit.*, pp. 389*ff*.
90. Lubove, *op. cit.*, pp. 140–2; Pearce, *op. cit.*, pp. 391–2.

manageability of any individual employer, whatever the incentives offered to him to regularize employment. However, as we shall see, this does not mean that other aspects of the Wisconsin approach were abandoned.

The first unemployment measure enacted in the United States was passed by the Wisconsin legislature is 1932. It had evolved from the model bill drafted by Commons for the AALL in 1921. The admirers of this Wisconsin Plan were very important in the deliberations leading to the unemployment provisions in the national level Social Security Act of 1935. They are also important evidence for the crucial role played by moderate big businessmen and liberal-minded lawyers from leading corporate firms. Among the people in the early discussions of the problem in Washington in the thirties were such AALL members as Louis Brandeis' daughter Elizabeth and her husband Paul A. Raushenbush, and big businessmen Henry Dennison (AALL, TCF) and Edward A. Filene (NCF, AALL, TCF).[91] (Mr. and Mrs. Raushenbush had drafted the Wisconsin bill.) This group was joined by three young New Dealers trained in corporate law who were to become prominent moderates within the power elite. They were Charles E. Wyzanski, Jr., Thomas H. Eliot and Thomas G. Corcoran. Wyzanski, a graduate of Exeter and Harvard, came from the prominent Boston law firm of Ropes, Gray, Boyden, and Perkins. Eliot, a product of Browne and Nichols preparatory school and Harvard, and the grandson of the former president of Harvard, had graduated from law school in 1932 and spent a year in a Buffalo law firm before joining the government. Corcoran, like his father, had graduated from Harvard Law School. Before going to Washington, he was with the New York corporate firm of Cotton and Franklin, which did much work for the finance house of Dillon, Read.

Work on an old-age pension plan was also proceeding,

91. Arthur M. Schlesinger, Jr., *The Coming of the New Deal* (Boston: Houghton Mifflin, 1959), p. 302.

led by Epstein and his association, which had been reorganized as the American Association for Social Security. However, Roosevelt decided that the social security program should be worked out as a single package, so he asked Congress to wait until the following year to consider such proposals. Schlesinger suggests that FDR's hand would have been forced if he had not taken such action.[92] In any case, he won the time he asked for, and in June, 1934, appointed a Committee on Economic Security, headed by Secretary of Labor Frances Perkins, and including Treasury Secretary Henry Morgenthau, Jr., Agriculture Secretary Henry Wallace, Attorney General Homer Cummings, and relief administrator Harry Hopkins. Miss Perkins, a "Brahmin reformer" with a "patrician Boston accent," had been involved in the National Consumers' League in New York since 1910, and was friends with President Roosevelt, Mrs. Roosevelt, Senator Robert Wagner, and other leaders of the New Deal.[93] Morgenthau, from a wealthy Jewish family, was a country neighbor of Roosevelt's. His father was very active in the big business community, and his sister was married to Maurice Wertheim, a member of a large investment house. Wallace, Cummings and Hopkins were from the middle ranges of society—a well-to-do farmer and journalist, a prominent local lawyer, and a social worker.

The Committee on Economic Security did not function alone or without guidelines. It set up a technical board to give it advice, and hired an executive director to direct a staff of research experts. (An advisory council also was appointed, but since its role was very minor it will be ignored here.) The head of the technical board, and a leader in organizing the whole program, was Arthur J. Altmeyer, an economist from Wisconsin who was closely identified with the AALL and the Wisconsin Plan. The technical board, drawn from personnel inside and outside the govern-

92. *Ibid.*, pp. 303–4.
93. *Ibid.*, p. 299.

ment, included committees on unemployment insurance and old-age security. The committee members were primarily economists, although Eliot, a lawyer, and Edward Jensen, secretary of the Business Advisory Council, were on the five-man unemployment insurance committee.[94]

The executive director who managed the research staff was Edwin Witte, a Wisconsin economist who had studied under Commons and was involved in both the AALL and Epstein's American Association for Social Security. Witte and his staff were responsible for a considerable amount of the detail work, although they had very little time in which to do it. However, as Witte emphasizes, the basic principles of the bill were determined by President Roosevelt's June 8, 1934 message to Congress which called for federal-state cooperation rather than a national plan, a contributory program as opposed to one based upon government subsidy funded by a general tax increase, and efforts to encourage the stabilization of employment.[95] This general outline was very similar to the AALL position. In fact, it is possible that the patrician Roosevelt, whose wife and friends were part of such moderate organizations as the AALL and National Consumers' League, utilized the general framework provided to him in conversations with Gerard Swope of General Electric and the AALL. According to Swope's biographer, Roosevelt "had given no indication to any of his close advisers that he was contemplating specific action [on social security] until he asked Swope to come to the White House for a private discussion of it over luncheon on March 8, 1934."[96] However, it is also the case that Roosevelt had been convinced of the need for social insurance for some time, and that he was generally in contact with many AALL-National Consumers' League members.

94. Edwin Witte, *The Development of the Social Security Act* (Madison: The University of Wisconsin Press, 1963), pp. 24–5.
95. *Ibid.*, pp. 18–19, 111.
96. David Loth, *Swope of GE* (New York: Simon and Schuster, 1958), pp. 234*ff*.

For example, AALL people such as Joseph Chamberlain had been involved in attempts to develop welfare programs for New York during Roosevelt's governorship.[97]

The Committee on Economic Security met formally eleven times before giving its report to the President on January 15, 1935. Five of the meetings came in December as the committee rushed to meet an extended deadline, and many decisions were made under time pressures. The committee report was based upon the work of the technical board committees and the research staff of executive director Witte. However, it did not escape without certain criticisms and changes by officials in the Agriculture and Treasury Departments before being sent to the President, who himself insisted on changes which would eliminate the necessity of a large deficit in the old-age fund after 1965. The various changes were made, and the President sent a special message based on the report to Congress on January 17, 1935.

Concurrently with the development of the report, the aforementioned Thomas Eliot was drafting "a bill to carry out the committee's recommendations."[98] Along with Altmeyer and Witte, Eliot appears to have been one of the most important people in the formulation of the details of the bill:

> Constitutional and legal questions were at all times considered to be the responsibility of the counsel of the committee, Mr. Thomas Eliot. Mr. Eliot also drafted the economic security bill and had direct charge of guiding this measure through Congress.[99]

The opposition came, as usual, from the NAM mentality, which coincided nicely with the small business and

97. Pearce, *op. cit.*, pp. 342–54, 393.
98. Witte, *op. cit.*, p. 76.
99. *Ibid.*, p. 33; perhaps the fact that only the President and Miss Perkins are indexed more times in the back of Witte's book may attest to his importance.

small-town outlook that has considerable influence in Congress. And, once again, this NAM opposition tends to be interpreted by many social scientists and historians as "business" opposition, thereby pitting "business" against the "liberals," who often remain unidentified sociologically. Schlesinger, for example, conveys this impression by noting the hostile views of men from the NAM, the National Industrial Conference Board, the Illinois Manufacturers' Association and the Ohio Chamber of Commerce. His comments from these gentlemen are preceded by the following introduction, which leaves little room for the notion that many powerful businessmen were for social security:

> While the friends of social security were arguing out the details of the program, other Americans were regarding the whole idea with consternation, if not with horror. Organized business had long warned against such pernicious notions.[100]

However, I believe Schlesinger overstates big business opposition, overlooking the moderate elements within the power elite. For example, he does not discuss the business involvements of the AALL, an organization he mentions only once in passing.[101] Most importantly, he does not note that the Business Advisory Council, made up of men from very large businesses all over the country, strongly endorsed the social security program, which one of its committees

---

100. Schlesinger, *op. cit.*, p. 311.
101. *Ibid.*, p. 301. All Schlesinger says about the AALL is that "From the onset of the depression it [social insurance] had been earnestly discussed among economists and social workers and within the American Association for Labor Legislation." His only hint of business leaders in the moderate camp is at the outset of the chapter when he notes that "In the fall of 1933 the Raushenbushes met in Washington (the meeting was in the Brandeis apartment; the Justice was absent) with a group of liberal businessmen, like Henry Dennison and Edward Filene, and young New Dealers, among them Charles E. Wyzanski, Jr., and Thomas H. Eliot of the Labor Department, and Thomas G. Corcoran" (p. 302). He does not connect Filene and Dennison to the AALL; nor does he note the backgrounds of the "young New Dealers" Wyzanski, Eliot, and Corcoran.

had followed very closely from the program's beginnings. The BAC position, which had been developed primarily in a committee headed by Gerard Swope of General Electric, and including Walter Teagle of Standard Oil, Morris Leeds of the AALL, and businessman Robert Elbert, was made known publicly when the following members of the council visited the White House to counter the sharp criticism of the President's program that was being mounted by the Chamber of Commerce.[102] The list includes some of the most powerful business leaders in the country:

Henry I. Harriman (retiring president, United States Chamber of Commerce)

H. P. Kendall (business leader in Massachusetts, spokesman for BAC)

Winthrop Aldrich (Chase National Bank)

James Rand (Remington Rand, Inc.)

W. A. Harriman (Brown Brothers, Harriman)

E. T. Stannard (Kennecott Copper Company)

F. B. Davis (United States Rubber Company)

Delancy Kountze (Devoe and Reynolds Company)

Charles A. Cannon (Cannon Towels)

R. R. Deupree (Procter and Gamble)

Gano Dunn (Grace National Bank, J. G. White Engineering)

Lincoln Filene (William Filene's Sons)

Lew Hahn (National Retail Dry Goods)

William Julian (Queen City Trust Company)

102. "Business Advisors Uphold President" (*The New York Times*, May 3, 1935), p. 1.

Morris Leeds (Leeds and Northrup)

Robert Lund (Lambert Pharmical Company)

A. P. Greensfelder (contractor)

George H. Mead (Mead Corporation)

Sidney Weinberg (Goldman, Sachs)

H. H. Heimann (credit association)

One other interesting effort by a leading institution of the power elite to further the social security program was made by the Rockefeller Foundation in 1933. The foundation brought Sir William H. Beveredge and Sir Henry Steel-Maitland from England to tell American business how pleased British business was with the social security system in that country. The twosome, both experts on such programs, met with business leaders, Rotary Clubs, and church organizations. According to Miss Perkins, they "did a great deal to allay the fears and doubts of the business and conservative part of the community."[103] Perhaps this was because, as Miss Perkins testified during the mid-thirties, the "English economists agree with employers and workers that [England's] ability to weather adverse conditions has been due in no small part to social insurance benefits and regular payments which have served to maintain necessary purchasing power."[104]

In short, contrary to the impression created by Schlesinger, there were differences of opinion within the power elite on social security. However, the differences do not seem nearly so serious as those we will see when we consider the recognition of labor unions. On the issue of social security, at least, it is clear that the moderate forces included

103. Frances Perkins, *The Roosevelt I Knew* (New York: Viking Press, 1946), p. 279.
104. Frances Perkins, "The Significance of Social Security," in *The New Deal: A Documentary History*, edited by William E. Leuchtenberg (Columbia, S. C.: University of South Carolina Press, 1968), p. 85.

some of the most powerful bankers and industrialists in the country. They also included such upper-class political leaders as Franklin D. Roosevelt and John G. Winant, the latter a trustee of the AALL and The Brookings Institution who became the first head of the Social Security Board.[105]

The administration bill, buttressed though it was by the work of experts from the executive branch and various research organizations, received rough treatment in Congress from the arch-conservatives and Southerners. Witte, who wrote the first part of the reports for both the Senate and House committees which discussed the bill, recalls that the House's bill draftsmen, in conjunction with Eliot, reworded the whole thing, and that it took considerable patience and guidance, in addition to pressure from the President and his cabinet, to get the bill through even in its modified form.[106] Harry Byrd of Virginia, whose upper-class credentials go back several hundred years, led a successful fight in the Senate to eliminate the setting of minimum state standards in old-age assistance. Among other things, the Congress also rejected the idea that states had "to select administering personnel on a merit basis."[107]

The Social Security Act, not particularly impressive to begin with, was even less impressive as it was finally passed. Benefits were minimal, with workers contributing half of the old-age pension funds, the employers paying for all of the unemployment compensation. In practice, the big corporations paid little or nothing, passing most of their costs along to the consumer.[108] And the tax burden, to the degree that it was a burden, was greater on small employ-

---

105. E. Digby Baltzell, *The Protestant Establishment* (New York: Random House, 1964), pp. 239–40, stresses the great prominence and respect Winant commanded within the upper class.
106. Witte, *op. cit.*, pp. 92–5; on page 97 he adds that the House bill "did not differ so very greatly from the original measure in content, but differed greatly in arrangement and language."
107. Schlesinger, *op. cit.*, p. 313.
108. *Ibid.*, p. 308; Loth, *op. cit.*, p. 238.

ers.[109] Nor were the rich taxed personally to help pay for the program (only the first $3,000 of a salary was taxed). The masses, in short, were being forced to save part of their incomes for a rainy day. Schlesinger concludes as follows about the employment portion of the bill: "It is hard to escape the impression that the Committee on Economic Security, correctly anticipating hostility in Congress and the courts and perhaps unduly influenced by the Wisconsin experience [read: AALL plan], felt obliged to adopt the least good of the plans of unemployment compensation before it."[110] As for the other key title in the bill, the old-age pension: "[It] left millions of old people uncovered, and in any case payments under old-age insurance would not begin till 1942."[111]

The development of the Social Security Act can be summarized as follows: There was considerable distress and discontent bubbling up from the lower levels within the depression-ridden society. This was producing expensive solutions such as the Townsend Plan to give every oldster $200 a month, and the economic system in general was being criticized. The moderate members of the power elite, with the help of academic experts, decided to accommodate these demands on the basis of plans developed by such elite-backed organizations as the American Association for Labor Legislation. These moderates carried their plans to a Congress that was more in sympathy with the less moderate NAM members of the power elite. Within Congress these moderate and conservative views reached a compromise that became the Social Security Act. The act was a far cry from what had been hoped for or demanded by the ex-

---

109. Arthur J. Altmeyer, "The Development and Status of Social Security in America," in *Labor, Management, and Social Policy,* edited by Gerald G. Somers (Madison: University of Wisconsin Press, 1963), p. 147.
110. Schlesinger, *op. cit.,* p. 314.
111. Arthur M. Schlesinger, Jr., *The Politics of Upheaval* (Boston: Houghton Mifflin, 1960), p. 40.

tremists, but it was probably their pressure that activated the moderate members of the power elite and enabled them to effect an improvement in the situation. While it is certainly true that many people benefited from the measure, which is what pluralists would quickly point out, it is also true that the result from the point of view of the power elite was a restabilization of the system. It put a floor under consumer demand, raised people's expectations for the future and directed political energies back into conventional channels. The difference between what could be and what is remained very, very large for the poor, the sick and the aged. The wealth distribution did not change, decision-making power remained in the hands of upper-class leaders, and the basic principles that encased the conflict were set forth by moderate members of the power elite.

## LABOR UNIONS AND COLLECTIVE BARGAINING, 1900–1937

The misunderstood story of how the power elite came to terms with labor unions, which is usually viewed as a complete defeat for big business, is a complex one that cannot be told in all its detail here. This is because there are several interacting factors that must be kept in mind, and an integrated account of what happened is almost unmanageable in a limited space. To reduce the problem to size, then, let me begin with certain generalizations that will become clear in the historical account which follows, an historical account which begins with the founding of the National Civic Federation in 1900 and ends with the Supreme Court's 1937 decisions upholding the Wagner Act, an act which recognizes, protects and enforces labor's right to organize and to bargain collectively with employers through representatives of its own choosing.

The first factor that must be kept in mind, and the one

most often overlooked, is that there was disagreement within the corporate elite as to how to deal with labor. On the moderate side were the big businessmen of the National Civic Federation, who from the start took a more conciliatory attitude toward labor organizations. They understood the conservative potential of American trade unionism. They sought to mold and strengthen conservative trends that were contending with socialistic ones. NCF members and the economists such as Commons who advised them were aware even then of what a recent account makes clear in retrospect: "The unionism that emerged was a mosaic of selfish sectional-minded groups, loosely organized in a relatively weak federation, hostile to the state, wedded to collective bargaining as the exclusive method of change, and frankly predicated upon a permanent acceptance of the capitalistic order."[112] As we will see, NCF leaders often accepted in principle the right of labor unions to exist and bargain, and on several occasions before the passage of the Wagner Act in 1934 they put these principles into practice in certain limited ways. Disagreeing with the NCF was the big business mentality symbolized by the National Association of Manufacturers, which adopted an anti-labor union stance in 1902 and maintained it vehemently from that time forward. The NAM was organized in 1896 to promote foreign markets, but in the early twentieth century its concern with organized labor became its most salient characteristic. (While there were other employer associations similar to the NAM, such as the National Metal Trades Association, which worked in close conjunction with it, the NAM will be used throughout this discussion as prototypical of the anti-union forces within the corporate community.) The conflict between moderate and conservative approaches was to continue throughout the pre-World War II decades. It is best exemplified by a court case in 1907, to be dis-

112. George H. Hildebrand, "American Unionism, Social Stratification, and Power" (*American Journal of Sociology*, Vol. 58, 1952–53), p. 387.

cussed below, in which some of the richest and most powerful members of the NCF financed and defended AF of L
president Samuel Gompers in the Supreme Court against
a suit brought by the president of the NAM.

And yet, to state the NCF/NAM split so cleanly and
simply is to immediately blur reality. First, many NCF
members were also in the NAM, and many of them seemed
to say one thing and do another. According to Commons,
for example, Mark Hanna played fair with labor, but some
of his fellow NCF members did not.[113] And it is certainly
the case that many NCF members had company-dominated
unions in their plants or fought unions by every means
available. Thus, in actual practice, and from the point of
view of the common worker, there was often very little
difference between the moderate and conservative approaches. Examples can be found of members of both
groups who dismissed workers for joining unions, hired
thugs to beat up striking workers, hired spies to report
union organizers, and indulged in other ugly practices that
call into question the image most members of the upper
class like to hold of themselves. However, the important
point here is that the moderate mentality was willing to
concede certain points *if* labor really showed major strength.
Its outlook is well summarized in the wisdom of J. P.
Morgan's lawyer, Francis Lynde Stetson: "The discontent
of the masses . . . 'is to be allayed not by a policy of stern
and unbending toryism,' but by flexibility."[114] In the meantime, adherents to the NCF approach tried to introduce the
necessary reforms to undercut unions even while they spent
some of their time talking to labor leaders and espousing
their commitment to labor peace. In short, carrot *and* stick
was the moderate policy, stick was the conservative policy.

113. Commons, *op. cit.*, p. 88.
114. Kolko, *The Triumph of Conservatism, op. cit.*, p. 164. The point of
much of the detail that follows in this essay is to show how this "flexibility" gradually led to the Wagner Act, which is so often hailed as a
complete victory for labor over an unbending business community.

The second factor that must be kept in mind in considering the way in which the power elite dealt with labor is their sense of the limits of their corporate-based power. That is, most union demands made headway during wars and depression, when the loyalty of labor to the overall system had to be insured. During World War I, for example, when socialist and anti-war sentiment were strong, the executive branch, imbued with the NCF mentality, gave labor the right to organize and bargain collectively. The amiable person dealing generously with labor was former President William Howard Taft, co-chairman of the War Labor Board. However, after the war the labor unions in most instances lost their gains and their membership declined considerably. One of the persons who hurt labor the most was the same William Howard Taft, functioning as Chief Justice of the Supreme Court. Similarly, it was World War II that saw the fading of the last serious resistance to the Wagner Act, but the war was followed in 1947 by the Taft-Hartley Act, which had widespread support in the business community and eroded certain of these gains. By the same token, the Wagner Act itself was passed at a time when organized labor was being decimated by the Depression and serious unrest was beginning to develop at the rank-and-file level and among unorganized workers. Correlating social conditions with legislative enactments, and comparing the actions of companies with the statements of their leaders, it is hard to escape the impression that most corporate leaders are coldly calculating in their relations with labor. This does not deny that some are more nobly motivated, but it seems that the benevolent have little success in persuading their corporate brethren except in times of crisis.

A third factor that must be considered, and that cannot be overestimated, is the role of the courts. This point has been developed by Richard Cortner in his account of the Wagner Act cases before the Supreme Court. Beginning his story in the last half of the nineteenth century, Cortner shows how business-dominated state courts had developed a body of precedent which left little room for organized labor.[115] These precedents were often built on the thinnest of tissue, but they did force the moderate members of the corporate elite to develop new constitutional avenues (rationalizations) when they decided that a more flexible policy toward organized labor was necessary. This in turn generated conflict over a larger issue, the role of the Supreme Court:

> The development of the laissez-faire Constitution following the Civil War, and the doctrines of legal realism which formed the language of dissent and the basis of the attack on laissez-faire constitutionalism, resulted in a broader conflict over the role of the Court in the government system which reached a crisis in 1937 in the Wagner Act cases and was the most important factor in their being decided as they were. These cases, therefore, determined not only the outcome of the union-employer struggle of the 1930's but also the outcome of the conflict over the constitutional system which had been created in the years since the Civil War.[116]

Constitutional law and the Supreme Court, then, are problems in their own right, and the struggle over unionism was complicated by this fact. Thus, the judicial system, usually staffed by older and more conservative members of the power elite, sets a framework for and often produces a time lag in corporate reactions to labor problems. As will be shown, however, cautious corporate lawyers serving as justices have been able to reverse themselves at critical turning points. Such was the case in 1937 when Chief Jus-

115. Richard Cortner, *The Wagner Act Cases* (Knoxville: The University of Tennessee Press, 1964), Chapter 1.
116. *Ibid.*, p. vi. A major theme of Cortner's book is that constitutional doctrine and Supreme Court decisions do not unfold in a vacuum, a point with which I heartily agree. The courts are one of the most important bastions of the governing class, legitimating and defending the "social structure" as it is embodied in laws. Members of the power elite are concerned to maintain its image as a high-minded, impartial arbitrator that is above any class interests.

tice Charles Evans Hughes and Associate Justice Owen Roberts, both leading corporate lawyers of the twentieth century, essentially reversed their opinions of one year previous in order to uphold the Wagner Act.

There are two other considerations which should be mentioned before the events leading to the Wagner Act are discussed in detail. First, the American rich learned a great deal from their British counterparts, whom they greatly admired and with whom they often interacted. For example, the British experience was often referred to at NCF meetings, or recounted by invited British guests. The fact that most labor problems happened earlier in Great Britain gave an added dimension to the deliberations of the American upper class. Secondly, it seems worthwhile to mention that large corporations are often in a different position vis-à-vis the demands of organized labor than were the smaller businessmen of the nineteenth century. For example, in certain industries where the demand was "inelastic," they often had enough market control to pass wage hikes along to the consumer in price hikes, especially in times of prosperity. More generally, from the point of view of the upper class, the wealth distribution has not been disturbed by unionism. Labor gains were made due to the general growth in wealth and at the expense of the consumer, which would mean small businessmen, pensioners, farmers, and nonunionized white collar employees. If we could force the general factors leading to the Wagner Act and collective bargaining into a single sentence, perhaps we could say the fact that final victory went to the NCF-type moderates within the power elite attests to their foresight in desiring to forestall class politics and political violence, their ability to profit from the British experience, their desire for stability and efficiency, and the oligopolistic position of their large corporations, which allowed them for several reasons to accede to certain labor demands at little or no cost to themselves. We can now turn to a detailed accounting of how the moderate position gradually developed and gained ascendancy.

The first major institutionalized response of the power elite to labor unrest was the National Civic Federation. It was more than symbolic that Mark Hanna was its first president and Samuel Gompers (president of the American Federation of Labor) its first vice president, for they had both worked for management-labor negotiations in the past. Gompers had abandoned his youthful radicalism of the early 1880's for two reasons. First, major labor defeats in the 1890's at the hands of corporation-dominated industries had convinced him that "in trustified industries unionism could exist only with the cooperation of the employers."[117] Second, he had come to believe that many corporate employers were willing to cooperate and to allow organized labor to exist: "The men who control wealth in this country are at bottom human and adaptable to the changed order of relations."[118] One of Gompers' reasons for this hope was the behavior in the 1890's of Mark Hanna, who entered into collective bargaining agreements and spoke highly of organized labor.

Within the NCF, then, the moderates of the corporate and labor communities got to know each other, and reached a sort of ideological bargain. From the side of capital, the concessions were collective bargaining (but no employer was to be forced by law to bargain), the right to organize unions (but no closed shops), protection against wage cuts, the possibility of gradual wage increases commensurate with increases in productivity and efficiency, and a real voice in the setting of working conditions.[119] The concessions concerning collective bargaining and organizing

117. Ronald Radosh, "The Development of The Corporate Ideology of Organized Labor, 1914–1933" (Unpublished Ph.D. dissertation, University of Wisconsin, 1967), pp. 6–7. I have drawn heavily on this excellent piece of research.
118. *Ibid.*, p. 9.
119. Jensen, *op. cit.*, p. 114.

were important ones for labor, but they were never much more than hopes until they were put into law in 1935, forcing all employers to comply with them. The benefits to capital were several: greater efficiency and productivity from labor, less labor turnover, the disciplining of the labor force by labor unions, the possibility of planning labor costs over the long run, and the dampening of radical doctrines. Again, while it is important to note how early this general arrangement was visualized, it is certainly the case that it was realized in practice only haltingly and unevenly until after World War II.

The general lines of this bargain were understood by many members of the NCF in the first decade of the century. However, this does not mean that all members of the corporate elite accepted it. Within United States Steel, to take one concrete case, there were some leaders who accepted it, some who did not.[120] Then too, big bankers seemed more open to these views than manufacturers. While bigness seemed to dispose a company toward more moderate views, the duPont-General Motors clique was to be a very large exception. There were also disagreements over the bargain within the working class. In 1901, for example, a steel union struck a subsidiary of United States Steel despite United States Steel's favorable arrangement with it. According to Radosh, the union had interpreted the company's friendly attitude as weakness. The somewhat moderate Morgan bankers were enraged, and dealt very severely with the union. Samuel Gompers also was angry about the tactics of this union—he condemned its actions in no uncertain terms, at the same time praising George Perkins of J. P. Morgan & Company.[121] Incidents such as this continued to fan the flames of mutual suspicion; both big labor and big business had to discipline the dissidents within their midsts.

In addition to discussing problems with labor leaders

120. Weinstein, *op. cit.*, p. 11.
121. Radosh, *op. cit.*, p. 18.

and arbitrating several strikes in the early years of the century, members of the NCF also displayed their willingness to deal with organized labor by starting a Trade Agreements Department in 1904, under the joint chairmanship of a coal company official and a labor union leader. Agreements were signed between union and management in several areas, including clothing, shipping, boilermaking, and coal mining. No argeements of any importance were effected in the mass production industries, however.

One of the most important NCF victories in its early years was in the anthracite coal strike of 1902. When coal operators refused to talk to union leaders, NCF members, especially Easley, Hanna and George Perkins of J. P. Morgan & Company, worked vigorously behind the scenes. They were especially concerned because the United Mine Worker president, John Mitchell, was a leading labor member of NCF. When their efforts with the coal operators were unsuccessful, they went to J. P. Morgan himself, who "promised to 'do what was right' when the opportunity for action came."[122] While wishing that Morgan had acted, NCF secretary Easley believed that he could not do so precipitously:

> I find that Mr. Morgan is a good deal in the same fix with these coal roads, as he was last summer with the Steel Corporation. He has a lot of unruly presidents on his hands who are willing to resign any minute if he undertakes to coerce them.[123]

When other efforts at conciliation failed, the miners went on strike in spite of opposition to such action by their leader, Mitchell. However, when the bituminous miners talked about going out in a sympathy strike, Mitchell and his NCF colleagues were able to convince them that it was better to live up to their contract. As the strike dragged on through

122. Green, *op. cit.*, p. 44.
123. *Ibid.*, p. 45.

the summer and into the fall, President Theodore Roosevelt became involved: "Morgan, Hanna, Easley, Mitchell, all had conferred with the President during the past months."[124] Finally, "On October 13, Morgan offered to the President, in the name of the operators, a proposition to turn over matters in dispute to a commission consisting of five men to be appointed by the President."[125] The men then returned to work, the union feeling that it had gained a moral victory. The commission, with John R. Commons of the NCF as one of its staff, issued a report in March, 1903. According to Green: "The decision of the anthracite coal commission was a vindication of the efforts of the National Civic Federation."[126] It urged recognition of the union and the formation of a board of conciliation with employer and union both represented. Among its observations were the following:

> Experience shows that the more full the recognition given to a trade union the more business-like and responsible it becomes. Through dealing with businessmen in business matters its more intelligent, conservative and responsible members come to the front and gain general control and direction of its affairs.[127]

Despite their favorable treatment within the NCF, labor leaders were uneasy because of their reception elsewhere. In particular there was the National Association of Manufacturers, its leadership taken over in 1902 by middle-sized, anti-union employers. The NAM leaders began an open shop drive which included several lobbying successes in Washington. They equated unionism and socialism, whereas NCF members such as Louis Brandeis believed that "the trade unions also stand as a strong bulwark against the great wave of socialism."[128] NAM members, in addition

124. *Ibid.*, p. 53.
125. *Ibid.*, p. 53.
126. *Ibid.*, p. 55.
127. *Ibid.*, p. 55.
128. Weinstein, *op. cit.*, p. 17.

to action in their plants and in Congress, also turned to the courts, asking for anti-labor injunctions which the courts usually granted. So successful were the courts and anti-union employers in their efforts that in 1906 a restive AF of L turned to political action. This meant the active backing of candidates who professed friendliness toward labor, and in some cases the running of labor candidates.

Members of the NCF were greatly upset by these developments. August Belmont thought it was a "matter of great moment when our workmen . . . become imbued with the idea that our courts are used by employers for partisan purposes."[129] Nor did they like the idea of labor entering into politics. Partly they just could not conceive of working men concerning themselves with any kind of politics, but mostly they feared that political activity would soon lead to the formation of a separate labor party, as had recently happened in Great Britain. Indeed, many had drawn a moral from the British situation, for the development of a labor party there, they believed, had been triggered by an anti-labor court decision in the Taff Vale case of 1902. Nor were NCF members unaware of socialist strength within the cautious AF of L. Pro-NCF leaders (such as Mitchell of the miners) had on occasion been displaced by the socialists, and a socialist-inspired resolution in 1902 calling for a labor party was defeated only 4,897 to 4,171 at the AF of L convention.[130] This now-forgotten socialist alternative was a very real concern to NCF leaders, and it probably inspired many of their conciliatory efforts.

However, even most NCF members were willing to go only so far with organized labor. For example, they did not want to meet labor's demand for exemption from the anti-trust laws. They felt such attempts were "class legislation" that should not be granted to labor unless they were also granted to business. As noted in the discussion of the origin of the Federal Trade Commission, the furthest they would go at this time was expressed in a clause they inserted into a series of amendments to the Sherman Anti-Trust Act which the NCF proposed in 1908. Included in these amendments was a clause guaranteeing the freedom of employees and employers in the collective bargaining process, and it was suggested that registered unions, like business corporations, "could apply for exemption from the restrictions of the Sherman Anti-Trust Law."[131] Unwilling to bend further, the NCF looked for other avenues to accommodate labor unrest, greatly increasing its concern with welfare programs and with social insurance.

The tug and pull between the moderate and conservative mentalities was symbolized by a court case which began in 1907. The clash concerned attempts by the AF of L to organize Buck's Stove and Range Company, whose president, James Van Cleave, was also president of the NAM. When Van Cleave refused to recognize the union, the AF of L called for a nationwide boycott of his company's products. Van Cleave turned to the courts, who granted an injunction, and Gompers and Mitchell fought the ruling to the Supreme Court. Many members of the NCF were annoyed by Van Cleave's action, and Easley was able to interest a number of big businessmen in seeing to it that Gompers and Mitchell had an adequate defense in their appeal to the highest court. Most of the money was put up by Andrew Carnegie, who was concerned only that Gompers abide by the decision of the court.[132] Gompers' lawyer was none other than Alton B. Parker, Wall Street lawyer, 1904 Democratic Presidential candidate, and future president of the NCF. In 1909 Gompers and Mitchell were sentenced to prison for contempt of court, but the legal battle over that penalty continued until 1914, when the court lifted the sentences on a technicality.[133] While hardly a victory for organized labor, the case does show the ultimate

131. *Ibid.*, p. 317.
132. Weinstein, *op. cit,*, p. 49.
133. Green, *op. cit.*, p. 196.

difference between the moderate and conservative methods of dealing with labor problems.

The moderate mentality demonstrated its willingness to deal with labor in one other way in the years before World War I. Continuing labor unrest, highlighted by the union dynamiting of an anti-union Los Angeles employer in 1911, had led reformers to appeal to President Taft to appoint a commission to study labor problems. Congress passed an act authorizing the commission, and Taft complied, but Woodrow Wilson was elected before the commission had time to organize. Wilson was able to appoint new members. The result was that the nine-member Commission on Industrial Relations had not seven but eight NCF members. From business there was Frederic Delano, president of the Wabash Railroad and uncle of the future President Roosevelt; Harris Weinstock, a San Francisco department store owner; and S. Thurston Ballard, a flour miller and president of the Louisville, Kentucky, Employers' Association. All three labor leaders were also members of the NCF. Two of the three "public" members were leading figures in NCF matters: economist John R. Commons of the University of Wisconsin and Mrs. J. Borden Harriman, wife of a prominent corporate leader and a friend since childhood of J. P. Morgan. The only non-NCF member was a middle-class lawyer and reformer, Frank P. Walsh. Walsh, the head of the commission, was a friend of Commons', and the two had worked out a plan for the commission before Walsh accepted the appointment.[134] The commission met for over a year. Walsh conducted a vigorous investigation which alienated many conservatives, including secretary Easley of the NCF. It included an embarrassing exposure of the complicity of the Rockefellers in the Ludlow massacre. Walsh produced letters showing that John D. Rockefeller, Jr. had lied in his first appearance before the commission;

134. Weinstein, *op. cit.*, p. 186.

Rockefeller knew and approved of the fact that his agent was pressuring Colorado's "little cowboy governor," as the agent called him, into using the militia to aid the coal companies.[135] Commons, on the other hand, and later his friend Charles McCarthy, were in charge of the commission's mundane research, and disliked Walsh's sensational methods. McCarthy, an old friend of Rockefeller's from college days, was particularly angry, and even counseled Rockefeller on how to handle the commission.[136] The result of the commission's work was not one but three reports. The first was signed by Walsh and the three labor members, but it was attacked by Mrs. Harriman and the business members as partisan to labor. The second was written by Weinstock for the business members, and the third was written by Commons and signed by Mrs. Harriman and the three business members. The Commons-Harriman report advocated a commission to establish codes and conduct negotiations, "a national labor board for collective bargaining."[137] The object was a nonpolitical governmental body to regulate labor relations: "As Commons put it when dissenting from Walsh's final report, the issue was 'whether the labor movement should be directed toward politics or toward collective bargaining.' "[138] Walsh and the labor representatives were for the former and Commons, Mrs. Harriman and the business representatives (and NCF) for the latter. It is therefore interesting that "Commons' thinking on the subject of capital-labor relations was similar to much that would later underlie New Deal legislation, including the National Recovery Administration and the Wagner National Labor Relations Act."[139] Collective bargaining was the moderate safety valve which

135. *Ibid.*, pp. 196–7.
136. *Ibid.*, p. 204.
137. Green, *op. cit.*, p. 358.
138. Weinstein, *op. cit.*, p. 202.
139. *Ibid.*, p. 208.

was preferred to potentially radical independent political action by organized labor.

Concern over the impending war pushed the commission and its report into the background, but the pressure of the war was to lead to the temporary adoption of many commission-NCF proposals:

> The code declared that workers had the right to organize in unions and to bargain collectively, and it pledged the Government would do its best to maintain existing industrial standards. The code that governed labor relations and that was used as a guide by the War Labor Board was drawn up by L. F. Lorree, C. E. Michael, Loyall Osborne, W. H. Van Der Voort, and B. L. Worden, men described by Secretary of Labor, William B. Wilson, as 'among the largest employers of labor in the United States.'[140]

The war, then, provided a precedent for working relationships between big businessmen and big labor leaders that was to be important in the twenties and thirties. In particular, Gompers became friends with Herbert Hoover, an important ally of the AF of L throughout the twenties. However, Gompers also had pleasant relations with Bernard Baruch, Daniel Willard (president of the Baltimore and Ohio), and Morris Cooke (a leader in the scientific management movement). Then too, it was during the war that Sidney Hillman of the garment workers became better known to more members of the power elite, and at the same time further moderated his views:

> The impact of the industrial experience of World War I, more than anything else, convinced labor leaders such as Gompers and Hillman that they could work with corporation leaders and obtain an equitable place for labor and unionism within the capitalistic political economy. . . . As such, they sought recognition for organized labor as a partner of the large corporation which they viewed as a rational and inevitable concomitant of modern industrialism.[141]

140. Radosh, *op. cit.*, p. 46.
141. *Ibid.*, p. 390.

The postwar years and the twenties were by and large difficult ones for organized labor. There was one legislative victory that was of use in the thirties as a precedent, and NCF committees continued to call for commissions and free collective bargaining, but the basic picture was one of decline for organized labor. Rather than recount the details of these lean years for labor, I will briefly summarize the situation at the outset of the New Deal:

1. There were some corporate leaders who were sympathetic to collective bargaining even while they worked to weaken unions through paternalistic and repressive measures. While I do not want to overestimate the number of such sympathizers, some of them were very large employers in very strategic positions, and I therefore think it is a mistake to equate business with the NAM and imply that it was against labor unions, as so many commentators tend to do.

2. Some employers were willing to deal with unions if they were organized on an industrial rather than a craft basis. They did not want to deal with dozens of craft unions. Edward A. Filene of NCF and the Twentieth Century Fund claimed that there was considerable sympathy for this view.[142] However, again, the vehemence of the reactions to the Wagner Act suggests that most employers just hated unions.

3. The Railway Labor Act of 1926, modeled on earlier NCF proposals, provided one legislative precedent for labor's right to organize, and the Norris-La Guardia Act had banned "yellow dog" contracts. Further, there were several endorsements of collective bargaining, such as the report of the Commission on Industrial Relations and the precedents of the War Labor Board.

142. Radosh, *op. cit.*, pp. 302–6.

4. With the exception of the 1930 decision upholding the Railway Labor Act, the courts and their precedents were not sympathetic to the goals of organized labor.

5. Organized labor, conservative though it was, was very weak. Membership had declined throughout the twenties and the early years of the Depression. The major industries were virtually without unionization, and the Railway Labor Act had not stopped most companies from their attacks on the railroad unions.

One of the New Deal's first attempts to deal with the Depression was modeled after the successful experience with the War Industries Board in World War I. Termed the National Recovery Administration (NRA), this business planning for business by businessmen was directed at its highest levels by men who had worked under Bernard Baruch on the War Industries Board. It is not my purpose here to trace the origins of the NRA, and there are minor variations in the various accounts of its development. However, most sources agree that Gerard Swope of General Electric, Henry I. Harriman of the United States Chamber of Commerce (a utilities executive and large landowner), Bernard Baruch, and Hugh Johnson were among the leading architects. According to Schlesinger, the details of the NRA were ironed out between a group headed by Hugh Johnson (a Baruch associate who was to become the NRA head) and another group headed by John Dickinson (a wealthy Philadelphian serving as under-secretary of Commerce) and Senator Robert Wagner.[143]

Among the provisions of the NRA was a clause guaranteeing labor's right to organize. However, section 7a (which embodied the labor clause) was not much use to organized labor. There was no enforcement provision, and employers were not required to bargain with the unions.

143. Schlesinger, *The Coming of the New Deal, op. cit.*, pp. 96–7.

Henry Ford, for example, refused to bargain collectively, and the auto industry in general held back. Company-dominated unions were quickly developed in the previously unorganized mass production industries. These unions were based upon plans developed and circulated by the NAM and the American Management Association. Steel, autos and rubber were the biggest offenders. The refusal to negotiate by Ford and other extremely conservative employers brings up a very important point in understanding the problem of labor recognition. From the point of view of the employers, it had to be an all or nobody proposition, for any holdouts would supposedly have the competitive advantage brought about by lower wage costs. Thus, the diehards held great power over the majority, making it ultimately necessary to legislate against them. Perhaps there is something to the claim that most employers would go along with union recognition if all their compatriots would. But not every employer would go along, which set the stage for the battle over the Wagner Act, a battle which precipitated a serious split in the power elite.

Labor's situation became more and more desperate. The decline from a unionization of 12% of the labor force in 1920 continued until it was at 6% in 1933. In early 1934, in Minneapolis, San Francisco and Toledo, there were serious strikes, and many big businessmen were determined to smash organized labor once and for all. However, Roosevelt, Frances Perkins, Swope and other moderate members of the power elite refused to be stampeded by calls for the troops, by claims of general strikes, and other such precipitous cries. By standing firm, they forced their counterparts into negotiation and compromise. For example, employers in Toledo finally agreed to federal mediation by Charles P. Taft II. According to Schlesinger, most of the union demands were then met.[144] In general, however,

---

144. Schlesinger, *op. cit.*, p. 393.

labor's record was one of defeat: "Labor failed in textiles, failed in the automobile industry, failed in rubber."[145] Nor were the failures simply due to business pressure. Some conservative union leaders, such as the head of the steelworkers, actually criticized local organizing efforts. Another called unskilled workers "rubbish."[146]

The official governmental agency dealing with labor disputes during this time of defeat for labor was the National Labor Board. The chairman was Senator Wagner, and there were three members from industry, two from labor, and one from the academic community:

Walter Teagle, president of Standard Oil, a member of the Business Advisory Council

Gerard Swope, president of General Electric, a member of the Business Advisory Council and the American Association for Labor Legislation

Louis E. Kirstein, a partner of Edward A. Filene of the Twentieth Century Fund and a member of the Business Advisory Council

Leo Wolman, Columbia University economist, an officer of the American Association of Labor Legislation, and a research director for Sidney Hillman's Amalgamated Clothing Workers

William Green, president of the AF of L

John L. Lewis, president of the United Mine Workers and a vice president of the AF of L

The executive secretary of the Board was William Leiserson, a long-time AALL member who had served under Commons on the Commission on Industrial Relations from 1914 to 1915, and the general counsel was Milton Handler, a

145. *Ibid.*, p. 394.
146. *Ibid.*, p. 411.

professor of law at Columbia University. In March, 1934, the board was expanded. The president of the Reynolds Tobacco Company, S. Clay Williams (a BAC member), and a Johns Hopkins economist, L. C. Marshall, were made vice chairmen. Also added were Pierre duPont (BAC), Henry Dennison (BAC, Twentieth Century Fund), Ernest Draper (vice-president of Hills Brothers, member of AALL), labor leader George L. Berry, and Dr. Francis J. Haas, director of the National Catholic School of Social Sciences at Catholic University of America.

There were also twenty regional boards under the national board. On them served "the most eminent citizens available in the various communities."[147] In Atlanta, for example, the head of the board was Marion Smith of a long-standing upper-class family. He was later to testify that the Wagner Act was a good, conservative bill that put labor in conservative hands.[148] Heading the board in New York was Jeremiah T. Mahoney, a one-time law partner of Senator Wagner's. A study of the members of these boards, and their subsequent views concerning the Wagner Act, might be useful in determining the degree of support within the power elite for the moderate position.

Despite the prestige of its members, the national board met with failure. The National Labor Board was an impotent agency. Chairman Wagner complained that it could rely only on the prestige of its members and upon appeals to public sentiment in obtaining collective bargaining. Many large corporations simply refused to abide by the board's rulings, and the board had no recourse. Aside from industry defiance, the board also was hampered because the NRA would not enforce majority rule. That is, the NRA would not agree that the organization that represented the majority

147. *Legislative History of the National Labor Relations Act,* Vol. I (Washington: U.S. Government Printing Office, 1949), p. 44.

148. *Legislative History of the National Labor Relations Act, op. cit.,* Vol. II, pp. 2707–8.

of workers had the right to bargain for all of them. Instead, it opted for proportional representation, which allowed the company-backed organizations to flourish.

The failure of the NLB convinced Wagner that further legislation was necessary. Addressing the Senate in March, 1934, he reviewed the frustrating experience of the labor board set up by the NRA, saying that its rulings had been ignored in several major industries. He then introduced legislation which gave labor the right to organize and bargain collectively, outlawing the unfair labor practices that were being used with increasing intensity. There was informative and bitter debate over Wagner's bill, but the effort came to nothing because President Roosevelt wanted to avoid a showdown with conservative businessmen. After a substitute proposal proved unsatisfactory, Roosevelt ended the matter for the time being in June, 1934, by calling his old friend and adviser Wagner to the White House and convincing him to substitute a compromise measure drafted by Donald Richberg of NRA and Charles Wyzanski. Termed Public Resolution No. 44, it created a National Labor Relations Board with some of the powers Wagner asked:

> The new Board had more status and power than the National Labor Board which it superseded. It was independent of NRA; it had explicit authority to interpret Section 7a and to hold elections; for this purpose, it could subpoena company payrolls, as its predecessor could not.[149]

Wagner was not so dismayed by this compromise as some of his more liberal colleagues. He was determined to try again the next year, and he felt his hand would be strengthened by the precedents set in recent amendments to the Railway Labor Act. Then too, the AF of L now had abandoned its emphasis on voluntarism, realizing it needed the help of the government if it were to survive.

149. Schlesinger, *op. cit.*, p. 397.

The National Labor Relations Board created by Public Resolution No. 44 met the same fate as its NRA predecessor, but it was important in setting the stage for the legislation that was to follow. The first head of the short-lived NLRB was a well-known young member of the upper class, Lloyd K. Garrison. The great-grandson of a famous Boston abolitionist and the son of a lawyer, he was married to Ellen Jay, a descendant of the first Chief Justice of the Supreme Court. A lawyer who had practiced on Wall Street for a short time during the 1920's as well as serving briefly in the Hoover Administration in the investigation of bankruptcy frauds, Garrison had gone to the University of Wisconsin in 1932 as dean of its law school. In the post-World War II era he was to be a senior partner in Paul, Weiss, Rifkind, and Garrison, one of the largest firms on Wall Street (and one of the few with a significant number of Jews and liberals). When Garrison resigned he was replaced by an even more eminent member of the upper class, Francis Biddle, former counsel for the anti-union Pennsylvania Railroad. Respected in his own right for his legal abilities, he was a member of one of the best-known of upper-class families. Biddle seems to have been aware of the prestige value of his name, even though I would substitute "the upper class" where he says "the country" in the following comment:

> Miss Perkins liked the idea chiefly because I was "respectable." Our firm represented solid interests, and the country would have a feeling that the appointment was that of a man who had dealt with the practical affairs of business, an experience generally believed to make him "safe," particularly in a position where the diverging conflict between labor and industry was at white heat.[150]

Despite the prestige of the board, and assurances that similar John R. Commons-National Civic Federation type

150. Francis Biddle, *In Brief Authority* (New York: Doubleday and Co., 1962), pp. 7–8.

of boards had worked well for business in New York, Pennsylvania, Wisconsin and Massachusetts, the board could not get compliance from some industrialists. Both the NRA and the Attorney General were reluctant to back up the board, and the NAM "urged all employers to disregard" an NLRB decision concerning majority rule in the recognition of unions.[151] NRA and the NLRB battled back and forth on a variety of matters, and in a case involving the unionization of newspapers, Roosevelt sided with NRA:

> . . . in January [1935] he sent Biddle a letter telling NLRB to stay out of cases where labor relations machinery existed under the codes. This included automobiles, newspapers, soft coal, and other industries. . . . But Biddle, judging the situation to be in flux, argued that there still might be value in a fight, and Senator Wagner backed him up.[152]

Biddle was correct in perceiving flux. First, he and many others were sure that the NRA was not working. He assumed that it "would be toppled over either by the Congress or by the courts."[153] Thus, new legislation would be necessary to guarantee labor the right to organize and bargain collectively. Second, Biddle had the feeling that President Roosevelt was only biding his time. FDR did not want to fight the employer battle with newspaper publishers, for obvious reasons:

> In a conciliatory note to me, a few days later, he scribbled after his signature: "You and I have had enough publicity." If a showdown was coming there was no use lining up the press against you before the time came.[154]

With no encouragement from President Roosevelt, who remained neutral, a new bill was drawn up by Wagner, Biddle, corporate lawyer Simon Rifkind (Wagner's secre-

151. Schlesinger, *op. cit.*, p. 398.
152. *Ibid.*, p. 400.
153. Biddle, *op. cit.*, p. 43.
154. *Ibid.*, p. 37.

tary and law partner), economist Leon Keyserling and lawyer Calvert Magruder. Biddle went on a speaking tour, outlining the basic problems to businessmen and unionists brought together by chambers of commerce and other economic forums.[155] Wagner also did a great deal of speaking in favor of the bill. The new act gave the National Labor Relations Board the power to prohibit unfair labor practices and to enforce its decisions. The emphasis was on the enforcement of rights rather than the mediation of disputes. The Interstate Commerce Commission, the Federal Trade Commission, the Securities Exchange Commission, and the Railroad National Mediation Board were cited as precedents. According to Irving Bernstein, the basic principles of this second attempt at a Wagner Act had been enunciated quite often before. The New Deal's collective bargaining legislation "gathered up the historical threads and wove them into law."[156] While I agree with that judgment by Bernstein, neither the National Civic Federation nor any big businessmen appear in his account of these precedents. It could not be guessed from reading his chapter on the "Sources of Ideas" for the Wagner Act that any corporate leaders or power elite organizations had a positive hand in the developments he discusses.

To understand the disagreement within the power elite on this issue, it is important to appreciate President Roosevelt's attitude toward the problem. He was not unsympathetic to labor, but had no great interest in labor unions. Moreover, he came out of the more paternalistic school of the National Civic Federation: "Reared in the somewhat paternalistic traditions of pre-war progressivism and the social work ethos, Roosevelt thought instinctively in terms of government's doing things for working people rather than of giving the unions power to win workers their own

155. *Ibid.*, p. 42.
156. Irving Bernstein, *The New Deal Collective Bargaining Policy* (Berkeley: University of California Press, 1950), p. 18.

victories."[157] On the other hand, he well understood the NAM mentality and was impatient with it: "I am fairly certain that the Manufacturers Association and some of that crowd did everything they could do to foment the general strike [in San Francisco], knowing that a general strike can never be successful and that when it failed it would end the days of organized labor."[158] Roosevelt, according to Schlesinger, "saw himself as holding the balance between business and labor," and it is here that Roosevelt, Schlesinger, and others have led us astray.[159] Roosevelt was not a balance between business and labor, but an integral member of the upper class and its power elite. However, he was a member of that part of the power elite that had chosen a more moderate course in attempting to deal with the relationship of labor and capital. He was a member of the tradition reaching back to the heyday of the NCF and some of the most prestigious members of the power elite (including his uncle, the aforementioned Frederic Delano). While he did not encourage unionism, as his record during the thirties makes very clear, he was nonetheless unwilling to smash it in the way the NAM had hoped to do since 1902. I believe we see here the importance of the ideas developed within the NCF in the pre-World War I years, ideas which Roosevelt encountered as head of shipyards during World War I and as a member of the NCF. When the time came for choosing, he and the moderate members of the power elite chose bargaining rather than repression.[160]

The hearings for the second attempt at a Wagner Act

157. Schlesinger, *op. cit.*, p. 402; however, "social work" ethos is really a little too middle class in its connotations to capture the flavor of the NCF-Roosevelt tradition on this matter.
158. *Ibid.*, p. 402.
159. *Ibid.*
160. Bernstein, *op. cit.*, p. 131, overlooks this difference within the business community when he says, "A basic problem for Wagner, however, was to convince the President that he should release himself from the viewpoint of business."

were a rerun of the hearings that had been held the previous year. Garrison, Biddle, Leiserson, Dennison, labor leaders, and one or two little-known, middle-sized businessmen testified in favor of it. Garrison's view was typical: Organized labor was a bulwark against radical movements; furthermore, it was necessary to increase the purchasing power of labor in order to get industry moving again.[161] Wagner also introduced a favorable report on such an act by a committee of the Twentieth Century Fund. The committee was chaired by William H. Davis, a New York corporation lawyer. Other members of the committee included Dennison, Leiserson, economist Sumner Slichter, and John G. Winant.[162] The latter, as noted in the discussion of the Social Security Act, was one of the most prominent and respected leaders within the upper class. The lineup against the bill was longer and more wordy. There was first of all the NAM and its affiliates, arguing at great length against the constitutionality of the bill. However, there was more than the NAM, for representatives of steel, autos, newspapers and textiles also spoke against it. Henry I. Harriman of the United States Chamber of Commerce, a moderate on some New Deal matters, was very much opposed. So was Alfred P. Sloan of General Motors.

In short, there can be no doubt that there was a deep and serious split within the power elite on how to deal with organized labor. According to a study by liberal businessman Edward Filene, in which he surveyed business conditions in fourteen large cities in 1934, it was New Deal labor policy that most annoyed big business.[163] Exposures of rigged stock markets and regulations against the unscrupulous were bad enough, but giving labor legalized rights to organize and bargain went too far. If a poll had

161. *Legislative History of the National Labor Relations Act, op. cit.,* Vol. I, p. 1505.
162. Eakins, *op. cit.,* pp. 248–9.
163. Schlesinger, *op. cit.,* p. 471.

been taken of the many thousands of members of the power elite at that time, many probably would have disapproved of the Wagner Act. However, the moderate clique within the power elite that held the political reins at that crucial juncture had had long experience in dealing with labor through the National Civic Federation, the American Association for Labor Legislation, the Women's Trade Union League, the National Consumers' League and the settlement houses, and it was this clique which chose a moderate course, appealing over the heads of their conservative brethren to the laborer, the farmer and the middle-class liberal.[164] Perhaps it is just such situations as this that political scientist V. O. Key had in mind when he wrote:

> The operation of democracy may depend on competition among conflicting sections of the "better element" for the support of the masses of voters. Hence, the workings of democracy require a considerable amount of disagreement within the upper classes.[165]

The battle over the Wagner Act did not end with its passage. Many expected the Supreme Court to agree with the NAM and the Liberty League as to its unconstitutionality. Indeed, Bernstein claims that many legislators voted for it with that eventuality in mind.[166] The Roosevelt forces also knew that the bill faced a tough hurdle in the courts, and they prepared carefully for the battle. Having lost NRA, President Roosevelt had worked closely with Senator Wagner between the time the NRA was declared unconstitutional on May 27, 1935, and the time he signed the Wagner Act on July 5. Among other things, changes were made in the wording in light of the recent court decision.

164. Arthur M. Schlesinger, Jr., *The Crisis of the Old Order* (Boston: Houghton Mifflin, 1957), pp. 24–5, recognizes the importance of the Women's Trade Union League and the National Consumers' League, but calls them "middle class" and pits them against "business."
165. V. O. Key, *Southern Politics* (New York: Vintage Books, 1949), p. 180.
166. Bernstein, *op. cit.*, p. 116.

Two other efforts were made to insure judicial victory for the pro-union forces. First, a fine set of lawyers was put in charge of finding and preparing the cases that would test the act before the court. The first important step in this direction actually had been taken in mid-March, 1935, when an ineffectual Solicitor General, who in one case had been asked by Chief Justice Hughes to be more clear as to "what you want this court to do," was replaced by Stanley Reed, a Kentucky corporation lawyer who played a key role in selecting and presenting the Wagner Act cases.[167] Reed was aided by Charles Wyzanski, Jr., an upper-class lawyer from a well-known Boston firm; by Charles Fahy, a middle-class lawyer who had practiced in Washington, D.C., and New Mexico; and by Warren Madden, a middle-class law professor who was serving as head of the National Labor Relations Board.

The second attempt to insure success was Roosevelt's famous proposal to "pack" the Supreme Court. Frustrated by the fact that he had not had the opportunity to make a Supreme Court appointment, and by the fact that the court was so conservative, Roosevelt suggested that additional justices be appointed to the court when those past retirement age did not retire. The plan was greeted with outrage in many quarters. The sanctity of the court had been questioned. Perhaps we will never know for sure what effect this proposal had, but shortly after it was made the court upheld four of the test cases in 5–4 decisions and one in a unanimous opinion. Voting on the side of the angels were the usual liberals: Benjamin Cardozo, Harlan Stone (a former partner in Sullivan and Cromwell), and Louis Brandeis. They were joined by the moderate corporation lawyers, Chief Justice Hughes and Associate Justice Roberts. Roberts—urbane, Episcopalian, and a director of City Trust Company of Philadelphia, Bell Tele-

167. Cortner, *op. cit.*, p. 67.

phone Company of Pennsylvania, Real Estate Title Trust Company, Franklin Fire Insurance Company, and Jefferson Medical College before his appointment to the high court—was mildly famous for being exposed as one of J. P. Morgan & Company's fifty-nine "preferred" customers allowed to buy good stocks at special low prices. Hughes and Roberts, in voting as they did, had taken back their views of one year previous.[168]

From a judicial point of view, the most important outcome of the Wagner Act cases was to remove the court as the final refuge in labor questions. The struggle was now assigned to the legislative process and, more importantly, to an administrative agency, the National Labor Relations Board. The right of unions to organize was to be "conferred in the public interest as a public right and that as such it was enforceable exclusively by the NLRB."[169] Once again, we see that favorite solution of the moderate members of the power elite, the "nonpolitical" administrative body or regulatory agency. Biddle makes clear the link to the Federal Trade Commission (and thus to the National Civic Federation) when he says: "The feature of the act attacked as the most radical was in fact the least novel—the provisions authorizing the Board to request a court to enforce its orders, which derived from the Federal Trade Commission Act of 1914."[170]

Even before the court decision, Roosevelt began to make moves to mend the rift within the power elite. Perhaps the most important overture was toward United States Steel, which was made through his friend Thomas Lamont, a partner in J. P. Morgan & Company. Lamont brought Roosevelt and US Steel president Myron Taylor together, and the two became very good friends.[171] United States Steel began secret negotiations with the CIO in January, 1937, and

168. Cortner, *op. cit.*, pp. 176–7.
169. *Ibid.*, p. 190.
170. Biddle, *op. cit.*, p. 50.
171. Perkins, *op. cit.*, p. 223.

signed a contract with the new union on March 3, 1937, a month before the court decision. Conservative steel diehards were enraged, which may have been why Taylor was replaced as head of the Iron and Steel Institute by Tom R. Girdler of Republic Steel. When the problem was automobiles, Roosevelt, Lamont and Taylor went to work on Bill Knudsen, head of General Motors, which was jointly controlled by the Morgan and DuPont interests. Roosevelt liked Knudsen and gave him important assignments during the forties (as he did Taylor).[172] Roosevelt also appealed to Walter P. Chrysler for support; Chrysler had given his support to Roosevelt in the 1936 election.

Roosevelt was not alone in these conciliatory efforts. According to Frances Perkins, she was able to call on some very important members of the power elite in effecting the new policy:

> Jesse Jones was also helpful. It may be surprising to some people to realize that men looked upon as the conservative branch of the Roosevelt administration were cooperative in bringing about a new, more modern, and more reasonable attitude on the part of employers toward collective bargaining agreements.[173]

She then lists Averell Harriman and Carl Grey of the Union Pacific Railroad, Daniel Willard of the Baltimore and Ohio, Walter Teagle of Standard Oil of New Jersey, Thomas Lamont of J. P. Morgan & Company, Myron Taylor of United States Steel, Gerard Swope of General Electric, and textile manufacturer Robert Amory (father of CIA leader Robert Amory, Jr., and writer Cleveland Amory) as among those whom she could call upon in difficult situations.

With war imminent, and industrial planning for it already beginning, the last serious resistances to organized labor disappeared for the time being in the early forties. Diehards remained, however, and Attorney General Francis Biddle had to have Sewell Avery of Montgomery Ward physically

172. *Ibid.*, p. 355.
173. *Ibid.*, pp. 324–5.

removed from the doorstep of his establishment. This director of a dozen companies was so angry that he called Biddle a name: "You New Dealer!"[174] But with prosperity returned after the war, Avery and the NAM received some relief, for, as we have already noted, everyone in the big business community from the CED to the NAM was in favor of most of the restrictions provided by the Taft-Hartley Act. Labor has been trying to get rid of that bill's "14b" ever since. I suspect they will have to await a crisis like war or depression, and that the first sign of hope will be found in a report from the CED, BAC, TCF, or a similar power elite organization.

A final question remains about the Wagner Act. If unions do not affect the wealth distribution, as they do not, and if many employers understand their usefulness as a conservative force, then why was the bitterness toward them so great? First, employers, due to their self-image and general ideology, preferred a paternalistic approach. They were willing to *give* certain things to labor, but they resented *demands* by organized labor. This paternalism, so obvious in the National Civic Federation, is also manifested in the sphere of charity and philanthropy. The rich do not like to be asked for money; they like to give gifts. It is striking how often biographies and autobiographies of the rich stress that they ignore pleas and requests, but turn around and give millions to some charity or cause of their choice. Second, the unions often demanded a voice in determining the production process. Most employers, again for ideological reasons, resisted fiercely. Working conditions they will discuss with the unions. Control of the production process is another matter.[175]

---

174. "You New Dealer!" (*Newsweek*, October 14, 1968), p. 36.
175. Several of the points in this paragraph were brought into meaningful relationships for me by conversations with economist Stanley Warner. He also made me aware of management's inflexibility on negotiating about the production process as contrasted with its relative flexibility about discussing working conditions.

All in all, organized labor, through the Wagner Act, did make some gains, particularly in its right to recognition, collective bargaining, and a voice in working conditions. The upper class, then, is not omnipotent; nor do all members appreciate what their farsighted leaders have done for them in channeling serious discontent into a moderate course. However, even after acknowledging that labor showed considerable strength in forcing the acceptance of the Wagner Act, the fact remains that the story of how labor acquired its rights is a very different one from what is generally believed. A powerful mass of organized workers did not overwhelm a united power elite position. Rather, moderate members of the power elite, faced with a very serious Depression, massive unemployment, declining wages, growing unrest, and spontaneous union organizing, and after much planning and discussion, chose a path that had been traced out gradually over a period of thirty-five years by the National Civic Federation, the Commission on Industrial Relations, and other pro-union forces within the power elite. By making certain concessions and institutionalizing their conflict with labor, they avoided the possibility of serious political opposition to the structure of the corporate system.

CONCLUSION

This essay began with a quote from the *Harvard Business Review* that well captures the flavor of the prevailing view about social legislation in this country. Our writer believed that "Business has not really won or had its way in connection with even a single piece of proposed regulatory or social legislation in the last three-quarters of a century," and from personal conversations I know that he is not alone in that view. I hope I have shown that the reality is quite otherwise. Members of the power elite have been intimately involved in shaping and developing the social legislation of the twentieth century. The power elite did not merely pervert and take over the regulatory agencies—they planned and developed them as an alternative to public ownership, destructive competition, and uneven state regulation. Workmen's compensation was not forced upon them—they forced it on labor to undercut political unrest and to eliminate lengthy and potentially costly litigation. Even the Wagner Act shows their considerable ideological influence, dating back to the turn of the century. And if, as I fully agree, the power elite have been reacting to pressure from "below" and granting some degree of satisfaction to the unhappy, I would emphasize that they have been doing so on their own terms. It is the power elite who take the overall view; it is the power elite who finance the long-range studies; it is the power elite who take advantage of the expertise trained at the universities they finance and direct. In short, it is the power elite that develop the plans to deal with the pressures of domestic discontent. Through organizations such as Brookings, CED and the various foundations, they control the inputs into the governmental process on social welfare matters; it is therefore not surprising that the outputs have maintained the wealth distribution intact, and with it the privileges, prestige and prerogatives of the few tenths of a percent of the population making up the American upper class. Pluralism lives on social welfare matters, but in cubbyholes, alleyways and interstices.

# CHAPTER SEVEN

# The Power Elite, the CIA, and the Struggle for Minds

Early in 1960, Robert A. Lovett (*Social Register*, New York), a leading figure in the power elite these past twenty-five years, testified before a Senate subcommittee seeking to improve the institutional structure for policy-making on national security. Lovett was certainly well qualified for this task. A general partner in the Wall Street investment house of Brown Brothers, Harriman (he married a Brown), and a director of the Union Pacific Railroad (as was his father before him), he has served as an assistant secretary of war, undersecretary of state, secretary of defense and special adviser to Presidents. Before turning his testimony to detailed matters of administrative functioning, he set the stage by painting the more general picture of national security. The United States faces a world, reported Lovett, in which rapid changes are occurring due to scientific and technological advances, growing nationalism, and the development of new countries in Africa and Asia. But most of all, Lovett warned, "our system of government and our way of life have come under direct and deadly challenge by an implacable, crafty, and, of late, openly contemptuous enemy of both."[1] After quoting Khrushchev's famous "We will bury you," he stated the basic premise that even today guides most of the policy decisions, foreign and domestic, that are made by the power elite: ". . . we are in a struggle for survival involving military power, economic productivity, and *influence on the minds of men in political, scientific, and moral fields . . .*"[2]

The theory this leading Cold War architect propounds is not an unfamiliar one despite the mild "thaw" of recent years. It is a concise statement of how leading members of the power elite view the world. Stripped of the rhetoric about the "Free World" (Spain? Portugal? South Africa?) and "free enterprise" (in the oil industry? price fixing? subsidies?), this power elite stance is succinctly described by sociologist Philip Rieff: ". . . a permanent war economy based on a negative ideology of an absolute enemy."[3] It is the kind of ideology that can justify any action, however contrary it may be to espoused moral precepts, because of the nature of The Enemy. It is the kind of ideology that can appeal to the "higher loyalty" which guides upper-class CIA agents when they undertake actions "contrary to their moral precepts."[4] In short, it is the kind of ideology tra-

1. Henry M. Jackson, *The National Security Council: Jackson Subcommittee Papers on Policy Making at the Presidential Level* (New York: Frederick A. Praeger, 1965), p. 76.
2. *Ibid.*, p. 76–7. Italics mine.
3. Philip Rieff, "Socialism and Sociology," *C. Wright Mills and The Power Elite,* G. William Domhoff and Hoyt B. Ballard, eds. (Boston: Beacon Press, 1968), p. 169.
4. David Wise and Thomas B. Ross, *The Espionage Establishment* (New

ditionally used by power elites to justify whatever actions are necessary to protect their privilege and position.

Now it is obvious to the naked eye that the power elite are competing with The Enemy in the military and economic spheres. The power elite have accepted and marketed a military definition of reality throughout the postwar era, raising their military establishment to a position of overwhelming prominence within the country and throughout the world. Closely tied to this is an increasing industrial capacity, encouraged by tax favors and nurtured by defense contracts. As everyone now knows, even President Eisenhower had occasion to make reference to the "military-industrial complex." What is perhaps not so obvious is that the power elite have been just as deadly serious about competing, as the quote from Lovett put it, for "the minds of men in political, scientific, and moral fields." That is, it was not so obvious until the mid-sixties, when the manipulation and infiltration of a variety of American and world organizations in these fields by the CIA was revealed to a surprised general population which very quickly got used to the idea and understood its necessity (in the name of "national interest" and "national security"). It turns out that the power elite, for all their sweet reasonableness and liberal rhetoric here at home, have their secretive, not-so-moral side.

The story of the CIA's ideological machinations has been told in bits and pieces in a variety of places. It would not be worthwhile to bring most of it together here if it were not clear at the outset that the CIA has become one of the most important organizations of the power elite, at home and abroad. Our research into the backgrounds of CIA

---

York: Random House, 1967), p. 293, quoting Richard Bissell, former CIA deputy director for plans. The son of an insurance company director, Bissell attended Groton and Yale, was a leading figure in the Committee for Economic Development during the early forties, and played a key role in the Marshall Plan and the invasion of Cuba.

leaders fully supports the following generalization by the country's most knowledgeable journalists on the "espionage establishment":

> Espionage establishments tend to attract the elite, privileged, and better-educated members of their society. In the West at least, intelligence officials often come from older, upper-class families whose scions, already assured of great wealth, are now more interested in public service [!] . . . And in both countries [England and the United States] there is a close relationship between the espionage establishment and what has come, loosely, to be termed the Establishment—that larger grouping of powerful men who, in any country, seem to control its affairs.[5]

Nor is this upper-class bias present only in the top leadership of the CIA. When we look at the lower levels and at specific operations—overthrowing governments in Iran and Guatemala, spying on Cuba, invading Cuba—we find some of the most respected and respectable members of the upper class doing the dirty work. From Boston there is an Amory, a Cabot, and a Saltonstall. From New York there are two Roosevelts. Until his death in the crash of a Kennedy in-law's airplane, the CIA office in St. Louis was headed by Lewis G. Werner—socialite, investment banker, and polo player. In the San Francisco *Social Register* we find Sherman Kent, a Yale professor turned CIA intellectual. These names are not exceptions; they are merely some of the better-known of the upper-class names in our CIA file.

Before turning to a discussion of where and how the CIA has entered the struggle for minds, it should be emphasized that the undercover work of that organization is not the first attempt by members of the upper class and their associates to have an impact in this all-important contest. Far from it. The attempts are legion. Members of the power elite, as individuals and as organizations, have purchased

5. Wise and Ross, *op. cit.*, p. 4.

newspapers and created magazines to promote their views and/or criticize and ridicule other views. They have withdrawn advertising from mass media to silence opinions they do not favor. They have created university chairs and research institutes to pursue topics of interest to them, at the same time playing an active role as university trustees in getting rid of professors with undesirable views.[6] They have written and caused to be written articles and books that present their side of every story as attractively and persuasively as is humanly possible. All this, and more, is well known. No one pretends that members of the power elite have no axe to grind. It is just that *Time, Newsweek,* the National Advertising Council, the Foreign Policy Association, centers for international studies and the Ford Foundation are there for all to see. Their trustees, officers, and projects are carefully chronicled in self-published annual reports.

Then too, the power elite have created and developed that wonderful field of public relations on an incredible scale. Some of the early practitioners of this art helped scrub up the images of the "Robber Baron" families; others specialized in the corporate image and the corporate conscience. Functionally speaking, the public relations departments of large corporations, in conjunction with the giant public relations firms that service many corporations, have become the early warning system of the upper class, picking up and countering the slightest remark or publication that makes funny lines on their sensitive radars. Thanks to them, public opinion is well-monitored, with an assist of course from the alert social scientists in certain university institutes financed by the big corporations and foundations. Wayward opinions, once detected, are duly corrected by a

6. Lionel S. Lewis, "The Academic Axe: Some Trends in Dismissals From Institutions of Higher Learning in America" (*Social Problems,* Fall, 1964), pp. 156–7; Lionel S. Lewis, "Dismissals from the Academy" (*Journal of Higher Education,* May, 1966), pp. 257–8.

barrage of printed matter and public pronouncements, unless the advisers consider the situation one in which replies should be avoided. More recently, the public relations firms are being used to foist political candidates on the bedazzled populace. Truly, the attempt to manipulate public opinion has become a conscious and full time profession. Perhaps its seeming success is really due to the nation's general prosperity over these past many years, but one has to admit that members of the power elite are in there selling every minute.

However, public relations efforts are well known too, even if their role in papering over cracks in the power elite image is not generally emphasized. What surprises some people within this pluralistic society is to find that the power elite have additional methods by which they carry on the ideological battle. That some of their members are underhanded and will stop at nothing is to be expected within a large collection of mere human beings. But to find out that the power elite as a group are intimately and intricately involved in secretive, manipulative and deceitful operations, and in the name of saving democracy and the open society, is to go beyond the peccadillos of a few personalities to expose another side to the *modus operandi* of the High and Mighty. Such is the import of the CIA revelations to be recounted below. They are of system-wide consequence, throwing floods of unwanted light on the activities and values of civic leaders who like to have themselves presented in a more glowing, more moderate, more philanthropic spotlight.

## STRAIGHTENING OUT STUDENTS

Young people between the ages of eighteen and twenty-five are terribly concerned with ideological matters. Worse, they are often in rebellion against the old ways as they struggle to establish their independence and self-identity. They are thus susceptible to people with persuasive arguments who want to enlist them in political causes. This is an important problem as more American and European youth are subjected to an even longer educational process that makes them even more irascible and even more interested in ideas and theories. Given the stakes, the youth battle could be a serious one to lose to rival ideologies. The danger seemed great in several allied nations. Leading members of the power elite decided not to take any chances. They therefore looked around for an effective way to combat the well-organized and well-financed communist youth groups in other countries. Working through the CIA, they found their mark in the National Student Association. Liberal, but anti-communist, the NSA had dropped out of the pro-communist International Union of Students after the Communist take-over in Czechoslovakia in 1948. Starting in 1950, apparently, the CIA began to help NSA.[7] Just a little at first, like the $10-$12,000 Frederic Delano Houghteling accepted on behalf of the NSA to send representatives to an international student meeting in Prague.[8] 1950 was also the year that eighteen national student groups met in Sweden to form a new international organization, the International Student Conference. NSA soon became the key organization in this international organization which had, as we shall soon see, considerable encouragement from America's power elite. In any event, the NSA-CIA relation-

7. The following account of the CIA and student groups is based upon three sources: Sol Stern, "NSA-CIA" (*Ramparts,* March, 1967); Stuart H. Loory, "How CIA Became Involved in NSA" (*San Francisco Chronicle,* February 28, 1967), pp. 1, 12; and the concise summary of all articles and letters on the problem in *The New York Times,* which appears on pages 1269–72 of *The New York Times Index,* 1967, Volume 55 (New York: The New York Times Company, 1968).

8. Loory, *op. cit.,* p. 12; Houghteling's father was a financial consultant who served in the Treasury Department during World War II. His mother was Laura Delano. Frederic Delano, be it recalled from an earlier essay, was Franklin D. Roosevelt's uncle.

ship grew more and more important. All in all, the CIA shelled out $4 million before an idealistic NSA officer finally blew the whistle in 1966. In some years 80% of the NSA budget was coming from the CIA. Most of the money was used for international programs, educational material, and student meetings.

Not everyone in NSA knew what was going on. In fact, only a handful did. Not only is the national leadership of the organization far removed from its grass roots, but the CIA was good at judging who and who not to "co-opt," to make "witty." Just a few were approached each year, usually the president and the international vice president. These witty lads would then graduate to the CIA, foundations, or more mundane government jobs. It was quite an operation, and it worked very well for sixteen years. The CIA made only one mistake—the 1965–66 president. It seems this president got to be too friendly with a radical, unwitty student who was in charge of raising money. When the unwitty one complained about the restrictions on his role, his president friend spilled the beans. After much soul-searching, the radical squealed. The CIA had been right about him; they had misjudged only the president.

What did the CIA get for its money? First, a flourishing anti-communist alternative with which other non-communist students could interact, particularly within the International Student Conference. Second, intelligence about the personalities and social backgrounds of foreign student leaders, which sounds harmless enough if it is not realized that such mundanities are the crucial stuff of espionage agencies. Third, some say-so in selecting officers and in shaping international programs. I should say "perhaps" on this third point because there are conflicting reports about it. In any case, it is not too important for my purpose in this essay, which is to show how the power elite encourage and use organizations and programs that fit their purposes.

NSA was not the only student organization utilized by the power elite. They also bought into the aforementioned International Student Conference, sponsoring its many programs of technical assistance, education, and student exchanges.[9] Then too, between 1961 and 1965 they spent $180,000 on the Independent Research Service, which sent American delegations to actively oppose the communists at communist-oriented youth festivals. Stern notes that the NSA as an organization remained aloof from such aggressive activities but that "important NSA officers and ex-officers were very active in the Independent Research Service activities in Vienna and Helsinki."[10] One Independent Research Service director became an NSA president, and then received a "scholarship" from a CIA "foundation."

The CIA was not alone in its manipulations. It was not so crude as to hand the money over directly. Frederic Delano Houghteling, for example, had to apply to two wealthy philanthropists, one in Chicago and one in Wilmington, for the $10–12,000 NSA received in 1950.[11] For later operations "foundations" were used. There are several, but only the two most important ones will be noted here. The first, the Independence Foundation, is a front in Boston about which little is known. Its address is the same as that of the large corporate law firm of Hale and Dorr. Moreover, one of that firm's partners, Paul F. Hellmuth, is an Independence Foundation trustee as well as a director of Cabot, Cabot, and Forbes, the Nickel Plate Railroad, the Urban League, and the University of Notre Dame. Another known trustee of the foundation is investment banker David B. Stone, a graduate of Milton Academy and Harvard. Between 1962 and 1963 this foundation gave $256,000 to the NSA. It also provided NSA with rent-free headquarters during the sixties.

9. Stern, *op. cit.*, pp. 30, 33.
10. *Ibid.*, p. 32.
11. Loory, *op. cit.*, p. 12.

Even more important than the Independence Foundation is the Foundation for Youth and Student Affairs, which is an above-board operation founded in 1952. In addition to giving hundreds of thousands of dollars to the NSA, it is also the primary support for the International Student Conference. Along with the San Jacinto Foundation set up by Texas oilman John Mecom, it gave the ISC $1.8 million between 1962 and 1964.[12] Some of its money comes from private sources, some from the CIA. Among its eminent trustees of recent years are five that are especially worthy of note here. The first two are Arthur A. Houghton and Amory Houghton, Jr., members of a prominent family that is in every way at the heart of the Eastern branch of the American upper class. Arthur Houghton, for example, is a Rockefeller Foundation trustee and a director of US Steel. Another interesting trustee is Frederick W. Hilles, a graduate of Taft School and Yale, and the vice president of the Yale University Press. Yet another is Robert E. Blum, a director of Federated Department Stores, Equitable Life Assurance Society and the Better Business Bureau, among others. Finally, there is Gilbert W. Chapman, a listee in the New York *Social Register* who graduated from Yale and is president of Pinnacle Press and a trustee of the New York Public Library. Then too, the executive secretary of the foundation, Harry Lunn, is a former NSA president. There can be no doubt about the respectability and importance of the Foundation for Youth and Student Affairs.

This brief recounting does not even begin to tap the involvement of the CIA and the power elite in student organizations all over the world. For example, it says nothing about the Institute of International Education, which brings many foreign students to this country, helps develop agricultural and business schools in foreign countries, provides counsel for corporations, and keeps track of

12. Stern, *op. cit.*, p. 33.

US students and scholars all over the world.[13] Two of its known sources of income are the gala Diamond Ball that kicks off the New York social season and the J. M. Kaplan Fund, one of many CIA conduits.[14] Detailed studies of the FYSA, IIE and their many sister organizations will have to be left to scholars wishing to research what C. Wright Mills called "the cultural apparatus" and what Marxists call "ideological hegemony." In the meantime, we can rest assured that the power elite are not neglecting young minds: "The American operatives were competing directly with Communist agents for the sympathy, loyalty, and support of the influential classes of the emerging nations."[15]

## REORGANIZING AND DISORGANIZING LABOR

Labor unions tend to become bureaucratic organizations controlled from the top by a pervasive ideology and a few leaders. They are a number one target for the communists, who think that the working classes will eventually bury capitalism. Although most American scholars deny the theory, members of the power elite do not want to count on theoretical arguments for their peace of mind. They actively support anti-communist trade unions throughout the world. This support consists of training non-communist leaders in the ways of American trade unionism and providing money and matériel for the propaganda pamphlets, offices, staff, and muscle men who are necessary for organizing a new union or causing a split in an existing union.

13. Michael Holcomb, "Student Exchanges Serve U.S. Policy" (*Guardian*, January 20, 1968), p. 6. One trustee of the IIE is Mrs. Morris Hadley. Her lawyer husband is the head of the Rubicon Foundation, which has served as a CIA conduit. One of his law partners is J. J. McCloy.
14. *Ibid;* "The Pass-Through: How the CIA Bankrolled Private Projects" (*Newsweek,* March 6, 1967), p. 31, a complex diagram which samples the interlocks among "fronts," "conduits," and "recipients."
15. Loory, *op. cit.,* p. 12.

However, the power elite have had considerable help in this effort. Since many American workers in the American Federation of Labor craft unions long have been xenophobic and anti-communist, their leaders were ready and willing partners in this venture. Indeed, they had been active in the organizing of foreign labor for some time.[16] This does not mean that industrial CIO unions were unwilling to be involved in such activities. Walter and Victor Reuther of the United Auto Workers, for example, took fifty thousand dollars in fifty-dollar bills from a CIA agent to pass out to anti-communist labor leaders in Europe in the early 1950's.[17]

At the present time the key organization in the AFL-CIO-CIA labor apparatus seems to be the American Institute for Free Labor Development (AIFLD).[18] Its chairman is J. Peter Grace of St. Paul's and Yale, whose many corporate directorships include companies with interests in Latin America. The vice chairman is Berent Friele, a corporation executive and a vice president and director of the Rockefeller-financed American International Association for Economic and Social Development. The president is George Meany, long-time head of the AFL-CIO. AIFLD tends to concentrate its efforts in Latin America, but there are other organziations for other areas, such as the African-American Labor Center and the Asian-American Free Labor Institute. The labor men who seem to be in charge of running these operations are Jay Lovestone, who was chairman of the Communist Party in the late twenties, and Irving Brown, who started out with the garment workers. The key man from the CIA side is

16. Thomas Braden, "I'm Glad the CIA Is 'Immoral'" (*Saturday Evening Post*, May 20, 1967), p. 14; Henry W. Berger, "American Labor Overseas" (*The Nation*, January 16, 1967), pp. 80–4.
17. Braden, *op. cit.*, p. 10.
18. Philip Reno, "The Ordeal of British Guiana" (*Monthly Review*, July–August, 1964), pp. 50–2; Richard Ward, "AFL-CIO Penetrates Latin America" (*Guardian*. August 24, 1968), p. 24.

apparently Cord Meyer, Jr., of St. Paul's and Yale. He is a former president of the United World Federalists. His mother is listed in the New York *Social Register*.

Certain labor leaders also help out directly through their unions. The International Oil Workers have spent CIA money in Indonesia. The Communications Workers of America have done their part, and so have the Food and Restaurant Workers Secretariat. One of the biggest operations is that of the American Newspaper Guild, which spent the million dollars given to it by CIA fronts to fight communism in journalism.[19] Another big CIA spender is the National Education Association (NEA), the company union of school teachers and administrators. It works closely with the World Confederation of Organizations of the Teaching Profession (WCOTP) in presenting an alternative to the Communist-oriented World Federation of Trade Unions. The money for NEA and WCOTP came primarily from the "Vernon Fund." A former NEA executive secretary joined with a Washington lawyer, Bryce Rea, Jr., in setting up the Vernon Fund.[20]

No one knows how effective these efforts are, but no one can deny that the CIA is giving it a good go. Budget estimates run to $120 million a year for labor operations. One of the few case studies available suggests that AIFLD, at least, is not entirely impotent.[21]

The CIA did not exhaust its labor organizing efforts with

19. Neil Sheehan, "News Guild Aided by Groups Linked to CIA Conduits" (*The New York Times,* February 18, 1967), pp. 1, 14. The American Newspaper Guild received money from the Granary Trust, whose known officer is lawyer George H. Kidder of St. Mark's School, Williams College, Harvard Law School, and the Boston *Social Register,* and from the Chesapeake Fund, whose known officer is lawyer George Constable of Princeton, Yale, and the Baltimore *Social Register.*

20. Gerald Grant, "2 Teacher Units Got CIA Funds" (*Washington Post,* February 22, 1967), p. 8.

21. Reno, *op cit.,* pp. 50–2; Berger, op. cit., p. 83; Neil Sheehan, "CIA Men Aided Strikes in Guiana Against Dr. Jagan" (*The New York Times,* February 22, 1967), p. 1.

its involvement in unions and training organizations related to the AFL-CIO. It also speculated in the activities of the "democratic left." Through the J. M. Kaplan Foundation, which was founded originally through the beneficence of the president of Welch Grape Juice Company, the CIA gave $1,048,940 between 1961 and 1963 to socialist Norman Thomas' Institute of International Labor Research, Inc. The money was used primarily to train democratic left unionists in Costa Rica and the Dominican Republic. Thomas reports that he didn't know the money was coming from the CIA, although he was somewhat suspicious. In any case, the CIA did not try to dictate policy.[22] However, the following story suggests that Norman Thomas was no stranger to the CIA and its long-time director, Allen Dulles (*Social Register,* New York; Sullivan and Cromwell). It seems that in the mid-fifties the head of the American Committee for Cultural Freedom was having trouble getting money for his projects. So he wrote to Edward Lilly, a member of a governmental agency for coordinating intelligence and psychological warfare operations, to plead his case. At the same time he wrote to Thomas, asking him to get in touch with Allen Dulles via telephone. Shortly thereafter the American Committee for Cultural Freedom received $14,000 from the Farfield Foundation and the Asia Foundation, important organizations with the most eminent of the eminent for directors. Thomas then wrote to the committee head: "I am, of course, delighted that the Farfield Foundation came through . . . I am happy to think I had a little to do with the proposition in certain quarters."[23] Dulles to Farfield Foundation to a committee to defend cultural freedom from totalitarians, with socialist Norman Thomas serving as greaser. Politics do make strange bedfellows. Maybe the CIA apologists are right

22. Steven Roberts, "Thomas Upholds CIA-Aided Work" (*The New York Times,* February 22, 1967), p. 17.
23. "The CIA Finds a Publisher" (*Ramparts,* November 30, 1968), p. 60.

when they say they had to sneak the money because Congress and its rightwingers wouldn't be able to comprehend that helping non-communist leftists was good strategy. After all, Barry Goldwater & Co. did complain about the funding of "leftists" when the CIA's activities in this area were revealed.[24] But if Norman Thomas and his democratic leftists manage to get to the left of the power elite on occasion, perhaps it is compensated for by the fact that the AFL-CIO is usually a bit to the right of the entire power elite on foreign policy. It's a tolerable kind of pluralism, financed from the wealthy "center." Now if only those rightwingers would wise up.

## PATRONIZING THE INTELLIGENTSIA

Intellectuals, which means writers, artists, critics, sophisticated journalists, and a few broad-gauge scholars, are a narcissistic bunch, full of their own self-importance. They love to talk, they love to see their words in print, and they love to be flattered. The power elite, through the CIA and other organizations, have been very accommodating about these intellectual needs. In fact, patronizing would be a better word. They have given American intellectuals money to start organizations, to hold conferences, and to publish magazines and books. They have encouraged them to meet with intellectuals from all over the world. The result is a series of CIA-financed associations, institutes, and magazines that provide opportunities for discussion, travel, pub-

24. Steven Roberts, "CIA Is Criticized by Conservatives" (*The New York Times*, February 23, 1967), p. 25; Roy Reed, "Goldwater Says CIA Is Financing Socialism in U.S." (*The New York Times*, February 27, 1967), p. 1. Actually, the ultra-conservatives have no reason to complain, for the CIA funneled money to their Christianform through Goldwaterite Peter O'Donnell's Jones-O'Donnell Fund. See Robert G. Sherrill, "Educational Pipelines: The Beneficent CIA" (*The Nation*, May 9, 1966), pp. 542–3.

lication, and mutual adulation. The CIA is seeing to it that rival ideologies do not go unanswered. It wants to be sure everyone who has anything to say against communism can get a hearing. No foreigners are going to outdo the US power elite when it comes to flattering the people who might, if frustrated enough, provide the catalytic words and programs for the socially disadvantaged.

American Friends of the Middle East, American-African Institute, magazines for Iron Curtain emigrés—there must be dozens of these organizations and publications which are aimed at the intelligentsia of the world. With few exceptions, very little is known about them, partly because they are not all that important, partly because they have not invited scholarly attention. Only the intemperate bragging of a former CIA agent has exposed one of them to the clear light of day. In what follows I will therefore focus on the Congress for Cultural Freedom, an organization which financed such avant-garde magazines as Great Britain's *Encounter* and included leading artists, writers and social scientists of the fifties among its members.

The CIA's relationship to the Congress for Cultural Freedom and *Encounter* was first noted in passing in one of a series of articles on the CIA that appeared in *The New York Times* (April 27, 1966). The mention brought heated letters. One was signed by economist-novelist-humorist John K. Galbraith, historian Arthur M. Schlesinger, Jr., physicist Robert Oppenheimer, and foreign service officer George Kennan.[25] The other was from Stephen Spender, Melvin Lasky, and Irving Kristol, all *Encounter* editors at one time or another.[26] The whole thing seemed to have

25. "Record of Congress for Cultural Freedom" (*The New York Times,* May 9, 1966), p. 38. The letter did not address itself to whether or not the CIA funded the Congress, but to the complete independence of the Congress' policy. There is a difference.

26. "Freedom of *Encounter* Magazine" (*The New York Times,* May 10, 1966), p. 44. This letter stressed editorial independence, but contained the sentence "We know of no 'indirect' benefactions."

blown over, when one year later an ex-CIA agent, Thomas Braden, apparently upset over criticisms of the CIA, stirred up the whole controversy again with his revelations in the *Saturday Evening Post*. Braden raised cain with the CIA critics who seemed to have forgotten the all-pervasiveness of the Moscow-directed Red Menace (some of the critics must be "naive," some "must be worse," some must be "pretending to be naive").[27] In the process he bragged about his role in putting CIA agents and money into the Congress for Cultural Freedom and *Encounter*. By the time the dust had settled the Congress had a new name (Association for Cultural Freedom) and a new director, Shepard Stone, director of internal affairs for the Ford Foundation, which assumed financial responsibility for the organization. Two *Encounter* editors had resigned in anger, and a third *Encounter* editor, Melvin Lasky, had admitted he was "insufficiently frank in explaining to Mr. [Frank] Kermode [Lasky's co-editor] what I had come to suspect had happened."[28] Galbraith, ever insouciant and unflappable, opined that "you could easily persuade me" that the letter to which he had attached his name was "much too fulsome." He even hinted he had known of the CIA involvement in the Congress since 1960.[29]

The financing for the Congress' programs and *Encounter's* articles came in large measure from two above-board CIA conduits. The first, the Farfield Foundation, is at the heart of the New York Establishment; the second, the Hoblitzelle Foundation, is in the same position in Texas. Among the Farfield trustees are publisher Cass Canfield (Harper & Row), publisher Gardner Cowles (*Look*), in-

27. Braden, *op. cit.*, p. 10.
28. Christopher Lasch, "The Cultural Cold War" (*The Nation*, September 11, 1967), p. 209; *The New York Times Index*, 1967, *op. cit.*, p. 1272; "Lasky Will Stay With *Encounter*" (*The New York Times*, May 9, 1967), p. 3; "Cultural Group Once Aided by CIA Picks Ford Fund Aide to Be Its Director" (*The New York Times*, October 2, 1967), p. 17.
29. Lasch, *op. cit.*, p. 209.

vestment banker Donald Stralem, investment banker William A. M. Burden (who is also a trustee for the Institute of Defense Analysis), and Godfrey S. Rockefeller. Karl Hoblitzelle of the Hoblitzelle Foundation is chairman of the Republic National Bank of Dallas, and a director of the Hoblitzelle Properties, Southwest Insurance, Texas Power and Light, and the Texas Research Foundation. Trustee James Aston is with the same bank and sits on the boards of American Airlines, Lone Star Steel, and the Texas Research Foundation, among others. Another trustee on whom we could find information, George MacGregor, is a director of four utilities companies. The final trustee we could identify is Judge Sarah T. Hughes, the judge who swore in Lyndon Johnson as President after the assassination of John F. Kennedy.

Many people concern themselves with the problem of which intellectuals "knew" and which were mere dupes, but that is of secondary importance. The point is that some men have views the power elite like, and some don't. The likable group gets financial, institutional, and mass media support (overtly and covertly) from members of the power elite. That is the "where it is at" of this subsection.[30] Establishment-oriented intellectuals are not bought. Indeed, they are not even very well paid.[31] They are merely patronized, flattered, and wittingly or unwittingly, used. In 1955 a New York Times editorial called the American Committee for Cultural Freedom "a most important front of freedom's defenders today" and praised it for its "key role" in the "struggle for the loyalty of the world's intellectuals."[32] Mighty fine praise indeed, if a little patronizing.

30. Jason Epstein, "The CIA and the Intellectuals" (*The New York Review of Books,* April 30, 1967), pp. 19–21.
31. Irving Kristol, "Memoirs of a Cold Warrior" (*The New York Times Magazine,* February 11, 1968), p. 91.
32. "They Speak for Freedom" (*The New York Times,* March 25, 1955), p. 22.

## USING THE EXPERTS

American academia at the major universities is in large measure a collection of experts, with each expert relatively confined to his particular specialty. Some of these experts are more useful than others. The more useful are housed in institutes as well as the traditional departments. They receive research grants from foundations, institutes, corporations and governments to further develop their expertise and train new experts. They often do consulting on the side for industry, government and power elite associations. Some are on yearly corporation retainer fees that can go as high as several thousands of dollars a year. Others work for $100–$200 a day (plus expenses) on a job-by-job basis. A very few are getting rich in conjunction with the investment bankers who finance them in a variety of enterprises. Experts, in short, seem to be a little more important than intellectuals.

CIA entanglements with the experts are several: hiring them as agents and analysts, supporting their research, financing the publication of their articles and books. The first well-publicized instance concerned CIA involvement in the Center for International Studies at MIT.[33] A second instance showed how the CIA and Michigan State University collaborated in propping up the American-created government in South Vietnam.[34] However, the case I would like to pursue here concerns an organization whose officers are functionaries in the American Political Science Association as well as close friends of former Vice President Hubert Humphrey. Operations and Policy Research, Inc., was

33. David Wise and Thomas Ross, *The Invisible Government* (New York: Random House, 1964), pp. 243–4.
34. Warren Hinckle, Sol Stern and Robert Scheer, "University on the Make" (*Ramparts,* April, 1966); Martin Nicolaus, "The Professors, the Policemen, and the Peasants" (Unpublished manuscript, January, 1966).

founded in 1955 as a "non-profit research organization set up to help the USIA [United States "Information" Agency] distribute literature in the United States and abroad and to advise on the selection of books to be sponsored by the USIA."[35] The executive director of the organization from the start has been political scientist Evron Kirkpatrick of Minnesota, a friend of Hubert Humphrey. Kirkpatrick had served in the Office of Strategic Services during the war and as a State Department intelligence officer after the war. The vice president of the OPR is lawyer Max Kampelman, also of Minnesota, who had served as a legislative counsel to Senator Hubert Humphrey. He is now a Washington lawyer and a director of a Minnesota company which he helped in "hoodwinking" the Agency for International Development out of $2.3 million.[36] In addition to aiding the USIA, Kirkpatrick and the many political scientists he has hired on a part-time and consulting basis were giving their services to the CIA. Probably the professors were unknowing dupes, but it seems likely that Kirkpatrick himself was "witty." What makes the OPR operation particularly interesting is that Kirkpatrick has been executive director of the American Political Science Association since 1955, while Kampelman is the association's treasurer and general counsel. They provide a double interlock between OPR and the APSA.

Four former APSA presidents investigated the situation and decided there was no reason for Kirkpatrick and Kampelman to sever one of their affiliations. A committee on professional standards was in general agreement.[37] Still, an enterprising student might want to try to trace the affiliations and beliefs of the men brought before the as-

35. Marvin Suskin, "Political Science: The Battle for Integrity" (*The Nation*, September 2, 1968), p. 179.
36. "The Vice President: Political Fallout?" (*Newsweek*, February 19, 1968), p. 26.
37. Surkin, *op. cit.*, pp. 179–80.

sociation by Kirkpatrick; apparently leaders of the CIA-financed Radio Free Europe were among them.[38]

The American Political Science Association felt compromised in only one respect. It *may* have received CIA funds indirectly from a conduit called the Asia Foundation. The connection is a highly significant one, however, for the Asia Foundation is a key outpost in the power elite network. It is symbolic of the whole operation. Founded in 1954, no information about it is listed in the *Foundation Directory,* a standard reference source on foundations. Its annual budget is $6 million, most of which is used for grants throughout Asia.[39] Among other things, the grants support Asian schools and libraries and travel grants for Asians to international conferences. Asia Foundation representatives are stationed in fourteen countries. Economist Clark Kerr, former president of the University of California, has been quoted as saying that "the Asia Foundation has more contacts with Asian intellectuals than any other American institution.[40] The Asia Foundation also has economic interests:

> Of late, the Asia Foundation has become increasingly interested in the expansion of Pacific trade. It has sponsored trade conferences and is underwriting trade advisors to Asian governments. It is assisting in the development of Asian commercial codes. In addition, the Foundation has taken an active role in exploring the avenues of economic and political regionalism in Asia.[41]

The president of the foundation is Dr. F. Hayden Williams, a former Deputy Assistant Secretary of Defense. The chairman of the board is Russell G. Smith, a retired vice

38. The Shadow, "Hubert's Advisors: Cold War Cronyism" (*Guardian,* August 24, 1968), p. 8.
39. Tom Caylor, "The Rising Tide of Pacific Business" (*Fortune,* June 15, 1968), p. 77. This article is part of a lengthy advertising section which extols San Francisco (and the heart of its power elite).
40. *Ibid.*
41. *Ibid.,* p. 78.

president of the Bank of America. The trustees are some of the most prominent men in the country, all of whom admitted in a signed statement they were aware the Foundation was receiving government money. Unfortunately, the assistant public affairs officer who released their statement didn't know whether or not they were aware that it was CIA money.[42] Among the fifteen trustees are the following:

Arthur H. Dean (*Social Register,* New York), lawyer, Sullivan and Cromwell, negotiator of the truce in Korea

Ellsworth Bunker (*Social Register,* New York), Ambassador to South Vietnam

Mortimer Fleishhacker, Jr., San Francisco philanthropist

Cyril Haskins, president, Carnegie Institution of Washington

Walter H. Mallory, executive director of the Council on Foreign Relations, and, he says, a twelfth generation descendant of a leader of the Pilgrims on the Mayflower

Mrs. Maurice T. Moore (*Social Register,* New York), chairman, Institute of International Education, wife of a partner in Cravath, Swaine, and Moore, and sister of the late Henry R. Luce of Time, Inc.

J. E. Wallace Sterling (*Social Register,* San Francisco), then president of Stanford University, which has a Stanford Research Institute doing yeoman work for the power elite in Thailand[43]

Grayson L. Kirk (*Social Register,* New York), then president of Columbia University

42. Wallace Turner, "Asia Foundation Got CIA Funds" (*The New York Times,* March 22, 1967), p. 17.
43. David Ransom, "Case Studies: The Stanford Complex" (*Viet Report,* January, 1968), p. 19; David Ransom, "Stanford's Warriors Invade Thailand" (*The Midpeninsula Observer,* January 22–February 5, 1968), p. 1.

Charles J. Hitch, then vice president, now president, University of California. Hitch is a former RAND Corporation economist and Defense Department consultant

Lucian W. Pye, professor of political science, MIT. Pye is one of the leaders of his profession

Three university presidents, a Carnegie foundation president, a Council on Foreign Relations executive, the chairman of the Institute of International Education, leading businessmen, corporate lawyers, and one of the bright young men of the political science field—together they direct a foundation with a $6 million-a-year budget derived in part from the CIA. The Asia Foundation and its projects are a microcosm of the relationship between the power elite and academic experts. Sociologically and ideologically, relationships such as these transcend the legalism and narrow professional standards that are used by the academic experts in discussing them.

FOUNDATIONS AND FRONTS

This essay has presented only a segment of the seamy side of the power elite. There are many other organizations and "fronts" in Houston, Detroit, and Cleveland that could have been used to make the same points. It is impressive to note, however, that this underside mirrors in structure and personnel the aboveboard foundations, associations, institutes, committees, commissions and civic organizations that the other essays in this book have discussed. Indeed, to focus too narrowly on the infrastructure of the seamy side and the minor conduit foundations is to miss the point, for they are really only a nicely circumscribed case study in a larger picture. *All* power elite foundations, institutes and associations, above ground and below ground, are involved in ideological combat. While reasonable critics are chiding CIA foundations as naughty fronts and criticizing ultra-conservative foundations as partisan and political, they are overlooking, and hence legitimating, the partisanship of the nonpartisan power elite groups that merely encourage us to be internationally-oriented in our thinking. They are missing the nefariousness of power elite groups that merely ask us to look at the facts and be practical. They are over-looking the fact that nonpartisanship and fact-finding are aspects of a low-key ideology of the status quo, as is that disarming Congress of Cultural Freedom-John F. Kennedy notion that ideologies are now passé and that all we need are a few experts to hone up the system. Imagine. After thousands of years of ideology they ask us to believe that ideology has suddenly ended—and in our own time, no less. Truly, it is one of the more subtle conservative ideol-ogies ever developed, a tribute to the sophistication of, among others, the National Bureau of Economic Research, the Bureau of Applied Social Research, the Congress for Cultural Freedom, and other such institutes and organ-izations in and around the MIT-Harvard-Yale-Columbia-Princeton-Johns Hopkins-University of Chicago complex that houses and generates the Eastern half of the American intellectual establishment.

The temptation to concentrate on CIA machinations and right-wing heresies and buy the power elite propaganda about non-ideology is very great. We hear it every day from the nicest people in the most respectable journals. But it must be resisted. Those who want to understand the power structure must stand back and assert in the face of all the power elite's kindness to academics, and all the intellectual establishment's objectivity and scientificality, that all power elite foundations, institutes, and associations are propa-ganda fronts which are involved in maintaining the legiti-macy and respectability of the present Establishment, even if in some cases this involves no more than giving some bright-eyed novice a few thousand dollars with which to amuse himself. If the Independence Foundation is a front, so is the Rockefeller Foundation, however unaware of that role some of its leaders and recipients may be. If the Farfield Foundation is a conduit, so is the Ford Foundation (which is also a tax dodge). If the Congress of Cultural Freedom fobs the illuminati, so does the holier-than-thou Foreign Policy Association and its dry-as-dust affiliate, the World Affairs Council.

## THE HIGHER IMMORALITY

When C. Wright Mills called the power elite "irresponsible" and accused them of practicing the "higher immorality," the Intellectual Establishment was annoyed. They momentarily forgot the white collar crimes of the big business world, not to mention the thugs and spies that are sometimes unleashed on new labor unions. Nor did the tax dodges, expense-account parties, expense-account vacations, and expense-account girls come into consciousness. No, all they could think was that Mills had once again gone too far, once again let jealousy and ill temper get the best of him.

Now, 13 years later, there can be little doubt about the validity of Mills' indictment, which certainly had a good basis in fact even then. The activities of the CIA at home and abroad in para-military and intellectual undertakings are in themselves enough to expose the power elite and their morality for all to judge. By either an absolute morality or the more mundane standards of their own moral claims, the power elite and their intellectual collaborators have reaffirmed an age-old axiom about governing classes and their word magicians. However much they may plead otherwise, they are primarily self-interested partisans, their horizons severely limited by the ideologies and institutions that sustain and justify their privilege, celebrity and power.

# Part Three

# CRITIQUES
# OF
# OTHER VIEWS

# Introduction

There is no need for a lengthy introduction to the two essays which comprise this final section. They are attempts to make my view of the power structure clearer by comparing and contrasting it with the views of ultra-conservatives and pluralists. In the process I will of course try to point out what I think to be the major weaknesses of these alternative positions. Critical essays such as these are seldom completely devoid of animus, but I have tried to direct such as remains into the channel of sarcasm. To remove all such references would have meant academic exercises without the cutting edge which transforms critiques into bearable reading.

# CHAPTER EIGHT

## *Dan Smoot,*
## *Phyllis Schlafly,*
## *Reverend McBirnie, and Me*

The picture of the American power structure to which I hold is shared by very few college-educated Americans, although it enjoys considerable popularity on lower levels of the socioeconomic ladder. For most relatively affluent people, two other views are more meaningful and coherent. The first is a set of propositions and images that can be classified under the term "pluralism," a term that I briefly mentioned in the introduction to the second section of essays. This view, which claims that different groups—business, labor, farmer, consumer—are powerful on different issues, and that no one group runs the country, is held by most American academicians and many middle-class liberals. The second widely held view of the American power structure is that of the ultra-conservatives, a view rarely encountered in the academic community but shared by perhaps five to fifteen million adult Americans. According to this view, the country is manipulated by a small, well-knit group of internationalists who operate in terms of a shared collectivist ideology which is contrary to everything America has stood for in the past. Due to their ideological predilections, these rulers are leading us in a direction we would not accept if we understood and realized what they were up to. Some of these misrulers are very rich, most are reputedly Eastern, most are well educated and friendly to academicians, and many travel under the label of liberals, but the important thing is the shared ideological program that supposedly motivates them.

As might be suspected, there is very little communication between the two views. The pluralist group calls the ultra-conservative view "paranoid" and absurd, the ultra-conservatives think the pluralists to be communists and socialists in disguise, or, at best, the unwitting dupes and carriers of socialist ideas which are subverting both American youth and a considerable percentage of the big business community. Certainly few social scientists have taken the ultra-conservative view seriously; it is rather an object for study, a weird exotica that is a nice topic for psychological research. Nor do the ultra-conservatives have anything but suspicion and disdain for the pluralists. In short, the two groups learn nothing from each other, and any discourse they have is of a purely *ad hominem* nature, whether it be the blunt accusations of the ultra-conservatives or the more subtle psychological "studies" quoted by the "non-ideological" social scientists. Needless to say, the pluralists usually win out in this sort of exchange, for they are witty, urbane, balanced, cool, reasonable and backed by the prestige of academic degrees.

Now, unlike the pluralists, I learned something from an ultra-conservative about a matter the pluralists never discuss. More specifically, Dan Smoot's *The Invisible Government* led me to a study of the power elite's discussion and policy-forming organizations, such as the Committee for Economic Development and the Council on Foreign Relations, which are important links between the corporations and the government. Furthermore, there are those pluralists who would suggest that my views are very similar to those of the ultra-conservatives, by which they mean that I too am "paranoid," forever lost in a "conspiratorial" view of history. Thus, it seems proper that I should not only give a serious hearing to the views of the ultra-conservatives but that I should let them and the pluralists know where and how my views are different.

Before discussing the ultra-conservative view, it is necessary to describe it more fully. Since there are many variations on the general theme, I have chosen to concentrate my remarks on the general picture found in books by three of its best-known spokesmen, Dan Smoot (*The Invisible Government*), Phyllis Schlafly (*A Choice Not An Echo*), and Reverend William S. McBirnie (*Who Really Rules America: A Study of The Power Elite*).[1] Smoot is a former FBI man from Texas who interrupted his graduate work in American Civilization at Harvard to join Hoover's agency at the outset of World War II. He remained with the FBI after the war, but finally resigned to become "an independent publisher and radio-television commentator," as it says on the back of *The Invisible Government*. What makes Smoot all the more interesting from a human interest point of view is that one of his high school friends was none other than C. Wright Mills. Writing in the high school paper, Smoot and a co-author admit that Charles Mills (as he was then known) was "not exactly gallant" and "far from suave," but they also note that he had "a wholesome

1. (Dallas: The Dan Smoot Report, Inc., 1962); (Alton, Illinois: Pere Marquette Press, 1964); (Glendale, California: Center for American Research and Education, 1968).

charm and a prevailing air of mental and physical clean-
liness . . . that makes one proud to call him a friend . . ."[2]

The second representative of the ultra-conservative view,
Phyllis Schlafly, found her book, *A Choice Not an Echo,*
a best-seller in the months of the Goldwater campaign of
1964 which it was intended to further. Mrs. Schlafly is a
conservative member of the American upper class. She
received her B.A. from hometown Washington University in
St. Louis and her M.A. at Radcliffe College. A member
of the D.A.R. and the Junior League, her Socially Registered husband comes from a family of bankers.[3] Our final
protagonist is a California religious fundamentalist, United
Community Church minister William S. McBirnie. The
author of over 125 books according to the back cover of the
book under consideration, Reverend McBirnie and his work
first came to my attention when several people told me he
was touting my book on his radio program. It turned out,
however, that he was actually plugging his own forty-page
book, which appeared several months after mine and was
entitled *Who Really Rules America: A Study of the Power
Elite.* Since the title of my book was *Who Rules America?,*
and since I never before have seen an ultra-conservative
publication use the concept "power elite," perhaps my un-
paranoid pluralist friends will forgive me if I indulge
myself in the tentative hypothesis that the similarity in the
two titles is no mere coincidence.

What is the view of the American power structure that

2. Evans and Smoot, "Visits with Interesting Personalities: Charles
Mills" (*Tech Talk Bi-Weekly,* Dallas Tech High School, 1933), as
quoted in Richard Gillam, "The Intellectual as Rebel: C. Wright Mills,
1916–1946" (Unpublished M.A. thesis, Columbia University, 1966),
p. 28.
3. The Schlafly family "empire" seems to consist of the Union National
Bank in East St. Louis (assets not listed), the Mountain Valley Spring
Company, the Potosi Ties and Lumber Company (makes railroad ties),
and the Hobbs Western Company. At least six Schlaflys are involved in
these companies as chairmen, presidents and directors, according to the
listings in the 1967 *Poor's Register of Corporations, Directors, and
Executives.*

emerges from these books? First, the country is ruled by a small band of "internationalists" who have "collectivist" if not communist proclivities. They are secretive and manipulative, and they are guiding us into "one-world" socialist entanglements that are antithetical to America's "traditional" disdain for foreign involvements. As part and parcel of this internationalist bent, these men are also destroying traditional American values, such as localism, minimum government, self-reliance, and independence. At home, the evidence for these collectivist sympathies is the welfare state, consisting of handouts to the poor which encourage dependency and irresponsibility, thereby further eroding the tough fiber that made America great.

There are minor variations on these themes. In Smoot's work it is clear that the Jews play a very large role in all this. For Schlafly, the emphasis is on the "Eastern Establishment" Republicans who manipulate the Republican Party and share many views with Democrats; she is a classic manifestation of rock-ribbed, isolationist Republicanism of the NAM-small business variety. For McBirnie, the emphasis is on just plain "bigness"—big labor, big religion, big business—and on the straying from fundamentalist, rural, small-town values. He seems to capture the concern of the "little man" from little towns who is shocked and dismayed when he encounters the big secular city. However, I do not want to push Reverend McBirnie's humbleness too far, for one of his arguments against the government guaranteed income is that it is already hard enough to hire gardeners, maids, and clean-up men.[4]

There are other aspects to the ultra-conservative view, but I am only focusing on its analysis of the loci and distribution of power in modern America. Where do the

4. William S. McBirnie, *Government Guaranteed Income? The Noose From Which There Is No Escape!* (Glendale, California: Center for American Research and Education, 1968), p. 7. "The government guaranteed income will make unemployables out of those whose services are needed. Try to hire a gardener, a maid, or clean-up man, even now!"

Smoot-Schlafly-McBirnie views on this topic touch base with mine? Well, we agree on who runs the country. I too think that David Rockefeller and the big businessmen who discuss problems at the Council on Foreign Relations are typical of the relatively small group of people who run this country. I too think that moderate Republicans are really bedfellows with the big businessmen who dominate the Democratic Party as it manifests itself in the executive branch of the federal government. I too think that these men are "internationalists." I even agree that some of the ultra-conservatives may have some justification for being angry about the welfare state, for they, not the big rich, are the ones who have to help pay for it.

Where, then, do I get off the boat? At a number of places, most of which can be made quite clear through a detailed analysis of the core of the ultra-conservative concept about the power structure, "the international Communist-Jewish conspiracy." Now, I am aware that not all ultra-conservatives hold in the same degree to each aspect of this concept, and that most, especially those in the John Birch Society, are coming to reject the Jewish factor, but it is nonetheless a useful starting point. Each word in the phrase will be taken separately and explained at length.

*International.* It is true that the men who run our country are "internationalists," but it is probably not correct to think that this is primarily because of political or psychological reasons. It is not communism or liberalism or a desire for greater power but business problems which make the majority of the power elite internationalists. American businessmen always have had an international orientation. However, in the last part of the 19th and early part of the 20th century, before businessmen knew how to use government to create consumer demand in this country, internationalism became even more important because many corporate leaders began to fear that their markets were drying up. They began to think they faced a crisis of overproduction. It is not important to know whether they were economically correct in assuming this; the important thing is that they believed it and acted as if it were true. They thus became very concerned about international markets. There were several symptoms of this increasing international emphasis in the first two decades of the century, but one of the first concrete evidences was the Council on Foreign Relations. Founded after the first world war, it billed itself as a nonpartisan discussion group whose aim was merely to make Americans more aware of international problems. Ultra-conservatives don't believe that is all there was to it, and I think they are right. The Council on Foreign Relations, for all its nonpartisanship and objectivity, is as much a propaganda organization as any of the foundations and institutes of the new rich Texas oil man H. L. Hunt and other ultra-conservatives. Just as Hunt and the ultra-conservatives are "isolationist," so is the CFR "internationalist." Through studies, articles, speeches, discussions and pamphlets over the space of nearly fifty years, it has helped to create a climate within which American leaders and scholars came to see an internationalist viewpoint as second nature; to question it was to be a little strange. I do not want to imply that the CFR was alone in this, nor that it met no opposition. During the Depression, for example, a heated debate occurred within the power elite as to what to do, with some having a "nationalistic" solution. In the early forties, however, a consensus began to emerge, and that consensus was to press for overseas markets and overseas investments.[5] The isolationist-NAM view did fight the CFR-CED-internationalist view on a series of issues during the forties, but it lost. Some of the flavor of this clash is captured in a study showing how the two views were presented at the time in Congressional hearings.[6] With the Marshall Plan as one important shoehorn, the growth of

5. David W. Eakins, "The Development of Corporate Liberal Policy Research in the United States, 1885–1965" (Unpublished Ph.D. dissertation, University of Wisconsin, 1966), pp. 296*ff.*
6. David S. McLellan and Charles Woodhouse, "The Business Elite and Foreign Policy" (*Western Political Quarterly*, March, 1960), p. 172.

American business involvement overseas during the fifties and sixties, particularly in Europe, was phenomenal. From only $1.7 billion in direct investments in Europe in 1950, the figure was estimated to be almost $20 billion in 1967.[7] Today, many of the biggest corporations depend upon their overseas sales and investments to permit growth and to improve profit margins. Consider these figures on one aspect, overseas sales, from the business magazine *Forbes*:[8]

| COMPANY | FOREIGN PCT. TOTAL BUSINESS | COMPANY | FOREIGN PCT. TOTAL BUSINESS |
|---|---|---|---|
| *Automobiles* | | *Capital Goods* | |
| Chrysler | 15% | Caterpillar Tractor | 45% |
| Firestone | 18% | International Harvester | 28% |
| Ford | 19% | Otis Elevator | 44% |
| General Motors | 16% | United Shoe | 54% |
| | | | |
| *Oil* | | *Office Equipment* | |
| Gulf | 32% | Burroughs | 26% |
| Socony Mobil | 59% | IBM | 29% |
| Standard Oil N.J. | 60% | | |
| Standard Oil (Calif.) | 43% | *Chemicals* | |
| | | Celanese | 26% |
| | | DuPont | 19% |
| *Food and Dairy* | | *Miscellaneous* | |
| Corn Products | 43% | Gillette | 31% |
| General Foods | 10% | Coca-Cola | 40% |

Nor are sales and profit margins the whole story. Direct investments are also important in themselves, particularly in important raw materials. Most of the bauxite essential to the aluminum and airplane industries comes from foreign sources, and the importance of such sources for iron ore is constantly increasing.[9] The staff of one Presidential commission of big businessmen wrote as follows in 1954:

7. Joseph D. Phillips, "The Dollar Invades Europe" (*The Nation*, September 18, 1967), p. 243.
8. "Taking in Partners" (*Forbes*, July 1, 1965), pp. 30–1.
9. Harry Magdoff, "The Age of Imperialism" (*Monthly Review*, June, 1968), pp. 30, 33.

Both from the viewpoint of our long-term economic growth and the viewpoint of our national defense, the shift of the United States from the position of a net exporter of metals and minerals to that of a net importer is of overshadowing significance in shaping our foreign economic policies. We have always been almost entirely dependent on imports for tin, nickel, and the platinum group of metals. In addition, our requirements for asbestos, chromite, graphite, manganese, mercury, mica, and tungsten have been generally covered by imports.[10]

One of the main charges made by ultra-conservatives against the internationally minded power elite is that it does business with the enemy, that is, with Yugoslavia, Russia, and more recently, other Eastern European nations. The ultra-conservatives believe that this is strengthening these countries so that they will ultimately bury the United States. They thus conclude, taking the pronouncements of both Russia and the United States seriously, that American power elitists must be either very stupid or secret agents of the communists. However, contrary to this kind of interpretation, I suspect the basic assumption of the American rulers is that by both standing firm militarily, as they think they did in Western Europe (forgetting that the communists also pulled back), and by developing trade relations in exchange for minor Russian concessions, they can eventually moderate the communist countries. And there is at least some reason to believe that their plan is working. One American Marxist, Paul Sweezy, believes that Yugoslavia, and perhaps other European Communist countries, may be drifting back to capitalism.[11] He also points out that the acceptance of European and American businessmen as

10. The Commission on Foreign Economic Policy, Staff Papers Presented to the Commission, Washington, D.C. (February, 1954), p. 224, as quoted in Magdoff, *op. cit.*, pp. 33–4. Pages 29 through 38 of Magdoff's article are a detailed discussion of the relationship of the several factors leading to a "Demand for External Sources of Raw Materials."

11. Paul M. Sweezy, "Czechoslovakia, Capitalism, and Socialism" (*Monthly Review*, October, 1968), pp. 11–12.

"partners" with communist state governments in certain big projects will move these countries in a less socialistic direction. Sweezy then quotes from a *New York Times* article as to how the Yugoslav government has taught the foreign businessmen to get control of companies which are theoretically controlled by the Yugoslav government. It may be that the American rich are neither stupid nor communist sympathizers, but that they know what they are doing:

> Investments by such diverse enterprises as Fiat, the Italian auto giant, and Printing Developments, Inc., of New York City, a subsidiary of Time, Inc., represent both the voracious demands of capital for new outlets and the conscious designs of a Communist state to accept a market economy and most of the trappings. . . . To them Yugoslavia is a pacesetter in the East as well as a show window for Western capital. Western companies operating here will have enormous competitive advantages once markets open up elsewhere in Eastern Europe . . . At first foreign companies were reluctant to get involved because the minority stake, they felt, would not give them any direct control over their investments. At seminars run for Western businessmen here, Yugoslav officials have been at pains to point out that ways can be found around this, for example, by vesting in the foreign investor control over the costs of production.[12]

But there is even more to the question of trade with Eastern Europe and Russia. Western Europe can use the Communist countries as an outlet for its products and as an area of investment. In other words, now that Western Europe has rebuilt from World War II, it is faced with the problems of overproduction and underconsumption. In many cases this European trade has indirect economic benefits for Americans. For example, Fiat, an Italian company, is building a big plant in Russia, but Fiat will get most of its machinery from American companies.[13]

12. *Ibid.*, p. 9, quoting from *The New York Times*, August 19, 1968.
13. "To Russia—Without Love: Not Many People Want to Talk About It, But the Fact Is That U.S. Industry Has a Major Role in the Soviet Union's Plans for a Vast New Automobile Industry" (*Forbes*, October 1, 1966), p. 19.

In short, I think ultra-conservatives must understand power elite relations with Communist countries in a new light. These relations are on the one hand business relations that are needed by Europe and lucrative to Americans. They are on the other hand attempts to moderate the Communist countries. It is a relatively conciliatory approach, and it is not readily understood if it is assumed that these men are psychologically motivated beyond the desire to maintain the corporate system in roughly its present form. More generally, it can be seen that my explanation of "internationalism" is essentially a socioeconomic one. I think it is largely a matter of dollars and cents for these men. It is my belief that they are cautious businessmen who think in terms of the health of their companies and the maintenance of the corporate system which they dominate. The power elite do not seem to be overly concerned with principles, ideals, or a desire for power; to the degree that anything can be inferred about their motives, which is always a risky undertaking, they are concerned with profits, stability, and the good life. This brings us to the second word in the phrase "international Communist-Jewish conspiracy."

*Communist.* Ultra-conservatives often assert that our rulers are communists, or the dupes of communists. While the ultra-conservatives base this charge on certain similarities between Russia and America, the situation deserves a closer analysis. Whatever we may say of him, David Rockefeller is not a communist. He is a multimillionaire banker and oil stockholder whose operations, holdings and life style are international in scope; he is probably sympathetic to many features of the welfare state; and he probably accepts Darwin's evolutionary theory. This makes him very different from most ultra-conservatives, but it does not make him a communist. To call him one, as so many ultra-conservatives do, is to lose the essential distinctions so necessary for a full understanding of this country. What, then, are the similarities between a David Rockefeller and a Russian communist that lead ultra-conservatives to equate the two? There are essentially four, each of which will be discussed in turn: Both are internationalists, both need large centralized governments, both accept the idea of government welfare to the needy, and both have a relatively scientific-secular view of the world.

As to the first similarity, their "international" frame of reference, I hope that I have shown already that the internationalism of a David Rockefeller is a pragmatic, business matter, and I will say no more about it. Let me turn instead to a detailed discussion of the acceptance of big government. Again, for David Rockefeller, and even the Russians, this is not a function of ideological beliefs, but of certain necessities. There are inevitable similarities in states made up of large corporations and large governmental agencies. For example, they are both overloaded with bureaucrats, forms, carbon copies, and red tape. But there are differences. Bertrand Russell once put one of them rather glibly: in Russia the politicians tell the corporate managers what to do, in America the corporate managers tell the politicians what to do. But why do the big rich of this country need a big government that is bureaucratic and centralized? They first of all need it because they decided to become "internationalists;" the state department has become a key coordinating agency for their overseas operations. They secondly need it to defend the American Way all over the world, that is, to defend and extend their overseas operations; the department of defense thus becomes an important part of the internationalist outlook. They thirdly need it to regulate themselves through commissions and agencies, taking business problems out of the arena of politics and the hands of states and counties, and putting them into the hands of neutral, qualified experts who understand the business viewpoint as well as the overall needs of the system. This strategy was discussed in the essay on "How The Power Elite Shape Social Legislation" (Chapter Six). The power elite fourthly need a big federal government to collect money from the rest of us so they can use it (a) for foreign aid and defense spending; (b) for research on new technologies and products; and (c) so that the government can help them avoid the kind of depression that almost wrecked the system in the thirties.

Since it is the desirability of government interference in the economy that is most questioned by ultra-conservatives, let me add a few more words about it. First, it was something the power elite came to reluctantly and grudgingly. Franklin Roosevelt himself was elected on a platform of economy and efficiency although he did talk about the need to increase consumer spending. However, when things continued in much the same vein, he started to experiment. As the economy began to pick up there was one more budget cut, but the system dipped again, and that made believers out of Roosevelt and many former conservatives. Even so, it cannot be overemphasized that this minor government spending was not enough to revive the economy. Only World War II brought this country out of eleven long years of depression. In this sense, the war was a blessing, but it was not an unmixed one from an economic point of view, for it led to the expansion of productive facilities and the potential for even greater overproduction and depression after the war. It was at this point that the CFR, CED, and other power elite organizations, fearing another depression, decided on overseas markets, government spending, and even limited planning as their only salvation.[14] Perhaps they were wrong economically, but the fear of a major upheaval in the face of another depression led them to choose what seemed most likely to insure the survival of their way of life. Apparently their general socioeconomic position was more important to them than any particular economic

14. See Karl Schriftgiesser, *Business Comes of Age* (New York: Harper & Row, 1960) and *Business and Public Policy: The Role of the Committee for Economic Development, 1942–1967* (Englewood Cliffs: Prentice-Hall, 1967) for a great deal of information that makes this point painfully clear.

theories. It was not stupidity or the influence of communist or Keynesian ideas that led them to make this choice; they merely preferred the path of least risk.

The desire to create consumer demand has been a major concern since the early thirties. It was one of the motives for social security then, and it is one of the motives for foreign aid now. For example, the Los Angeles *Times* noted in 1963 that the US foreign aid program "has become another subsidy built into the US economy . . . ", and then added that "Labor leaders and businessmen in export industries have long appreciated this—and so have their Congressmen."[15] *Forbes* explains further by showing that the money never leaves home; it goes to American businessmen. It tells how a group of big businessmen quietly lobbied for the 1965 foreign aid bill, explaining to Congressmen that foreign aid creates jobs for Americans and creates markets and good will in the recipient countries: "The businessmen recognize, as few Americans yet do, that since 1960 the foreign aid program increasingly has become aid to US business."[16] Actually, foreign aid played this role for American business long before 1960, but not so deeply and obviously as it does now when over 90% of the aid money is spent directly in this country. Even poverty programs are thought of in terms of maintaining the economy. Douglass Cater wrote as follows on the origins of the "war on poverty":

> This one seems to have had at least partial beginnings in the Council of Economic Advisers, where it was stimulated not so much by any sudden sympathy for the poor but by tough problems of fiscal policy. . . . But as Council Chairman Walter Heller began to look beyond the tax cut and ponder the inevitable downturn in the government's rate of spending for defense, space, and related activities, he recognized the

15. Ernest Conine, "U.S. Aid Program—Another Subsidy" (Los Angeles *Times,* August 25, 1963), p. G-1.
16. "The Money Never Leaves Home" (*Forbes,* May 1, 1965), p. 15.

combined advantages of a broad attack on the deep-seated economic problems that economists describe as "structural" . . .[17]

However, "pump priming," as it is sometimes called, is not the only reason for power elite acceptance of the welfare state. Let me assume that it is now clear that a David Rockefeller is not a communist because he and his friends need big government to further their huge fortunes, and turn directly to the third similarity with the Russians, the use of the state to provide for the young, the old, and the sick. From the point of view of the power elite, the welfare state consists of a set of minor concessions which are thought to make the overall corporate system more stable and efficient. Furthermore, it costs members of the upper class virtually nothing. They do not pay for social security or medicare out of their dividend checks, nor do they pay a greater percentage of taxes to provide the other services. The lower classes pay for the welfare state. Again, a pragmatic course has guided the power elite in the slow development of the "welfare state," as I hope my essay on "How The Power Elite Shape Social Legislation" (Chapter Six) made clear.

Internationalism, acceptance of big government and acceptance of the welfare state are three characteristics of present-day big business thinking which lead ultra-conservatives to compare a corporate America with the realities of Soviet Russia. There is a final rough similarity. The big businessman of today does not have a religious outlook on the world. Although he probably belongs to a church (usually Episcopalian or Presbyterian), he has a secular view of the world, based upon his liberal and scientific education in a nondenominational university. That he probably believes in evolution and other scientific theories is evidence to many ultra-conservatives of his Godless materialism, or

17. Douglass Cater, "The Politics of Poverty" (*The Reporter*, February 13, 1964), p. 16.

communist ideology. Once again, there is a certain similarity with the communist which makes both very different from the religious fundamentalist who is an anti-evolutionist, but it is not due to any influence of communism. Instead, the rise of science and technology, based on an intellectual tradition of which Marxism is but one small offshoot, and the confrontation with other cultures and religions due to improved transportation and communication networks, have led many twentieth-century urban Americans to this secular view.

Let me summarize my comments on this second word, "communism." I have tried to show that there are certain points of general similarity between the power elite and communist views, but I have stressed that in each case—internationalism, acceptance of big government and the welfare state, secularism—the power elite came to its views on the basis of its needs and national history, and not on the basis of any contamination or influence by communism. Big businessmen created big government, and they can live with the welfare state. However, ultra-conservatives cannot seem to bring themselves to criticize big businessmen as businessmen. They usually see these men as subverters of the true business ideology (laissez-faire), as men who have consciously or unconsciously selected a foreign ideology. Thus, the men they criticize are seen not as businessmen but as traitors or the unknowing dupes of liberal and collectivistic intellectuals. This latter point is an especially interesting one. Rather than criticizing the big businessmen who espouse the views, some ultra-conservatives prefer to concentrate on the scholars who often advise the rich.

*Jewish.* Some ultra-conservatives still think that it is Jews who propagate the internationalism and collectivism that are eroding the Eastern Establishment. Alas, nothing could lead them further from the possibility of coming to grips with the power structure they wish to understand. *Fortune Magazine* told it all many years ago, in 1936.

Surveying the entire economy industry by industry, it found that there were a significant number of Jews only in the waste products industry (e.g., scrap iron, cotton rag), in clothing, in tobacco buying and in New York department stores.[18] As to banking, well, there are a few Jews in investment banking, but they are a distinct minority, and practically all of them of any significance are mentioned by Dan Smoot in *The Invisible Government,* where they are given a prominent place.

There is one more thing I should say about this handful of upper-class Jews: They are more upper class than Jewish. As a book such as Stephen Birmingham's *Our Crowd* makes clear, these people often try to play down and de-emphasize their Jewishness.[19] Many start reform synagogues, others go to ethical culture schools, and to the degree that the prejudiced WASPS will let them, they join the social institutions of the upper class. They send their children to private schools, they found "parallel" city clubs and country clubs when they are excluded from the WASP clubs, and they intermarry into the upper class in a great many cases. One of the questions I asked in my questionnaire to psychoanalysts was "Do [wealthy Jews] have a tendency to play down their Jewishness and become merely upper class?" Of the twenty-six psychoanalysts who had seen such patients, eleven answered that "many of them" did, ten said some of them did, and only five said that none of them did. A very sophisticated sociologist, E. Digby Baltzell, tells us what we need to know to explain this phenomenon: at the lowest levels of American society a person is a member of an ethnic group; at the middle levels he is a member of a religious group; at the highest level he is first of all a member of his social class.[20]

18. "Jews in America" (*Fortune,* February, 1936), pp. 133–4.
19. (New York: Harper & Row, 1967.)
20. E. Digby Baltzell, *The Protestant Establishment* (New York: Random House, 1964), pp. 52–3, 62–5.

*Conspiracy.* A conspiracy, says my college edition of *Webster's New World Dictionary of the American Language,* is a "planning and acting together secretly, especially for an unlawful or harmful purpose, such as murder or treason." Well said, and that ultra-conservatives believe America is run in such a conspiratorial way fills the pluralists with dismay. It is just too manipulative, they say, and it assumes a unity of purpose and plan that couldn't possibly exist. In fact, to believe such is to be a nut, and if you can succeed in getting the label "conspiratorial thinker" attached to a person, you have ended all possibility that he will be taken seriously in the academic community.

Before comparing my position on conspiracies with that of the ultra-conservatives, let me state the pluralist view. While there is no one place to quote from, it seems to add up to something like this: History is made by and large by impersonal physical and social forces that are beyond the control of any one group of men, however conscious and manipulative. As to the role of businessmen, they have a certain general common interest, and a certain rough ideology, but they also have a great many differences. Furthermore, they do not meet and plan together in secret little gatherings, and even if they did, there are other groups which can checkmate business power.

In many ways this view is the antithesis of the ultra-conservative view, which sees a small group of men meeting and carefully planning as to how to manipulate society toward certain agreed-upon goals. As for myself, I am a moderate on this question. That is, I take a position between the two sets of extremes, the ultra-conservative and pluralist views. On the one hand, I believe that the power elite are more aware of their interests, and do more planning and talking about them than any pluralist ever dreamed of daring to consider. However, I do not believe that history is one big conspiracy, or even a lot of little ones. I agree with the pluralists that it is mostly millions of people doing their thing alone and in groups, within the context of interacting, impersonal variables which no one fully understands, let alone controls. However, if it was not conspiracy that led to the medical, scientific, technological, communication, and transportation advances that have shaped the twentieth century, it was nonetheless a relatively small number of very rich people and their academic advisers who met together in various interlocking social and policy-forming groups to decide how best to make money from and take advantage of these developments for their own narrow ends. If the power elite cannot make history just the way they want, there is still reason to assert that they are successful in realizing their wishes far beyond the modest limits claimed by pluralists. If it is true, as I believe, that the power elite consist of many thousands of people rather than several dozen; that they do not meet as a committee of the whole; that there are differences of opinion among them; that their motives are not well known to us beyond such obvious inferences as stability and profits; and that they are not nearly so clever or powerful as the ultra-conservatives think—it is nonetheless also true, I believe, that the power elite are more unified, more conscious, and more manipulative than the pluralists would have us believe, and certainly more so than any social group with the potential to contradict them. If pluralists ask just how unified, how conscious, and how manipulative, I reply that they have asked a tough empirical question to which they have contributed virtually no data—at the same time pointing to findings such as I have presented throughout this book.

What are the main attributes of the conspiratorial view when it is applied to the structure of power? How can we recognize it in ourselves or others? First, it tends to project omnipotence onto the ruling group. *They* are seen as so powerful that *they* can do anything *they* want to, and are thus blamed for anything that goes wrong. The claim, "Dean Acheson lost China," is an example of this imputation of omnipotence. It implies that Dean Acheson alone could have prevented the Chinese Communists from taking over that vast land of 500 million people if he had wanted to do so. The facts are that Dean Acheson represented the predominant view among leading members of the power elite at that time; after pouring millions of dollars into China and sending many task forces and investigating teams there to assess and advise, they concluded that Chiang Kai-shek and his regime were so weak and discredited that America could not save China without a tremendous infusion of troops and money. They felt they did not have the power to make this fight, given their problems in Europe at that time, and they were probably right. But even if they weren't, the point is that there are limits to the powers of any ruling group, and to overextend yourself is to invite defeat. The problem of respecting these limitations is not acknowledged by those who project omnipotence onto the "villain." In short, the smug Dean Acheson, whose British mannerisms so annoy many ultra-conservatives, no more lost China (the ultra-conservative delusion) than the boorish Lyndon B. Johnson, so distasteful to cultured types, personally decided to escalate the Vietnam War (a common liberal delusion). Acheson's decision represented considered opinion within the moderate wing of the powerful, just as Johnson's decisions to escalate and then to de-escalate were made with the advice of very important members of the higher circles.[21]

A second attribute of the conspiratorial view is that it

21. Johnson's secret advisers at the time of the de-escalation, known as the "Senior Informal Advisory Group," were corporate lawyers Arthur Dean (Sullivan and Cromwell), Dean Acheson (Covington and Burling), Cyrus Vance (Simpson, Thatcher, and Bartlett), and George Ball (now with Lehman Brothers investment firm); investment banker C. Douglas Dillon of Dillon, Read; Ford Foundation president McGeorge Bundy (Boston Social Registerite); and former generals Matthew Ridgway, Maxwell Taylor, and Omar Bradley. Stuart H. Loory, "Secret Session: How Advisers Changed LBJ's Mind on War" (*San Francisco Chronicle*, May 31, 1968), p. 1.

attributes omniscience to the leaders. They know every-thing and never make mistakes. "Mistakes" are clever and deeply-motivated plans. This is seen, for example, in those few ultra-conservatives who argue that the power elite planned the invasion of Cuba so that the American people would think they were doing something about communism, but purposely made it fail because they are really com-munists who welcome Castro in Cuba. It is seen in those postwar liberals who saw every foreign demonstration or disturbance as evidence for the cleverness and world-wide intelligence of the Russians. In short, the ultra-conservatives make our power elite more clever and manipulative than they really are, just as the liberals make the Kremlin and Peking more clever than they are. In my view, our power elite are more sensible and manipulative than pluralists would have us believe, but they are also human, ruled by their impulses and subject to errors of judgment and execu-tion. Furthermore, while they plan further ahead and un-derstand the system better than most of us, thanks in part to their academic advisers, they do have their limits, their ideological blinders. Once again, a reading of the reports and histories of the organizations Smoot pinpoints would make clear that they are more clever than most people think.[22] But they are not *that* clever.

A third characteristic of the conspiratorial view is that it makes the whole thing more secretive and organized than it is in reality. Secrecy is not the reason why *they* rule. Nor are they really very secret. Dan Smoot got his information from articles in *Harper's Magazine* and from the annual reports of the organizations themselves. And if CFR re-ports do not reveal what everyone said at the meetings, they do record every group that met. They also give a distillation of the groups' wisdom in articles in *Foreign Affairs* and in books published by CFR.

22. Eakins, *op. cit.*; Schriftgiesser, *op. cit.*; and the essays in Part Two of this book.

An example of this attempt to make something secret out of something that isn't can be seen in Mrs. Schlafly's dramatic chapter called "Who Are the Secret Kingmakers?" Here she tells us how she "stumbled on clear evidence that very powerful men actually do meet to make plans which are kept secret from American citizens."[23] She found this conspiracy while visiting Sea Island, Georgia, an upper-class resort area where rich people such as Mrs. Schlafly often vacation. At any rate, she tells of the elaborate security precautions she encountered, and then names the rich and well-born from the United States and Europe who were at the meeting. She next tells us "Yet, there was not a word in our press."[24] Unfortunately, she did not check very far. We found the meeting reported in *The New York Times* (February 16, 1957). Furthermore, attentive ultra-conservative readers may recall that they read a lengthy report on the matter, mostly based on *The New York Times* article, in the July, 1957, issue of the *American Mercury* which, characteristically, put Felix Frankfurter and Arthur Hays Sulzberger (both Jews) at the top of the list of plotters and tried to tie the meeting to international monetary difficulties.[25]

What did Mrs. Schlafly actually discover? According to *The New York Times*, the informal discussion group called the Bilderberg (after the hotel in which it first met) was called together by Prince Bernhard of the Netherlands to talk about how "mutual understanding for each other's [Europe and the USA] viewpoint [can] be promoted. . . "[26] This 1954 report noted that former government leaders from European nations, as well as David Rockefeller and former Eisenhower adviser C. D. Jackson, would be among

23. Schlafly, *op. cit.*, p. 103.
24. *Ibid.*, p. 105.
25. Paul Stevens, "Money Made Mysterious; Part IX, Planned Bankruptcy" (*American Mercury*, July, 1957), p. 135.
26. "Prince Bernhard Invites West Leaders to Parley" (*The New York Times*, May 18, 1954), p. 6.

those present. The result of the meeting was general agreement that the West must stand together in fighting Communism, and that political and economic action had to accompany military resistance.[27] The 1957 article which Mrs. Schlafly overlooks gives a more general picture:

> An unpublicized backdoor approach to better relations among nations of the North Atlantic Treaty Organization is getting its first tryout on United States soil. . . . The meeting is the fifth by an informal association called the Bilderberg group and organized by Prince Bernhard of the Netherlands, who is presiding. . . . Bilderberg group members include selected public officials, economists, professors, publishers, industrialists, and some labor leaders. . . . Most of the ninety-one members are from abroad.[28]

The 1964 meeting of this discussion group was duly noted as follows in the American Establishment's major means of communication:

> Ninety-five representatives from the United States, Canada, and Western Europe ended the thirteenth annual Bilderberg Conference on international affairs here yesterday. A statement issued at the closing said the topics discussed in the three day meeting included new developments in the Soviet Union, Communist China, and other Communist countries; East-West trade and political, military and economic relationships within the Atlantic community. The chairman was Prince Bernhard of the Netherlands, who has served as chairman since the first parley ten years ago at the Bilderberg Hotel in Oosterbeek, the Netherlands.[29]

27. "Bernhard Parley in Accord on Reds; Leaders Agree All of West Shares Peril—Rifts Laid to Lag in Conferring" (*The New York Times,* June 2, 1954), p. 4. This follow-up article adds that publisher Barry Bingham, investment banker Paul Nitze, and industrialist J. D. Zellerbach (head of CED from 1955 to 1957) were among those present.
28. "Views Exchanged on NATO Policies: Informal Session in Georgia, First in U.S., Is Forum for Leaders of Nations" (*The New York Times,* February 16, 1957), p. 10.
29. "Talks on World Affairs Are Closed in Williamsburg" (*The New York Times,* March 23, 1964), p. 36. An earlier dispatch (March 15, 1964, p. 49) told of the arrival of Prince Bernhard to chair the "thirteenth session in a series of informal meetings on international affairs."

Clearly, then, the Bilderberg group is not quite the secret Mrs. Schlafly thinks it is. It is merely one of many, many get-togethers by business leaders and government officials. While such informal gatherings are important in cementing the group and ironing out differences, they are not summit conferences, and the fact that they occur should surprise only those among the pluralists who do not believe that big businessmen maintain a variety of intimate, off-the-record contacts with each other and public officials. Mrs. Schlafly does us a service in pointing out these informal links between the corporations and the government that are all but ignored by the pluralists, but she makes too much out of them.

Conspiratorial theorizing such as is found in the work of Smoot and Schlafly is the essence of what Richard Hofstadter has called "the paranoid style" in American politics.[30] While Hofstadter notes that "it is admittedly impossible to settle the merits of an argument because we think we hear in its presentation the characteristic paranoid accents," he immediately adds in a footnote that "while any system of beliefs can be espoused in the paranoid style, there are certain beliefs which seem to be espoused almost entirely in this way."[31] Then too: ". . . the paranoid style has a greater affinity for bad causes than good"[32] I would like to register a dissent to Hofstadter's style in talking about a paranoid style. First, I think it tends to turn people away from the merits of the argument despite Hofstadter's mild warnings against such an eventuality. Second, such articles are seldom written with the humility of giving one's own style a clinical label. I am often left with the feeling that the style that is not paranoid is somehow more healthy or more objective, and therefore not needful of clinical

---

30. Richard Hofstadter, *The Paranoid Style in American Politics* (New York: Knopf, 1965).
31. *Ibid.*, p. 5.
32. *Ibid.*

examination. Such is not the case, in my opinion, and to redress this imbalance, I would like to consider briefly a clinical characterization of much academic thinking.

The title of my comments could well be "The Compulsive Style in American Social Science." The compulsive style is narrow, restrictive, highly phobic about flights of fancy, and usually partial to the status quo.[33] Ritual is highly important, as rules make everything just routine.[34] There is a need to categorize, weigh, and label phenomena in order to bring them under mental control. This style tends to see everything in shades of gray, perhaps under-emphasizing where the paranoid style over-emphasizes. In general, this style has a strong tendency toward the insignificant, a "displacement" on to small details.[35] Despite its love of system, its use of the defense mechanism of isolation keeps it from seeing events as connected:

> Isolation frequently separates constituents of a whole from one another, where the noncompulsive person would only be aware of the whole and not the constituents. Compulsion neurotics, therefore, frequently experience sums instead of unities, and many compulsive character traits are best designated as "inhibition in the experiencing of *gestalten* [wholes]."[36]

The point I have tried to make in using Hofstadter's method of distilling a clinical style from the similarities of one clinical group to one intellectual approach is that there are styles and there are styles, and that one group is as justifiably psychologized as any other. To delineate a paranoid style while neglecting others is to be one-sided, inviting *ad hominem* thinking about one group but not another. Furthermore, the paranoid style may sometimes

33. Otto Fenichel, *The Psychoanalytic Theory of Neurosis* (New York: W. W. Norton & Co., 1945), pp. 284–6, 297–8, for a discussion of compulsive characteristics.
34. *Ibid.*, p. 285.
35. *Ibid.*, pp. 285, 290.
36. *Ibid.*, p. 288.

occasion discoveries or emphases that are not open to other clinical styles. Maybe this style brings to awareness things that are little known because another style does not consider them important or encourage research on them. As Freud suggested, even "persecutory paranoics" do not "project it into the blue, so to speak, where there is nothing of the sort already. They let themselves be guided by their knowledge of the unconscious, and displace to the unconscious minds of others the attention which they have withdrawn from their own."[37] In other words, such people are often blind to their own motives, but they are not bad at searching out those of others. On the other hand, there are good things about the compulsive style too. Since words and thoughts are important in it (as a substitute for action), intellectual abilities are highly developed. Thus, it is not surprising that people with such a style would find academic pursuits congenial. Since reaction formations against impulses are frequent, control, logic, caution and orderliness are often prominent features of this style, while its tendency to doubt leads it to check and re-check its claims. Then too, coldness and lack of emotional feeling lend this style to highly abstract and impersonal thinking:

> The retreat from feeling to thinking succeeds, as a rule, in one respect: compulsive thinking is *abstract* thinking, isolated from the real world of concrete things. Compulsive thinking is not only abstract, it is also general, directed toward systematization and categorization; it is theoretical instead of real.[38]

Having shown, as Freud warned, that the use of psychoanalytical findings in arguments cuts both ways, I now

---

37. Sigmund Freud, "Some Neurotic Mechanisms in Jealousy, Paranoia and Homosexuality (1922)," *The Standard Edition of the Complete Psychological Works of Sigmund Freud* (London: The Hogarth Press, 1955), Vol. 18, p. 226. In one of his final works, "Constructions in Analysis" (1938), Freud speaks of the "kernel of truth" and "fragment of historic truth" in delusions. Sigmund Freud, *Therapy and Technique, Collected Papers* (New York: Collier Books, 1963), pp. 284–6.
38. Fenichel, *op. cit.*, p. 297.

return to the core concept of ultra-conservative thinking about the power structure, "the international Communist-Jewish conspiracy," and compare it with my view. For "internationalist" I would substitute "interested in overseas sales and investments." For "Communist" I would substitute "big businessmen with needs that lead corporate America to some similarities with the Russian state." For "Jewish" I would substitute "urbane," "liberally educated," "secularized," and "accepting of the welfare state to provide stability and consumer demand." For "conspiracy" I would substitute "aware of their interests," "far-seeing," "willing to meet and plan with other rich men and corporate leaders," and "willing to use scholars as consultants." In my view, then, there is nothing like an international Communist-Jewish conspiracy, although I do not dismiss the notion out of hand because it is supposedly an emanation of a particular style which is said to be more associated with some ideas than others and with more bad causes than good ones. In my view, the country is run by a group of very rich, cosmopolitan big businessmen with international business interests. They are part of, or employees of, a social class making up about a few tenths of a percent of the population. Many of them meet together in a variety of groups and try to figure out how to react to and capitalize upon the problems and opportunities that the forces-tides-drift-winds-exigencies of history (pick your own favorite impersonal term) bring to them. They are a group of relatively pragmatic multimillionaries and their employees, with at least some sense of the limits of their power. They are rational, reasonable, and forward-looking within the context of their big-business, upper-class mentality.

In short, the American rulers are not secret communists conspiring with Russian Communists, but wealthy men trying to reach a limited accommodation and détente with a rival power group that they cannot militarily destroy except at great risk and cost. They are not driven by internationalist or collectivist ideological principles, but are seeking to solve their problems and enhance their fortunes through overseas sales and investments. They are not liberal or socialist ideologues wanting to give a break to the poor and elderly, but corporate leaders who accept the welfare state as a potential solution to the problems of stability and consumer demand at very little cost to themselves. They are not treacherous traitors to the ideals of individualism, self-reliance, and laissez-faire, but the operative heads of a technologically-based urban society of 200 million people who have different problems from the small businessmen, small farmers, and pioneers who espoused those ideals in an earlier epoch.

To conclude, I hope ultra-conservatives will consider seriously this effort which takes them seriously, and that pluralists will not avoid coming to grips with my views by calling them conspiratorial and paranoid. Moreover, I hope I have shown that my views, to say the least, have several major divergencies from those of the ultra-conservatives as well as the pluralists, and that *ad hominem* arguments, even when wrapped in clinical discussions of style, are as useless to serious discourse about social and political issues as they were when Aristotle ruled them out of logical order 2,200 years ago.

# CHAPTER NINE

# *Where a Pluralist*
# *Goes Wrong*

Differences between those who do and don't think the power elite dominate the political process, which is the distinction between my view and that of the pluralists, have existed for a very long time. These disagreements often reflect differences in style, temperament and degree of satisfaction with the status quo as well as more intellectual differences concerning the structure and distribution of political power. Within the United States in the early part of the twentieth century the "governing class" type of argument was carried by well-known radicals such as Thorstein Veblen, while the pluralists were represented by less-known, but highly-respected political scientists.[1] During the Depression

1. Robert A. Dahl, "Business and Politics" in *Social Science Research on Business* (New York: Columbia University Press, 1959), pp. 18, 36.

the "governing class" position was upheld by people such as Marxist Anna Rochester and radical journalist Ferdinand Lundberg; among those on the other side were two authors who were to become very well known in the academic community, A. A. Berle, Jr. and Gardner Means.[2]

The postwar era saw new protagonists enter the lists. On the pluralist side were David Riesman with his popular *The Lonely Crowd* and David Truman with his well-received political science textbook.[3] On the other side was C. Wright Mills, the first academic person since Veblen to make a strong case, in slightly modified form, for the idea that the "corporate rich" (aided by the "warlords" and the "political directorate" as partners) dominate the American scene. Mills was joined by sociologist Floyd Hunter and Marxist Victor Perlo, although there were of course differences among the three on many points.[4]

Pluralists launched strong arguments against Mills and Hunter in the late fifties and early sixties. Most of the criticisms were of a theoretical or methodological nature, suggesting that the considerable amount of empirical information these two men had collected did not have all the implications Mills and Hunter claimed it did. While most of these criticisms were considered well-taken within the academic community, no pluralist came forth with a book which was an attempt to present a picture contrary to that of Mills and Hunter for the national level. Instead, pluralists concentrated on studies of the local level, testing the "power elite" thesis in New Haven, Chicago, and other cities.

2. Anna Rochester, *Rulers of America* (New York: International Publishers, 1936); Ferdinand Lundberg, *America's Sixty Families* (New York: Vanguard, 1937); A. A. Berle, Jr. and Gardner Means, *The Modern Corporation and Private Property* (New York: Macmillan Co., 1932).

3. David Riesman (with Reuel Denney and Nathan Glazer), *The Lonely Crowd* (New Haven: Yale University Press, 1950); David Truman, *The Governmental Process* (New York: Knopf, 1951).

4. Floyd Hunter, *Top Leadership, USA* (Chapel Hill: University of North Carolina Press, 1959); Victor Perlo, *The Empire of High Finance* (New York: International Publishers, 1957).

The pluralist case, then, rested for some time on introductory political science textbooks, such as that of David Truman, critiques of Mills and Hunter, such as those of Robert Dahl, and case studies of local issues, such as those by Dahl and Edward Banfield.[5] This situation finally was remedied in 1967 with the appearance of the late Arnold M. Rose's *The Power Structure*.[6] The product of a distinguished sociologist with a great many publications and honors in addition to experience as a state legislator, the book presents an empirically based pluralistic view of the national power structure as well as a running critique of the work of Mills and Hunter. As might be expected, the book was an instant success as a classroom text, for it filled a longstanding need for a source that presented the pluralist view in a way that would be useful to upperdivision undergraduates and beginning graduate students in political science and sociology. There are few findings, arguments, or references from the twentieth-century pluralist literature that are not presented or footnoted.

The book also received generally favorable comment from reviewers. *The New Yorker's* brief review called it a "first-rate work."[7] A short notice in *The New York Times Book Review* said it was a "useful contribution."[8] Reviewers in two major sociology journals were almost ecstatic. One said "we cannot fail to be impressed with the indictment [of the Mills-type thesis, for] the case is marshalled with great skill [and] argued calmly and dispassionately."[9] The other went so far as to say that it was a "splendid book,"

5. Truman, *op. cit.*; Robert A. Dahl, "A Critique of the Ruling Elite Model" (*American Political Science Review*, June, 1958); Robert A. Dahl, "Top Leadership, U.S.A." (*Journal of Politics*, February, 1960); Robert A. Dahl, *Who Governs* (New Haven: Yale University Press, 1961); Edward Banfield, *Political Influence* (New York: The Free Press, 1961).
6. (New York: Oxford University Press, 1967.)
7. *The New Yorker* (August 5, 1967), p. 83.
8. *The New York Times Book Review* (July 9, 1967), p. 20.
9. John Porter, "The Power Structure" (*American Sociological Review*, April, 1968), p. 301.

with both "a political and a sociological sophistication," which would appear to be a complete refutation of the fanciful notions of Mills and other conspiratorial thinkers.[10] While two other reviewers remained unconvinced, the consensus within the academic community seems to be that it is a representative book.[11] For example, political scientist Philip Green, who has criticisms of both pluralist and power elitist views, notes in passing that it is "the best recent work in the [pluralist] genre."[12]

Because of its favorable reception, wide classroom use, and attempt at comprehensiveness, *The Power Structure* is an ideal case study for an attempt to demonstrate the shortcomings of the pluralist position. Indeed, the critique of the pluralistic position that I was slowly developing could be applied almost word-for-word to Rose's work. In what follows, however, I will concentrate my remarks almost exclusively on *The Power Structure,* leaving it to readers to decide how much of what I say about Rose's "multi-influence" perspective is applicable to specific works by other pluralists. It is important to emphasize this, for I would not want to claim that each person fitting the general classification "pluralist" can be criticized on every point that I raise about *The Power Structure.* I know full well that there are many differences among pluralists, just as I hope they realize there are many differences between my work and that of Mills or Hunter, even though it is not unfair to place me in the same general tradition with them.

Although I will make some remarks that may be considered methodological or theoretical, I will concentrate

10. Robert Bierstadt, "The Power Structure" (*The American Journal of Sociology,* March, 1968), pp. 635–6.
11. Leonard Reissman, "The Power Structure" (*Annals of the American Academy of Political and Social Sciences,* January, 1968), p. 233; Robert Heilbroner, "Who's Running This Show?" (*The New York Review of Books,* January 4, 1968), pp. 20–1.
12. Philip Green, "Science, Government, and the Case of RAND" (*World Politics,* January, 1968), p. 306*n.*

my attention on what I hope to be empirically answerable problems, purposely avoiding the philosophical and ideological conflicts that are not easily resolved by social science research. In doing this I am agreeing with Anatol Rapoport that good descriptive studies are what are needed in the social sciences, and that the tendency to premature grand theorization and overgeneralization may be a drawback in this field.[13] Nor will it be my purpose to defend the views of Mills and Hunter. I will develop a critique of Rose's multi-influence hypothesis rather than writing a critique of his critique. Furthermore, any contrasts that I draw will be with my own perspective, not those of Mills or Hunter. However, this does not mean that I necessarily agree with all of Rose's criticisms of those two theorists. As will be seen, some of my arguments against certain of Rose's views support by implication some of their views.

The fact that I will be focusing on where a pluralist such as Rose goes wrong does not mean I disagree with him on every point he raises. There are areas of agreement between us, and on certain questions our disagreement is primarily one of degree. For example, just *how* conscious, *how* united, *how* rich, and *how* successful does a social upper class have to be before we call it a "governing class"? It may be that Rose would use that label for a closely-knit .3% of the population that has 50% of a country's wealth and provides 75% of its governmental leaders, whereas I would be tempted to use it if the .3% has 22% of the wealth, 60–70% of the corporate stock and contributes merely many times more than its share (a disproportionate number) of decision-makers. Then too, if Rose and I agree that the role of the Executive branch has increased at the expense of Congress and local governments, there is still

13. Anatol Rapoport, "A System-Theoretic View of Content Analysis." In *The Analysis of Communication Content,* George Gerbner, Ole R. Holsti, Klaus Krippendorff, William J. Paisley, and Philip J. Stone, eds. (New York: John Wiley & Sons, 1969), pp. 28–9, 35.

the problem of just how much it has increased. To make the areas of commonality clear before I chastise Rose as strongly as I am going to, let me register my essential agreement with the following points in *The Power Structure:*

1. There are great difficulties with the "reputational" method of studying power (wherein you ask various people, supposedly in a position to know, who has power). This is a good part of the message in Chapters Eight and Nine. I have not used this method in developing my views of the power structure, although I learned a great deal about certain elements of this power structure from Hunter's interviews with big businessmen in his reputational study, *Top Leadership, USA*.

2. The military is subordinate to the "political elite" and is not monolithic. This is the essence of the first section of Chapter Four.

3. Independent regulatory agencies tend to be controlled by those who are supposed to be controlled by the agencies (100, 485).[14] However, Rose thinks this point can be pressed too far (21).

4. Lawyers are often the "leading instruments" of the "economic elite" (160). More exactly, I would say many members of the social upper class become corporate lawyers and play an essential coordinating and political role within it.

5. A small group of people controls foreign policy (488). However, members of the Council on Foreign Relations and the Foreign Policy Association are a little more than "experts" as Rose calls them.

6. Speaking of businessmen involved in foreign policy, Rose asks and answers: "Whose interests then do they

14. All numbers in parentheses in this essay refer to pages in *The Power Structure*.

promote? They promote, in my opinion, *their conception* of the national interest in foreign affairs" (93). (Italics mine.)

7. It is probably true that most politicians do not take pressure groups very seriously in most cases (58, 69).

8. "Bought" legislators probably are less important to businessmen than those who are closely affiliated with one or another economic interest group (470) or have "business-oriented" ideologies (119).

9. There are differences between the Republican Party and the Democratic Party (66).

10. One of the key cleavages in interest and power is between bigger and smaller businessmen, and there is a split in the Republican Party which largely overlaps this split (91).

11. Money is very important in getting the Presidential nomination, although it is not the only factor (397). More generally, heavy money is a very important upper-class resource for influencing politics (459–63).

12. There are various types of power structures at the local level, and many important decisions are made outside the local communities by state and federal agencies, nationally-based corporations, and labor unions (297). The importance of local power structures has been "significantly eroded" since the thirties, although they are still important for the individual citizen (253). It should be added that Rose raises several good questions about the standard pluralist views on community power research.

13. Corporations can influence local and state policy merely by threatening to relocate (102–3).

14. The American public divides along many lines other than class and ideology, and this has many political implications (63).

15. Most people probably have only vague and inarticulate views on "the power structure," and the image that is held varies from social group to social group. This is the burden of an overly-long and redundant Chapter Ten that seems mostly irrelevant to the main thrust of a discussion of power structures. It can be added that an earlier study shows that people at different levels of the social structure also have very different notions of what constitutes the upper class in American society.[15]

16. The general public has no frame of reference for its views on foreign policy and is dependent on the mass media in this issue-area (93*n*).

17. Most people are not hostile to big business (114–15). Nor are very many dissatisfied with the general nature of the government, if we can believe questionnaire studies (175).

Looking over this list of agreements, one might be inclined to suspect that Rose has conceded many points of interest to the governing-class theorist. This is not entirely the case, however, for his primary concern is to put the "economic elite" (his term) within a total perspective that shows the constraints on this elite and the powers of other groups. I now turn to a sketch of his "multi-influence" hypothesis, using several quotes as a safeguard against bias. The second paragraph of *The Power Structure* "states our general hypothesis," says Rose. What emerges from

15. A. Davis, B. B. Gardner, M. R. Gardner, *Deep South: A Social Anthropological Study of Caste and Class* (Chicago: University of Chicago Press, 1941), as summarized in David Krech, Richard S. Crutchfield, and Egerton L. Ballachey, *Individual in Society* (New York: McGraw-Hill, 1962), p. 19.

that paragraph is a picture in which "there are several economic elites," "two political parties which have significantly differing programs," a lack of cohesion in the political parties, and a federal government where "there is significant political control and limitation of certain activities over the economic elite" (2). Rose does not deny the importance of the economic elite, but he does claim that things are more complex than be believes Hunter and Mills think they are (3). A few pages later he suggests there are several "elites" which are not united, some with economic power, some with political power, and others based on "military, associational, religious, and other controls" (6). The picture is filled out a little more when he lists the constraints on economic elites: large-scale historical forces, cultural values, the American creed (e.g., liberty, equality, fair play), "the Constitution and other forms of law," "counter elites (such as civil-rights groups, youth groups, and trade unions), kinship and friendship loyalties, public ' opinion, and voluntary associations" (18–19). Voluntary associations are very important in Rose's view as evidence against the charge that the masses are impotent and alienated and manipulated. He devotes an entire chapter to them, in the process of which he reports that it is mostly "the upper-middle-class associations which show concern for the state of the community and conduct activities designed to do something about it" (224); that lower-class people tend not to participate in them (227); that rich people tend to belong to many and poor people usually belong to none (235); and that the PTA, NAACP, Farm Bureau Federation, League of Women Voters, American Civil Liberties Union, American Legion, and the labor unions are examples of voluntary associations which exert social power (236–45).

Rose returns to general statements of his position in the final chapter of the book. There are many power structures, and their power is primarily in their own specific domain

(483–5). Congress and state governments are far from powerless despite the increasing ascendancy of the federal government in general and the executive branch in particular (486). Voters remain a "restraining and modifying power over the elite"—"most governmental elections accord a good deal of power to the electorate" (484, 205, 27). He closes with a summary in which he asserts:

> . . . [the] power structure of the United States is highly complex and diversified (rather than unitary and monolithic), that the political system is more or less democratic (with the glaring exception of the Negro's position until the 1960's), that in political processes the political elite is ascendant over and not subordinate to the economic elite, and that the political elite influences or controls the economic elite at least as much as the economic elite controls the political elite. (492)

Contemplating this picture, it can be seen that it is generally reasonable and balanced. The economic elite, divided though it is, is given its due, but there is no need for the strident tones of a C. Wright Mills in talking about it. The structure of power is so complicated that the "top businessmen scarcely understand it much less control it" (490). Furthermore, when they are involved in government they often try to act in terms of their conception of the national interest rather than narrow economic motives (23, 93), and their degree of importance has been declining since 1933 rather than growing (490). As to the rest of us, most people feel they have a piece of the action, and Rose presents evidence that he believes to be support for this belief. True, there are problems, but there has been progress over the past one hundred years (250), and more recently on medicare and civil rights (487). All that is needed to improve things even more is to increase public awareness and citizen participation (475–82).

Where does *The Power Structure* go wrong? Certainly not in gauging the beliefs of many Americans, and certainly not in claiming that there are many local power structures and that voluntary associations of a wide variety can be effective in getting specific actions, whether it be better recreational facilities (233), changes in the local schools (237), or rights for minority groups (239–44). On these points Rose seems to be on relatively firm ground, and I do not want to enter into a discussion of them that would be a matter of details and emphasis. Here I only will note that I think the framework which determines the limits and strategies within which local structures and voluntary associations can function is developed at the national level by the power elite. I will therefore concentrate on where I think Rose goes very wrong, namely, his misunderstanding of the nature of the economic elite and its relationship to the national government. My remarks will be developed under the following points:

1. *The Power Structure* lacks an adequate conception of the economic elite, which is nowhere defined.

2. *The Power Structure* does not point out the several ways in which members of the power elite formulate and communicate policy to the various aspects of the federal government. It does not spell out their several direct involvements in the political process.

3. *The Power Structure* is deficient in its understanding of how foreign policy is made.

4. *The Power Structure* neglects the role of moderate big businessmen in the shaping of domestic legislation.

5. *The Power Structure* does not look closely enough at the political elite in terms of its effectiveness in controlling the economic elite. Nor does it inquire into the social and occupational backgrounds of members of the political elite.

6. *The Power Structure* overemphasizes the role of Congress and underestimates the predominance of the economic elite within it.

## THE ECONOMIC ELITE

In the introduction to *The Power Structure* Rose tells us that one of the unique features of his book is that it attempts to infuse the pluralistic position, which is usually guided by political science theory, with sociological theory. It is my judgment that Rose falls down very badly on this when it comes to his understanding of the economic elite. Indeed, he gives us virtually no information of any kind about the economic elite, let alone puts them in any sort of a sociological context. Who are the economic elite? Are they men worth $10 million or more? Or are they men who own and manage businesses of a given size? Do they know each other? Rose is silent on these questions. He thus violates Dahl's first canon for discussions of the "ruling elite" hypothesis: The putative ruling elite must be clearly specified.[16]

The difficulties with Rose's failure to specify the economic elite can be seen in his comments about Presidents Theodore Roosevelt, Franklin Roosevelt, and John F. Kennedy (35). According to Rose, the two Roosevelts were of the "upper upper" class, but Kennedy was the only President who was "very wealthy." The problem is made more complex by the fact that Herbert Hoover, a self-made multimillionaire who was quickly assimilated into the highest circles is not mentioned as either a "very wealthy" or an "upper upper" President. The arbitrariness of these classifications is seen when Rose says that Franklin Roosevelt, Kennedy, Averell Harriman, Senator Joseph Clark, Senator Herbert

16. Robert A. Dahl, "A Critique of the Ruling Elite Model," *op. cit.*, pp. 463–4.

Lehman, Senator Stuart Symington, and former Michigan Governor G. Mennen Williams are of the "upper economic class" (28). Franklin Roosevelt, earlier not of the "very wealthy," is now of the "upper economic class."

Rose's first problem, then, is his failure to specify and to describe his economic elite. He does not explore the possibility that the economic elite is a sociological group that is a specific social stratum as well as a catalogue of rich men. Nowhere does he discuss even the best sociological work on the economic elite as a social class, that of E. Digby Baltzell. Baltzell's first book, *Philadelphia Gentlemen,* appears in one footnote, where it is merely noted as one of five books critiqued by the witty polemicist Irving Polsby (281). Baltzell's second book, *The Protestant Establishment,* is mentioned only once, and then to support the pluralist argument by showing the distinction between the "aristocratic" and "caste" mentality within the upper class (91–2). Even here, Rose goes wrong in claiming that this is simply a distinction between the "old aristocrats" and "new" businessmen, which is not my reading of the thesis.

There is no better example of Rose's failure to understand the economic elite as a social class, and to specify its major institutions, than in his use of the phrase *nouveau riche* in discussing John F. Kennedy and his background (35). By my reckoning, Kennedy was a completely integrated member of the upper class. The son of a multimillionaire who had himself gone to Boston Latin School and Harvard, Kennedy was a product of Choate and Harvard.[17] His friends were fellow scions from all over the East Coast, and he married into a family (the Auchinclosses) that Stephen Birmingham puts at the very heart of the "right people."[18] But Arthur M.

---

17. It was the longtime headmaster of Choate who used to say, "Ask not what your school can do for you, but what you can do for your school."

18. Stephen Birmingham, *The Right People* (Boston: Little, Brown, 1968), pp. 322, 331.

Schlesinger, Jr., who knew Kennedy fairly well, best captures the point I want to make. While admitting that his "Irishness remained a vital element in his constitution," Schlesinger also points out that in most respects Kennedy did not fit Irish-American stereotypes: ". . . he was reticent, patrician, bookish, urbane—much closer, indeed, to a young Lord Salisbury than to a young Al Smith. . . "[19] A little later Schlesinger notes that Kennedy "lived far away from the world of the Holy Name societies, Knights of Columbus and communion breakfasts," and that he was "a Catholic as Franklin Roosevelt was an Episcopalian—because he was born into his faith . . ."[20] In other words, Kennedy was a full-fledged member of the American upper class.

Amazingly, Rose makes no use of the wealth distribution in talking about the economic elite. He mentions it briefly in an appendix to Chapter Three, where he misinterprets it in a way that fits nicely with his belief that the power of businessmen is declining (131–2). Lest I be accused of making too strong an accusation, let me quote the words which I find somewhat misleading:

> During the Great Depression and second world war period, from 1929 to 1949, differentials in wealth and income in the United States were diminishing. Both poor economic conditions and government controls (including rising income taxation) created pressures on upper income brackets, and the new welfare, social security, and labor organization developments of the 1930's as well as the full employment of the 1940's set floors under and pushed upward the lower incomes. But since 1950 there has been a reversal of trend, though wealth differential *is not nearly as great* in the 1960's as it was during the 1920's or earlier. (131) [italics added]

Now, Rose may be right about the fact that social security and unemployment compensation have put some floors under the lower levels, but let it be clear that nothing has

19. Arthur M. Schlesinger, Jr., *A Thousand Days* (Boston: Houghton Mifflin, 1965), p. 78.
20. *Ibid.*, p. 107.

changed at the top levels, where taxes are easily avoided. Indeed, a study published in 1965 suggests that the trend toward further concentration noted by Rose had reached the point by 1958 where there was virtually no difference between the 1920's and the present.[21] I believe it is misleading, then, to say that the "wealth differential is not nearly as great in the 1960's as it was during the 1920's or earlier." It is true that the American pie is getting bigger and the standard of living is going up (some would say at the expense of the rest of the world), but the wealth distribution has remained virtually the same. The big rich are still super rich, with 200,000 households owning 22% of all wealth as of 1962.[22]

In any event, it would seem to me that any discussion of an economic elite should include mention of the wealth distribution and try to ascertain who are the persons making up the few tenths of a percent who own an amazing proportion of the country's wealth in general and an even more incredible proportion of its corporate wealth. Such an investigation would lead directly to members of the upper class and their high-level employees. This would then give Rose several means by which to specify the economic elite even though this group has been relatively successful in keeping from us the economic information that would be necessary for a really precise study.

Although Rose does not directly define the economic elite, it is very clear whom he means. He has defined the term by specifying instances of it in a variety of places, and in each case he points to the same organizations: the National Association of Manufacturers (NAM), the U.S. Chamber of Commerce, and the American Medical Association (AMA). There are three places where he makes

21. James D. Smith and Staunton K. Calvert, "Estimating the Wealth of Top Wealth-Holders from Estate Tax Returns" (*Proceedings of the American Statistical Association,* 1965).

22. Ferdinand Lundberg, *The Rich and The Super-Rich* (New York: Lyle Stuart, 1968), p. 23.

this absolutely clear, and no place where he contradicts it (30, 71–2, 400–2). The first instance is worthy of a rather lengthy quote as it expresses a painfully embarrassing myopia about the big business community:

> The economic elite in fact does often expound its wishes— in the programs and campaigns of the National Association of Manufacturers, the United States Chamber of Commerce, and more specialized groups such as the American Medical Association. As we shall see in subsequent chapters the President and the majority of the Congress more often go against these programs than support them, although the businessmen are more likely to get their way when they seek narrow economic advantages from the independent regulatory commissions and the military procurement agencies. Are the National Association of Manufacturers, the Chamber of Commerce, and the American Medical Association merely engaging in window dressing to fool the public as to their true wishes when they come out with a program or campaign? (30)

The first difficulty in Rose's specification of the economic elite via its organizations is that no one I know of ever claimed that the American Medical Association was part of the governing class or power elite. True, there are upper-class people who become physicians, and most physicians come from the middle and upper-middle classes, but the AMA is hardly an association which is concerned with the interests of the upper class. Physicians are by and large highly-paid professionals who have bid their price up by the tried and true craft union strategy of limiting the number of practitioners. Physicians could be reduced tomorrow to the more mundane financial status of other highly-trained professionals without changing the position or status of the upper class one iota. If anything, such an eventuality would be in the interests of the power elite if it were accompanied by improved and less costly medical care for the underlying population. Defeats of the AMA prove nothing about the power of the power elite. My own impression is that a good part of its seeming power derives from the economic concerns of the insurance and drug companies and from the ideological concerns of the NAM and Chamber of Commerce.

As to the NAM and Chamber of Commerce, they are merely the more conservative element of the economic elite, including certain very large firms and more of the smaller of the big businesses. Indeed, a good part of Rose's failure is wrapped up in this one simple fact, for by quoting NAM pamphlets and leaving the President and the backers of progressive legislation unspecified socioeconomically, he can pose the bad-guy businessmen (economic elite) against the good-guy liberals (who are often Democrats besides). However, I should immediately add that Rose is not alone among pluralists in his failure to take into account the more powerful moderate element within the big business community. In general, it is one of the major errors of all pluralists. Where, then, is the rest of the economic elite that takes an active interest in the political process? On foreign policy they are in the Council on Foreign Relations and the Foreign Policy Association, among other organizations too numerous to mention. On domestic policy they are in the Committee for Economic Development and the National Planning Association, among others. On cultural, educational and welfare matters they are in the big charitable foundations and various civic organizations. None of these receives any serious attention in *The Power Structure*. The CFR and FPA are mentioned in passing on one page as sources of expertise on foreign policy, but one would never know they were organizations of the power elite (488). The Committee for Economic Development appears twice, once in a quote from Floyd Hunter, once as the source of a report showing that bankers don't think Congress pays enough attention to them.

Foundations are dismissed in a single page. Although some may say the foundations are powerful because they have "funds to give away," this is not so at all (162). Public and congressional criticism have made foundations very cautious, and since they want to keep their tax-exempt status they stick to contributions to education and scientific research, which "are certainly not the avenue for exercising power in the society." The next sentences in his account are somewhat surprising:

> Whatever the merits or defects of the philanthropic foundations, they cannot be considered great centers of power in the United States. This is especially true of the national philanthropic foundations, like the ones bearing the names of Ford, Rockefeller, and Carnegie. (162)

It turns out, however, that some of the local ones are pretty powerful, like the Kansas City Association of Trusts and Foundations, whose director, trained as a social worker, "has achieved a national reputation [is Rose resorting to the sinful reputational method?] for local power" (162).

I do not think Rose could be more wrong about the power of the Ford, Rockefeller, and Carnegie foundations in that they have the prerogative to back some educational and scientific ventures, and not others.[23] However, that is a mere interpretation. What is not in question are all the projects he overlooks. Simply put, these foundations finance many of the projects of the Council on Foreign Relations, The Brookings Institution, the Committee for Economic Development, and the National Planning Association, among other power elite groups. In short, they do involve themselves in matters of considerable importance to the po-

---

23. According to Robert A. Dahl, "The Behavioral Approach in Political Science" (*American Political Science Review*, December, 1961), p. 765, his brand of political science could not have developed without extensive support from the big foundations: "If the foundations had been hostile to the behavioral approach, there can be no doubt that it would have been very rough sledding indeed. For characteristically, behavioral research costs a good deal more than is needed by the single scholar in the library—and sometimes, as with studies of voting in presidential elections, behavioral research is enormously expensive."

litical process, a fact which Rose simply overlooks. The foundations are an integral part of the power elite in other ways too, and to dismiss them as casually as Rose does, and without relating them to the economic elite, is a very grave error.

Most of the things that Rose says about the NAM-Chamber of Commerce wing of the power elite are correct, but they are not accurate in general for any group resembling what Mills, Hunter or I would mean by an economic elite or power elite. For example, Rose tells us that the economic elite is for the balanced budget (31). A reading of the work of Karl Schriftgiesser shows that this is not so for the Committee for Economic Development, a big business organization that has been much more important in the postwar years than the NAM.[24] He also tells us that "false consciousness" is more often found in the economic elite than in the lower classes (32). Again, all this means is that the NAM mentality is somewhat shortsighted, but it is hard for me to believe that the CFR-CED-NPA outlook, informed as it is by the Harvard-Yale-Princeton-Columbia social scientists who dominate their fields, is more confused in its understanding of the system than people of the middle and lower classes. While these two examples are not all-important in and of themselves, they make the point that almost anything Rose says about the economic elite is likely to be inaccurate. He simply has not studied the economic elite, not even as it is portrayed in the business magazines and *The New York Times*. His portrait of the economic elite is "distorted," a "caricature," to borrow the terms he uses to describe Mills' portrait of the American power structure.

Rose stresses that the economic elite is not united. It should be clear by now that he could not know it if it were,

24. Karl Schriftgiesser, *Business Comes of Age* (New York: Harper & Row, 1960); Karl Schriftgiesser, *Business and Public Policy* (Englewood Cliffs: Prentice-Hall, 1967).

but the interesting thing is that he asserts this without any data. He is just not inclined to believe that Mills' reasons for saying there is some unity to the power elite—"psychological similarity," "social intermingling," and "coinciding interests"—are compelling:

> While our own *inclination* [italics mine] is to believe that the United States is too large and too heterogeneous to permit the economic leadership to be as integrated, in any of the three respects, as Mills says it is, we shall not present any direct data on these matters. We shall, however, consider how the political elite is subject to diverse pressures, to external limitations not subject to control by the economic elite, and to tendencies which on many occasions resist the interests of the economic elite (18).

Simply put, Rose skirts the question and rests his case on his own opinion, which should not be satisfactory to anyone who values data. I think my own work, and that of Baltzell, has shown that the economic elite is more united than Rose would ever imagine, but I will not try to repeat those analyses here. Instead, I want to note how quickly Rose dismissed perfectly respectable arguments. As to "coinciding interests," I think it is arguable that millionaires have more interests in common with each other than they do with blue collar and white collar workers. They seem to be able to get together on a great many things. As to "social intermingling," social scientists seldom deny that social groups which attend the same schools and clubs and resorts develop some commonality. At least I have never noted that they do so when discussing the working classes or middle classes. Nor are "psychological similarities" such a daring inference to make on the basis of "social interaction from childhood on" (18). There are plenty of data to support such inferences on middle and working class children. Why, in the absence of data indicating otherwise, should we deny that this is also the case for the upper class? Indeed, the few studies we have comparing the upper and middle classes suggest that there is every reason to make such claims.[25] Neither Mills nor I am saying anything stunning or new in talking about "coinciding interests," "social intermingling," and "psychological similarity" as bases for unity. We are merely saying about the highest level of society what most social scientists say about other levels of the social ladder. If anything, we are on more solid ground than those who make these statements about the other strata. The upper class is smaller, attends separate schools, plays different sports, has more money, and is buried in different cemeteries. The question of the unity of the power elite is of course one of degree, but I think I have said enough to suggest that Rose has created an entirely wrong impression and dismissed out of hand some very real evidence, not to mention arguments that others listen to respectfully when they are made about the middle and working classes.

Actually, Rose does give us an opportunity to contradict him factually about the degree of cohesiveness, for at one point he hints that he might be impressed by interlocking directorates: "Interlocking directorates, where they occur in the larger corporations, give them a high degree of cohesiveness" (133). Although he notes government studies from 1947 and 1950 which suggest a considerable amount of interlocking, I think he puts in the phrase "where they occur in the large corporations" because he believes that such interlocks do not occur very often. I infer this from an earlier passage where he says: "Management often controls a majority of the directors, so that interlocking direc-

25. Charles McArthur, "Personality Differences Between Middle and Upper Classes" (*Journal of Abnormal and Social Psychology*, March, 1955); Harold M. Hodges, Jr., *Peninsula People: Social Stratification in a California Megapolis* (Mimeographed). Hodges characterizes the .2% making up the upper class in the San Francisco area as "insouciant," tradition-oriented, often given to "inconspicuous" consumption, less permissive than upper-middle-class parents, and conservative yet non-conforming.

torates are the exception rather than the rule" (92). Rose
believes this because he has misunderstood an inadequate
and out-of-date study that is also the basic reference used
by Dahl when he gives what I think to be very wrong impressions about the nature of control in corporations.[26]
What Rose's source says is that in many cases top management chooses the directors.[27] It also says that in thirty-five
of the 155 corporation boards studied there were as many
"inside" (employees of the given company) as "outside"
directors, and that thirteen of the 155 companies had 75–
100% "inside" directors.[28] I think Gordon is wrong about
management control of directors, but in any case none of
this has anything to do with interlocks. A management-
selected board or an "inside" board could have many interlocks if these men were directors of other companies.
Indeed, the one table Gordon presents which is at all related
to interlocks shows the presence of fifty-one commercial
bankers and thirty-eight investment bankers in his sample
of thirty-five typical corporate boards.[29]

There have been several studies which show the very
complex interlocks that weld together the big business community.[30] More recently, my own work has shown the large
number of bankers and insurance men who interlock with
each other and many industrial concerns. As far as industrial concerns themselves, let me use examples from our
study of 1963 directorships that I have not used before.
The five outside directors and the chairman of Standard Oil
of California bring that firm into contact with seven banks,
fifteen industrials, two insurance companies, one railroad,

26. Robert A. Gordon, *Business Leadership in the Large Corporation*
(Washington: The Brookings Institution, 1945), Chapter VI; Dahl,
"Business and Politics," *op. cit.*, pp. 8–9.
27. Gordon, *op. cit.*, p. 109.
28. *Ibid.*, pp. 118–19.
29. *Ibid.*, pp. 122–3.
30. *Interlocks in Corporate Management* (Washington: U.S. Government Printing Office, 1965) summarizes previous information and references as well as presenting new data.

three utilities, and two universities. People who sit on the board as outsiders at IBM also belong to the boards of thirteen banks, twenty-three industrials, three insurance companies, one oil company, one railroad, and five utilities. There are also three interlocks with foundations and six with educational institutions.

In the future, then, any pluralist wishing to test the power elite hypothesis should, as Dahl warns, clearly specify the supposed "ruling elite." Just as Dahl used the New Haven Lawn Club as his indicator of upper class, so should future pluralist investigators consider corporate boards, social registers, clubs, and private schools as possible indicators of membership in the economic elite. They also should immerse themselves in the considerable non-academic literature on the subject (by journalists and biographers and company historians, among others) so that they have a feel for the group they are studying. They also should be aware that there are a large number of foundations, institutes, and associations that are a part of this group. They should recognize that it has a moderate and a conservative wing that do not agree on each and every issue.

## THE ECONOMIC ELITE AND THE GOVERNMENT

Rose does not seem to have a clear notion of how the big businessmen relate to the government. However, we should not be overly critical of him on this point, for Dahl has pointed out that political scientists, who should show the way, have done virtually no research on this problem.[31] They have managed to restrict their attention to government regulation and "pressure groups." Rose is aware of their research on these topics, admitting that businesses have a

31. Dahl, "Business and Politics," *op. cit.*, pp. 3–4.

good deal of influence on the regulatory agencies while at the same time claiming that "pressure groups" and "lobbyists" do not seem to be very important (58, 69, 100). Casting about for yet another possible link between business and government, he looks at the role of "company agents" in Washington and finds it to be minimal, which no one ever really doubted (71). Having exhausted the standard possibilities of links between business and government, Rose writes as follows about the power elite hypothesis:

> This assertion might have a degree of plausibility if empirically supported explanations were offered as to the means of linking the conspiracy to the observable facts of power. But the conspiracy theorists who adopt the economic-elite-dominance hypothesis do not offer such explanations as far as the observable facts of political power are concerned. (4)

> I understand these and other statements by Mills to mean that the economic elite has taken over control of the executive branch of the government. But just exactly how they have done that, he does not say. (23)

Rose is not alone in these criticisms, for they are among the most important raised by pluralists. Pluralists are not willing to infer power from wealth—they are interested in the political *process*, in how things work. They want to be shown the means by which the big businessmen supposedly rule. The challenge is a fair one that can be readily met. I will list the major links between big business and the government, and then briefly discuss each one in turn:

1. Organizations such as the Council on Foreign Relations, the Business Advisory Council and the Committee for Economic Development.

2. Presidentially appointed task forces and commissions.

3. Special committees that advise the various departments of the executive branch.

4. Appointments to the executive branch.

5. Campaign funds.

6. Lobbying.

## Institutes and Associations

The moderate element of the power elite, which by and large means owners and managers of the biggest and most international corporations, has developed a variety of organizations that are very much involved in the governmental process. Since I have talked at length about these organizations in earlier essays in this book, I will make no effort to cover the same ground here. I think I have shown that these organizations serve as training grounds for future government appointees, as discussion centers where future policies are formulated, and as meeting places where corporate leaders get to know each other and their academic advisers. Pluralists who wish to study the decision-making process would be advised to compare the reports and statements of these organizations with what finally emerges as governmental policy on a given issue. To take one small example not used before, there is a considerable similarity between a Committee for Economic Development paper on what should be done in Latin America and the Alliance for Progress:

> CED completed its work on this statement just before President Kennedy sent his Alliance for Progress program to Congress. The parallels between the two were striking, no doubt in part because some of CED's top advisors for this project also were members of Kennedy's "Alliance" task force.[32]

There is one function of these organizations that I did not stress enough in the previous essays, where I concentrated on showing their complex involvement with the

32. Schriftgiesser, *Business and Public Policy, op. cit.,* p. 140.

executive branch: they are major suppliers of expertise to Congress. For example, we can recall the Senate's use of these power elite organizations when it decided to get an "independent assessment" of foreign policy matters so that it would not have to rely entirely upon the executive branch for its information.[33] We also have seen that the National Planning Association and Committee for Economic Development provided the major in-puts for the Employment Act of 1946, and that The Brookings Institution and the National Association of Manufacturers probably supplied the drafts for the Taft-Hartley Act of 1947.[34]

## Commissions and Task Forces

Presidentially appointed commissions often recommend new policies that eventually become government policy. Again, earlier essays have shown that these commissions and task forces are dominated by corporate leaders and their academic advisers, especially corporate leaders and academic advisers from institutes and associations such as the Council on Foreign Relations and the Committee for Economic Development. In the pre-inaugural period President-elect Kennedy set up a number of such task forces to help "chart the main directions of policy."[35] Corporate lawyers Adlai Stevenson and George Ball drafted a report on foreign policy; Stuart Symington, big businessman and Social Register listee turned Senator, headed a task force on the defense establishment. Paul Nitze (formerly of Dillon, Read), David Bruce and Roswell Gilpatric, all listed in the Social Register, were the main members of a committee on national security. Corporate lawyer A. A. Berle, Jr., the chairman of the Twentieth Century Fund, headed

33. H. Field Haviland, Jr., "Foreign Aid and the Policy Process: 1957" (*American Political Science Review*, September, 1958), pp. 691–2.
34. "How the Power Elite Shape Social Legislation," pp. 188, 191, 196.
35. Schlesinger, *op. cit.*, p. 155.

the task force on Latin America.[36] The expenses of one of the task forces were met "by a grant from the Edgar Stern Foundation."[37] Thus, decision-making studies not only should compare government policy with institute and association proposals. They also should study the reports of special government commissions and task forces, which seem to be one of the main methods by which the thinking of the institutes and associations gets passed on to the government.

## Special Committees of the Executive Branch Departments

During World War II many advisory committees made up of big businessmen were established to furnish expertise to the government about specific industries. With some interruptions in the late forties, such committees have existed ever since. They primarily involve the Commerce, Interior, Defense, and Treasury Departments. In the case of the many Commerce Department committees, political scientist Grant McConnell calls them "a direct 'pipeline' to government for businessmen."[38] To elaborate:

> The Department of Commerce network of committees and task groups, the employment of WOCs [Without compensation governmental appointments from business], and the holding of conferences of industry groups (sometimes with WOCs from those industries as presiding officers for the government) constituted perhaps the most remarkable venture of government-industry collaboration to occur in peacetime.[39]

The Interior Department has such committees, too, notably the National Petroleum Council. McConnell suggests

36. *Ibid.*, pp. 155–7.
37. *Ibid.*, p. 160.
38. Grant McConnell, *Private Power and American Democracy* (New York: Knopf, 1966), p. 269.
39. *Ibid.*, p. 271.

the membership of this oil committee is so impressive that "it is difficult to imagine Interior Department officials, even if they wanted to, ever taking positions contrary to those adopted by the industry in its own organizations . . ."[40] The Department of Defense has the largest list of such committees, while the Treasury Department openly drew its committees from such private associations as the American Bankers Association.[41] McConnell stresses that some of these committees are of little or no importance, and that it is hard to know for sure how important many of them are, but he does believe that "some of these groups have achieved a strong degree of influence over—even control of—public policy in particular areas."[42] At any rate, here is a concrete link between business and government on the kind of specific and day-to-day issues so essential to big business that is not even noted by *The Power Structure*.

## Appointments to the Executive Branch

Members of the power elite do not merely appear in Washington as heads of State, Defense, Treasury, and Commerce. They are also appointed to assistantships and advisory positions in these departments. Many of these appointees are from the large corporate law firms whose major clients are the big banks and industrials. Rose can still counter that it must be shown that these men act in their own interests when in government—I will merely note that sociological and psychological studies suggest that it is very hard to transcend one's background and implicit assumptions. Be that as it may, Rose is wrong to say that such appointments are only of major importance in Republican administrations (122–3). It is an empirical fact that the executive branch always is honeycombed with members

40. *Ibid.*, p. 273.
41. *Ibid.*, pp. 274–5.
42. *Ibid.*, p. 275.

of the power elite: rich stockholders, corporate managers, corporate lawyers, and former employees of power elite institutes, foundations, and associations.

## Political Campaign Funds

*The Power Structure* concedes considerable importance to campaign funds as a major means of business involvement in the political process, so I will not belabor the point. However, the information available merely gives the general picture. (Rose quotes one source ($459n$) which says that 1% of the people give 90% of the money for federal campaigns.) The information also tends to concentrate on Presidential campaigns. There is a need for detailed studies of the financial backing of every member of Congress. Then too, the possible influence of such general fund raisers as businessman George Allen, responsible for many years for Democratic congressional campaign funds, should be checked with care.

## Lobbying

The effects of lobbying are hard to assess, for the process often is more subtle than it supposedly used to be. However, it is certain that various business groups and their Washington lawyers are the most prominent lobbyists, even when they do not bother to register as such. Reporter Richard Harris has provided an impressive case study of the drug industry's influence; political scientist Robert Engler has provided another for the oil industry.[43] Consumer crusader Ralph Nader has been developing several striking examples.[44] In addition to talking to Congressmen, lobbyists also give a great deal of campaign money, directly and by their

43. Richard Harris, *The Real Voice* (New York: Macmillan, 1964); Robert Engler, *The Politics of Oil* (New York: Macmillan, 1961).
44. Ralph Nader, "The Great American Gyp" (*The New York Review of Books*, November 21, 1968).

attendance at $100-a-plate and testimonial dinners. Many times the lobbyists who give money ask for nothing in return—perhaps they merely understand the potency of gift-giving.[45]

Concluding this specification of six concrete links between big business and the political process, it should be obvious that Rose did not search far enough before concluding that none of importance was present. It also should be clear that it is not anything like the secret little conspiracy Rose caricatures it to be. Links between big business and government abound, and let us hope that pluralists will join in the prolonged research effort necessary to spell them out in detail. As Dahl says:

> The difficulty in choosing among these views [Mills-Hunter and the pluralists], or even in developing another variant, is that we do not have anything like enough carefully formulated case studies of the roles of businessmen in politics. To be sure, library shelves sag with cases in law, business and public administration. But few if any of these cases are useful for testing hypotheses about influence, for the relevant questions were not in the minds of the authors.[46]

## THE MAKING OF
## FOREIGN POLICY

*The Power Structure* is at its worst on foreign policy. Rose concedes that foreign policy is made by a small group that is relatively unresponsive to a public that is not well informed on foreign problems anyhow (92–3, 488). He also knows that the Council on Foreign Relations is an important aspect of this foreign policy elite (488). From there he goes astray, by calling the CFR members "experts," and by saying that the economic elite, other than military sup-

---

45. Marcel Mauss, *The Gift* (Glencoe: The Free Press, 1954); Norman O. Brown, *Life Against Death* (New York: Random House, 1959), Chapter 15.
46. Dahl, *op. cit.*, p. 36.

pliers, has no more influence on foreign policy "than the workers organized into trade unions, especially when they engage in shipping boycotts" (488). In fact, as I have shown in "How the Power Elite Make Foreign Policy" (Chapter Five), the big rich are very much involved in the making of foreign policy, and the Council on Foreign Relations is one of their major instruments in this area.

Rose also makes the mistake of detaching certain CIA activities from foreign policy by saying that the CIA is not always controlled by top policy leaders because "they are often too busy to do so" (158–9)! One difficulty with this view is the intimate involvement of the CIA leaders and foreign policy leaders. People switch from one group to the other with great ease at the higher levels of the two groups; they interact at CFR study groups; they know each other socially. I do not think the works of Wise and Ross sustain Rose's view.[47]

One of Rose's most interesting interpretations in the area of foreign policy concerns government insurance of American investments overseas. It seems that a business gets 90% of its investment back from the American government if its overseas operations are confiscated. This is evidence to Rose of government control because the government gives this handsome guarantee only if the business meets certain government standards (129). An alternative interpretation of such a benevolent insurance might be that the government is under the control of big business. Those who can't make up their minds between the two interpretations might want to do a detailed study of (a) the nature of the controls and (b) the enforcement of the controls. For myself, I will assume that the big-business dominance hypothesis is the more likely until such time as a study shows that the controls are both significant *and* enforced.

47. David Wise and Thomas Ross, *The Invisible Government* (New York: Random House, 1964); David Wise and Thomas Ross, *The Espionage Establishment* (New York: Random House, 1967).

## BIG BUSINESS AND
## DOMESTIC LEGISLATION

One of Rose's major evidences against the economic elite dominance hypothesis is the existence of welfare and labor legislation that the NAM and the Chamber of Commerce usually opposed (27, 73, 115, 153, 485–7). It is true that these groups opposed this legislation, and succeeded only in watering it down, but it is also the case that the moderate element of the power elite was very important in shaping this legislation. Once again, Rose's limited conception of the economic elite leads him astray. Nor is there any evidence that he studied this legislation in any detail. For example, he might not have included the Securities Exchange Commission Act on one of his lists (73) if he had read the case study on this act, for it shows quite clearly that the moderate elements of the power elite, including Wall Street lawyers, created the agency which polices the worst abuses of the stock market.[48] Indeed, its first head was one Joseph P. Kennedy, a Wall Street speculator of some renown.[49] Nor was the Public Utility Holding Company Act very restrictive.[50]

Pluralists such as Rose rely on case studies of the decision-making process as their major means of deciding who governs. They conduct interviews and read old newspapers and government reports and then determine who is powerful and not powerful on the basis of who initiates, vetoes and carries through ideas and programs. Most pluralists admit that such studies are very difficult to do well, for there is always the possibility that some essential factor or person might be overlooked. Rose attempted one major decision-making analysis in the area of domestic legislation.

48. Ralph F. DeBedts, *The New Deal's SEC* (New York: Columbia University Press, 1964), Chapters Two and Three.

49. Richard J. Whalen, *The Founding Father* (New York: The New American Library, 1964), pp. 138–41.

50. DeBedts, *op. cit.*, Chapter Five.

It concerned the passage of the Medicare Act, an act that hardly would be judged by most observers to be a threat to the power elite. In any event, I do not think Rose's case study is a good one. My understanding of the Social Security Act suggests that he does not appreciate the role of corporate moderates in formulating this type of legislation. I also suspect from his list of the supposedly few economic elitists who supported the Medicare provisions—Marion Folsom of CED and the BAC, Nelson Rockefeller, Clifford Case, *Business Week*—that he did not go beyond the surface of the question. On the basis of these two criticisms alone, not to mention all the weaknesses of his conception of the economic elite that I have outlined, I think the study is disqualified as a case that could be used one way or the other in the pluralist-governing class controversy. I think certain domestic legislation can be used to demonstrate the limits on the powers of the economic elite. However, the inadequacies in such legislation due to the pressures of the power elite, and its NAM-Chamber of Commerce wing in particular, should not be ignored either.

## THE POLITICAL ELITE

The central problem with which *The Power Structure* wrestles, according to Rose, is "the relative power of the economic and political elites" (456). His conclusion is that the political elite—the government—controls the economic elite (2, 3, 21, 485). The heart of Rose's contention can be found in the following quote. It follows a quote from Mills in which Mills claims that in "virtually every case" the regulatory agency becomes a "corporate outpost":

> He ignores the numerous and powerful governmental restraints and limitations on corporations—through the power to tax, to license, to set rates in interstate commerce, to control conditions of marketing (of securities as well as of products), to control the accuracy of labeling and adver-

tising, to set the conditions of collective bargaining and the labor contract, and dozens of lesser governmental powers. It is of course true that in some of these areas (particularly rate-setting and licensing), the economic elite has found means of influencing the government administrators, but even here the fact that they must work through the government administrators (appointed by the President with the consent of the Senate) is a limitation on their power. (21)

I think there are three questions concerning the political elite that Rose does not probe deeply enough to make his conclusions at all meaningful:

1. Are the controls significant?

2. Are the controls enforced?

3. What are the social class and occupational backgrounds of those who are the political elite?

## The Significance and Enforcement of Controls

Almost anything that can be said on the first two questions is a matter of degree. Take the example of the regulatory agencies. Of course the government now officially controls many businesses through regulatory agencies. But how significant are the controls? Rose says the hearings Mills refers to on regulatory agencies "show the persistence of business monopolies in the face of antitrust legislation; they do not show that there is no effective regulation and limitation of business and industry in other spheres" (21*n*). But Mills did not use this source "to support this statement" (21*n*). Rather, he says, "See, for example . . .", which makes clear that this is one of many sources that could be cited.[51] In his nit-picking, a common enough failing among pluralists in general, Rose overlooks the fact that on page 258 of *The Power Elite* Mills quotes John Kenneth Galbraith as saying that regulatory agencies "become, with some exceptions,

51. C. Wright Mills, *The Power Elite* (New York: Oxford University Press, 1956), p. 391.

either an arm of the industry they are regulating or servile." Mills was stating conventional wisdom; his mistake was in daring for a minute to be like Galbraith in using few supporting footnotes.

Regulatory agencies aside, what of legislative controls? Rose mentions control of "the accuracy of labeling and advertising," by which he may be referring to the "Truth in Packaging Bill." But that bill gives control in name only. The big companies were successful in gutting the bill.[52] Rose gives other examples. They may or may not support his position. The point is that he treats them so casually and superficially that we do not know whether or not they have the implications he claims. There is reason to believe that many do not. Ralph Nader, a crusading lawyer who has been looking into such matters, is somewhat more pessimistic about government control than Rose. Although he believes some useful precedents have been established, and that there is some recent stirring of interest on the part of the public, he suggests that businesses do as they please even when legislation is passed. For example: "So far, most state and Federal efforts to set meaningful safety standards and enforce them have failed miserably."[53] Bills passed concerning flammable fabrics and oil pipelines were never enforced. The National Highway Safety Bureau has no facilities for determining whether or not automobiles meet its safety standards. Then too, the penalties for violating various governmental controls are virtually nil. The Federal Trade Commission, the major government watchdog of corporations, has a minuscule staff and budget, and "anemic enforcement powers" that it costs very little in fines to flaunt.[54] Even if we are generous and grant for the moment that legislation has theoretically corrected the worst abuses

52. "How the 'Truth in Packaging Bill' Was Gutted by an Industry Lobby" (*I. F. Stone's Weekly,* October 10, 1966), p. 4. If he was referring to the already existent powers of the Federal Trade Commission, he was referring to less than nothing in the way of enforcement.
53. Nader, *op. cit.,* p. 31.
54. *Ibid.,* pp. 29, 31.

of the power elite, and that the occasional sensational cases such as the price-fixing prosecution in the electrical equipment industry keep big business on its toes, the overall picture of governmental control of the economic elite is not in my judgment the impressive feat Rose celebrates.

## Social and Occupational Backgrounds of the Political Elite

Rose does not look in detail at the social and occupational backgrounds of the political elite. For example, he identifies McGeorge Bundy, the son of a corporate lawyer and an old-line member of the upper class, as "a Republican without business connections" (126). Dean Rusk, for eight years the president of the Rockefeller Foundation, came to the State Department "from a career in government and education" (123). Luther Hodges, a businessman all his life before becoming governor of North Carolina in the fifties, is not one of the three members of the Kennedy Cabinet who had "primarily business backgrounds" (123).[55] John W. Gardner is not identified as the president of both the Carnegie Corporation and the Carnegie Foundation for the Advancement of Teaching, Nicholas Katzenbach is not identified as a member of the upper class, and Willard Wirtz, Henry Fowler, and Abraham Ribicoff are not noted to be corporation lawyers (123-4).

Closely related to this failure to make class and occupational identifications is Rose's failure to trace the political careers of any members of the political elite. For example, to trace the careers of Woodrow Wilson, Dwight Eisenhower, Lyndon Johnson, and Richard Nixon is to see how intimately involved at least some key politicians are with big businessmen. Further examples will be presented when I discuss Congress.

55. However, three pages later Rose says that Hodges has "strong business ties" (126).

Rose claims that there were few big business appointees in the Truman and Roosevelt Administrations except during World War II (122). This is only true in contrast to the Eisenhower Administration and in terms of a narrow definition of the economic elite. Certainly it was not true of the Johnson Administration. The kinds of people Johnson's "headhunter" sought for sub-Cabinet appointments were "men who hold middle-level executive positions in big corporations or law firms and obviously are headed for the top."[56]

Rose also presents figures on the dramatic difference in the percentage of businessmen in the Eisenhower and Kennedy administrations (123). Unfortunately, his figures are drawn from a very, very inadequate study by economist Seymour Harris. Harris compares his findings on Eisenhower appointees with the brief "occupation before appointment" information on Kennedy appointees that appeared in two *Congressional Quarterly* listings.[57] We re-did Harris's study, and our findings suggest a somewhat different picture.

First, Harris says there were only twelve businessmen (6% of the appointees). We found in a more serious search that at least sixteen more of these people were primarily businessmen. Harris classifies most of them as "government officials" because that was their most recent affiliation. However, this hardly does justice to a man who becomes a governor after a long business career; or to C. Douglas Dillon of Dillon, Read, or oil multimillionaire George McGhee. In short, Harris's figure is much too low.

The line between businessman and other occupations is sometimes a vague one. For example, thirteen of the lawyers in the group were corporation officials or corporate directors, and perhaps they should be added to our total. It

---

56. "Help Wanted" (*Forbes*, July 15, 1965), p. 33.
57. Seymour E. Harris, *The Economics of the Political Parties* (New York: The Macmillan Company, 1962), p. 25.

seems to me that they, as well as many other corporation lawyers not formally affiliated with a given company, are part of the corporate elite. A businessman/lawyer dichotomy, as used in so many studies, is very deceptive if the role of corporation lawyers within the big business community is overlooked.

It is also worthy of note that three of the academicians in the group were directors of businesses. Two were directors of Sprague Electric, whose chairman was involved in the defense planning of the late fifties. Then too, two of Kennedy's science appointments were directors of the Aerospace Corporation, a non-profit research and planning organization with several ties to the corporate world. Other of the academic appointees had consulted for major firms or for such organizations as the Ford Foundation and Committee for Economic Development.

According to Harris, only 15% of the Kennedy appointees came from the field of law. This is a surprising statement, for we found that 42% had law degrees. Even if we ignore the lawyers working as government officials or as law professors, there are still well over 15% who are lawyers who have spent most of their lives in private practice. Several are with leading corporate firms in New York and Washington. However, a precise determination of the percentage who are primarily in private practice is somewhat arbitrary, for many of these men are in and out of government service throughout their careers.

## THE ROLE AND CONTROL OF CONGRESS

There are two difficulties with Rose's discussion of Congress as a pluralistic body of considerable importance in the national government. First, most people do not think it is that important. Second, it is dominated by the conservative element within the power elite.

## The "Power" of Congress

The "power" of Congress is a relative matter both historically and as compared to other branches of the federal government. Establishment journalist Stewart Alsop answers his question: "How much power does Congress have in the American governmental system?" with the words "less and less."[58] He is not alone in this belief. Even Rose concedes that there has been some decline (486). The following types of evidence have been brought forth to support this thesis:

1. The growth in size and scope of the executive branch.

2. The removal of many congressional prerogatives to the executive branch (e.g., tariff policy, treaty ratification, declaring wars).

3. The growth in importance of expertise, which is monopolized by the executive branch. The executive branch simply overwhelms Congress with its testimony and reports.[59]

4. The encroachment of regulatory agencies on congressional territory.[60]

Rose claims there are still some bills "that are originated by the Congressmen themselves," but he cites no examples (28). Douglass Cater, on the other hand, says that most bills come from the executive branch, and that "A bill initiated by the individual congressman faces giant obstacles unless it has been submitted first to the President's

58. Stewart Alsop, *The Center* (New York: Harper & Row, 1968), p. 281.
59. *Ibid.*, p. 308–9.
60. *Ibid.*, p. 309.

Budget Bureau for 'legislative clearance.' "[61] Political
scientist Dahl also points to the initiatory role of the executive branch: "It is the President, not the Congress, who
determines the content and substance of the legislation
with which Congress deals."[62]

The most recent general discussion of congressional
power by a leading pluralist is that by Dahl in the introductory political science textbook just cited. Characteristically,
his three-page discussion (pages 139–42) of "Has Congress Declined as a Policy Maker?" begins by noting that
the question "is not as simple as most observers assume."
However, he does detect within the bewildering complexity
"two kinds of historical changes in the character of congressional control." First: "In the twentieth century not only
has the President broken the monopoly of Congress over
policy—and, of course, over appointments—but, as we
have seen, he has also largely taken command over the
initiation of new policies." On the other hand, Congress is
"far more active" than it used to be, and the matters it con-
siders "affect all of us, and the whole world, to an incom-
parably greater extent today than in the nineteenth century."
Thus, the decisions it ponders are of great significance, and
in that sense Congress has gained power:

> In sum, in the post-Civil War period, Congress enjoyed a
> monopoly control over policies mostly of trivial importance;
> today Congress shares with the President control over policies
> of profound consequence. Congress has, then, both lost and
> acquired power.[63]

Whether or not it is agreed that the decisions of the late
nineteenth century were mostly trivial, it must be admitted
that Dahl's view is balanced. And it does concede the very
important point concerning the initiation of policy.

61. Douglass Cater, *Power In Washington* (New York: Random House,
1965), p. 7.
62. Robert A. Dahl, *Pluralist Democracy in the United States* (Chicago:
Rand McNally & Co., 1967), p. 136.
63. *Ibid.*, pp. 139–42.

## Who Runs Congress?

Rose does not discuss the members of Congress. Others do. Donald R. Matthews, who most emphatically does not believe there is any such thing as a governing class in America, summarizes a considerable amount of empirical data by saying that "incumbents in the top offices are mostly upper- and upper-middle-class people."[64] Alsop notes that it is becoming a fact of life that a man has to be rich or have rich friends to be elected to Congress. He believes there are at least a half-dozen multimillionaires in the Senate, with many more who have "capital in the high hundred thousands."[65] Another report out of Washington pegs the millionaires in the Senate at from one-fifth to one-third of the total group.[66] Among the less well known of the big rich are Wallace F. Bennett, Senator from Utah and former president of the NAM; lawyer-financier Hiram Fong of Hawaii; B. Everett Jordan of North Carolina; and lawyer-plantation owner James O. Eastland of Mississippi.

The careers and connections of the legislators also are ignored. It is of more than passing interest when Democrat Claude Pepper, a director of the Washington Federal Savings & Loan Association of Miami Beach, introduces two bills that benefit savings and loan associations.[67] It is also worthy of note that Senators Edward Long, Sam Ervin, and John McClellan are bank directors, that Senator Jennings Randolph is an insurance company director, and that many congressmen are involved financially in broadcasting stations and savings and loan associations. Then too, little has been

---

64. Donald R. Matthews, *The Social Background of Political Decision Makers* (New York: Random House, 1954), p. 32. See the tables on pages 23 and 30 for the details on congressmen.
65. Alsop, *op. cit.*, pp. 284, 291.
66. "One-Fifth of Senators Are Millionaires" (San Francisco *Chronicle*, March 9, 1968), p. 12.
67. Dom Bonafede, "Our Sideline Congressmen" (*New York Herald Tribune*, June 9, 1965), p. 1. This is the first in a series of six articles.

done to develop the corporate connections of the law firms from which many legislators come. Thomas Dodd, who has many rich patrons, is the counsel for a firm which lists ten insurance companies as clients. The corporate connections of former Florida Senator George Smathers' law firm are quite interesting in terms of the legislation he sponsored.[68] After noting that in the mid-sixties 305 of the 535 congressmen were lawyers, Washington reporter Dom Bonafede writes: "Seldom does an attorney completely abandon his legal practice upon entering Congress. The majority retain a connection with law firms in various ways."[69]

Senator Jacob Javits continues to draw a salary from his corporate law firm; Senator Everett Dirksen was counsel for a firm which includes International Harvester, Pabst Brewing, National Lock, and Panhandle Eastern Pipeline among its clients. Some law firms become two firms when a member is elected to Congress. One firm retains the congressman's name, the other does not. They usually have the same office and telephone number, however. Reporters Drew Pearson and Jack Anderson studied fifty "typical" law firms that have partners serving in Congress:

> These have a remarkable similarity of clients. They represent the vested interests of America: the banks, insurance companies, gas and oil interests, great corporations. Of the fifty law firms in the survey, forty represent banks, thirty-one represent insurance companies, eleven represent gas and oil companies, ten represent real estate firms. Some of the biggest corporate names in America are listed as clients of congressmen's law firms in such out of the way places, say, as Nicholasville, Kentucky and Pascagoula, Mississippi.[70]

Pearson and Anderson go on to note a number of interesting coincidences between certain congressmen's views

68. Robert G. Sherrill, "The Power Game: The Golden Senator from Florida" (*The Nation*, December 7, 1964), pp. 427–31.
69. Bonafede, *op. cit.*, June 13, 1965, p. 14.
70. Drew Pearson and Jack Anderson, *The Case Against Congress* (New York: Simon and Schuster, 1968), p. 102.

and what would appear superficially to be the "natural interests" of some of their law firms' major clients.[71] Now, pluralists will say that it is necessary to show that such ties are "significant," but it is interesting that Rose never even mentions them or raises the possibility of their potential importance.

Nor has Rose or anyone else done much research on the small group of backers with whom most legislators are involved. One observer who spent ten years as an administrative assistant to congressmen speculates as follows on this question as far as the House of Representatives is concerned:

> Most Congressmen are elected only with the active assistance of two or three giant economic forces in their districts . . . Each Congressional district has its own internal Establishment—usually a combine of industrialists, financiers, businessmen, newspaper publishers, television owners, corporate lawyers, powerful ministers or priests. When the Congressman returns home these are the people he sees at civic-club luncheons and country clubs; these are the people whose lobbyists entertain him in Washington—and then report back to their superiors whether the Congressman deserves to prosper.[72]

Who is "in" Congress is not in and of itself an answer to "who runs Congress?", for most legislators do not count. Congress is run by an establishment consisting of the key committee leaders and party leaders in the two houses. The houses are leadership-dominated clubs in which one goes along with the leadership if he wants to get along to a position of importance. There are four major statements that can be made about this establishment:

1. It is generally very conservative, at least more so than the executive branch.

71. *Ibid.*, pp. 103–27.
72. Larry L. King, "Inside Capitol Hill: How the House Really Works" (*Harper's Magazine*, October, 1968), p. 68.

2. It has "mild, but only mild, overtones of plutocracy."[73]

3. "Patrician" Senators held 17% of the Senate committee chairmanships from 1947 to 1957 even though they are only 7% of the membership.[74]

4. Southern congressmen head many of these committees, and even Rose admits that many of these Southerners are very much involved with the big business point of view (120). Open-ended questionnaires that I sent to journalists, Republican state chairmen, and Republican national committeemen to find out more about the Democrats also point to the role of big business in the Democratic Party in the South. V. O. Key gives earlier evidence.[75]

Looking at both the legislative establishment and congressional members in general, it is my conclusion that the NAM-Chamber of Commerce perspective is predominant in Congress. Congress reflects conservative elements within the power elite and represents their short-run interests in specific geographical areas. The executive branch, on the other hand, is permeated by the CED-CFR outlook and is usually concerned with the corporate system in general and its overall functioning. There is thus conflict between the two branches of government, reflecting the two tendencies within the power elite. Organized labor, farmers, and other groups can get their way with Congress only when they can convince the executive branch, that is, the moderate

73. Joseph S. Clark, *The Senate Establishment* (New York: Hill and Wang, 1963), p. 22. Clark, in his patrician way, is very polite and understates the case.
74. Donald R. Matthews, *U.S. Senators and Their World* (Chapel Hill: University of North Carolina Press, 1960), p. 163. "Patricians" are in effect men from "old" upper-class families who have been in the Senate for a long time.
75. V. O. Key, Jr., *Southern Politics* (New York: Random House, 1949).

members of the power elite, to go along with their wishes.[76]

Does the evidence warrant the importance Rose gives to Congress as a bastion of the pluralist society? Each reader will have to weigh the evidence for himself, particularly in the light of my comments in earlier essays on the two books most often quoted by pluralists on the functioning of Congress: Stephen Bailey's *Congress Makes A Law* and Raymond A. Bauer, Ithiel de Sola Pool and Lewis A. Dexter's *American Business and Public Policy*. Four conclusions emerge for me that are contrary to Rose's contentions:

1. Congress is declining in its importance. It is mostly a delaying, veto, watchdog organization.

2. The men who dominate Congress come from a very narrow band of the social structure.

3. Rich men are the friends, retainers and backers of a great many congressmen.

4. The conservative, NAM-US Chamber of Commerce-American Farm Bureau mentality predominates in Congress.[77]

CONCLUSION

I am aware that I have not in this brief essay dealt with every example of pluralism presented by Rose, nor even answered every general question usually raised by pluralists.

76. Edward Malecki, "Union Efforts to Influence Non-Labor Policies" (Unpublished M.A. thesis, University of Illinois, 1963). I should add that the American Farm Bureau Federation is a conservative big business organization that teams with the NAM and US Chamber of Commerce in providing the right anchor of the power elite. See also Robert G. Sherrill, "Harvest of Scandal" (*The Nation,* November 13, 1967).

77. I now think I conceded too much to the pluralists concerning Congress in *Who Rules America?* (pp. 111–14). The foregoing represents my new position on the "role" and "control" of Congress.

For example, because most pluralists do not take the wealth distribution or business activity very seriously, they will ask, like Rose, for evidence that the power elite rule in their own interests (28, 473). Pluralists also will note, as Rose does, that the people have the vote, by which they ratify foreign policy decisions (92) and place a "significant restraint" on government officials (27, 205, 484). For now, I will leave it to readers to judge the significance of these questions in the light of the description of the power elite and the political process that is presented throughout this book.

Nor have I dealt with the methodological and philosophical questions that can be raised about the pluralist position. Are case studies of the "decision-making process" necessary to support a power elite position?[78] Are meaningful decision-making studies even possible?[79] Are some of the difficulties with the pluralist position due to the fact that its criteria of evidence are based upon one particular philosophy of science within the British tradition, an experimentally oriented philosophy of science (based upon the model of physics) that is being called into question for the social sciences by other scientifically oriented philosophers and by some biologists and social scientists? Merely to raise these difficult questions without discussing them is to indicate that the last word in pluralist/power elite arguments will be a long time coming. In the meantime, let me agree with the pluralists that the world is complex, and that life is a struggle besides. The forces of history do carry us along, people are sometimes blind to their interests, and not everybody in the upper class is acquainted and in agreement with every other member. The world, then, is pluralistic, a real hodgepodge. So is the American power structure—if we take a very short time span, deal with a myriad of specific

78. G. William Domhoff, *Who Rules America?* (Englewood Cliffs: Prentice-Hall, 1967), pp. 6–7, 143–6.
79. Raymond Bauer, "Social Psychology and the Study of Policy Formation" (*American Psychologist,* October, 1966).

issues of varying importance on a moment-by-moment basis, make little or no attempt to interrelate interest groups or identify the social standing and occupational backgrounds of the "actors," and, most important of all, ignore a wealth distribution in which 200,000 households have 22% of all wealth and 60–70% of the corporate wealth.

# Index

## ABOUT THE AUTHOR

G. WILLIAM DOMHOFF is Associate Professor
of Psychology, Cowell College, University of
California, Santa Cruz. He is the author
of *Who Rules America?*, co-editor of
*C. Wright Mills and the Power Elite*, and
author of essays on applied psychoanalysis
and research papers on dream content.

# VINTAGE WORKS OF SCIENCE
## AND PSYCHOLOGY

# VINTAGE BIOGRAPHY AND AUTOBIOGRAPHY